IMAGES
of America

CALIFORNIA STATE FAIR

I0806321

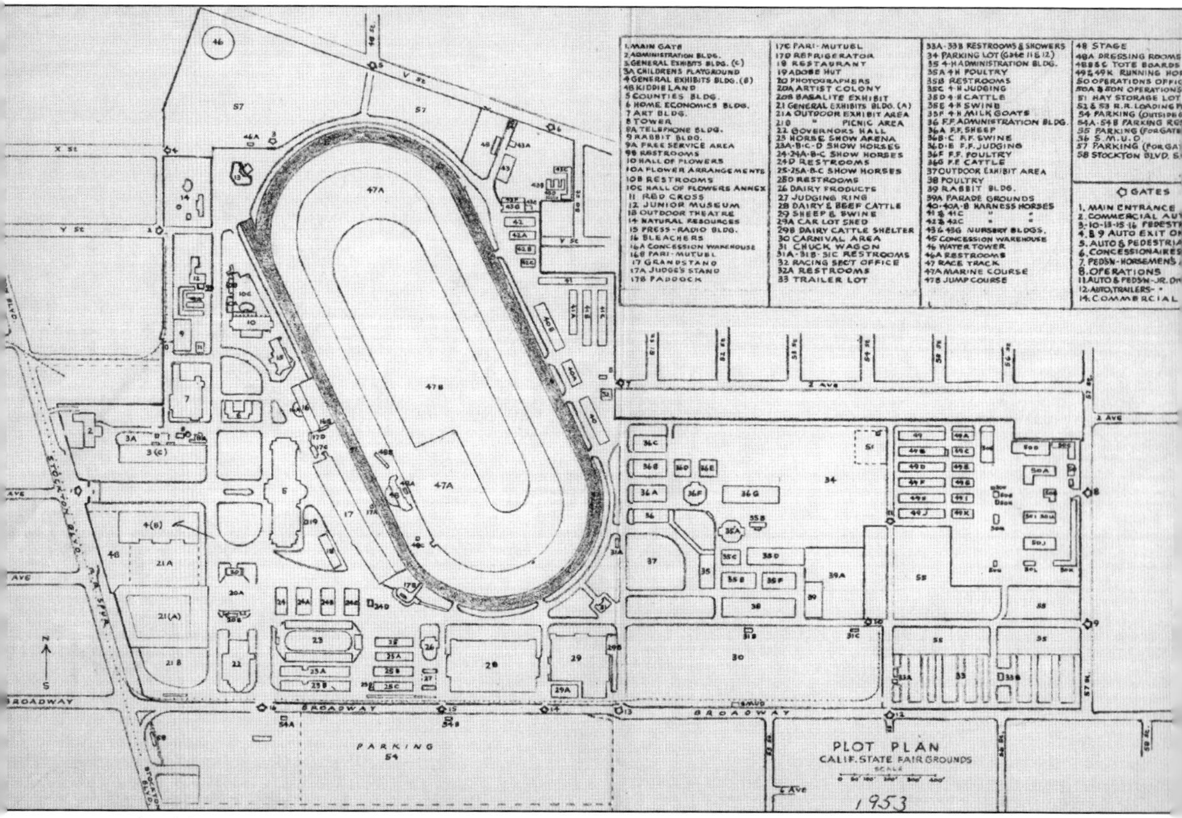

This blueprint copy of the plot plan of the California State Fairgrounds is from 1953. Unlike the maps in the rest of the book, this is drawn to exact scale. The State Fair took up just over 200 acres at the Broadway and Stockton Boulevard site, and one can see here how tightly packed the venue became. By comparison, Cal Expo uses about 350 acres and has room to grow. (CSH.)

On the cover: What could be more fun than watching children take part in a parade at the California State Fair? The yellow-and-black-clad troupe of baton twirlers, seen here on September 3, 1961, is the Sacramento Saddle-Ites. In the wagon behind them are the Sacramento Banjo Band and a tumbling team from Lea Beth Dance Studios. (CSH.)

IMAGES
of America

CALIFORNIA STATE FAIR

Carson Hendricks

ARCADIA
PUBLISHING

Copyright © 2010 by Carson Hendricks
ISBN 978-0-7385-8089-0

Published by Arcadia Publishing
Charleston, South Carolina

Printed in the United States of America

Library of Congress Control Number: 2010921988

For all general information contact Arcadia Publishing at:
Telephone 843-853-2070
Fax 843-853-0044
E-mail sales@arcadiapublishing.com
For customer service and orders:
Toll-Free 1-888-313-2665

Visit us on the Internet at www.arcadiapublishing.com

To Lanie, we land where we need to be.

Contents

ACKNOWLEDGMENTS

Books are never done by just one person. While it is true that the name on the cover is mine, I could never have accomplished this without the help of quite a few people. First and foremost, I would like to thank my friends and colleagues at the Center for Sacramento History (the former SAMCC): Patricia Johnson, *the* finder of really cool stuff; Dylan McDonald and Rebecca Crowther, whose ability to scan photographs and put up with my requests is truly unmatched; Lisa Prince, whose eye should always be trusted; and their manager, Marcia Eymann, who said "yes" in the first place and is able to keep the whole thing running smoothly, which is no small feat. And a special thank you to Bill Gaylord for reading most of this first. The images from the center are credited "CSH."

I would like to thank the staff of the Sacramento Room at the Sacramento Public Library—Clare Ellis, Tom Tolley, and James Scott—for their enthusiastic support of this project and love of Sacramento history. Thank you to Linda Johnson and Jeff Crawford and the rest of the staff at the California State Archives. Conducting research there is always enjoyable, and they are a big reason why. Thank you also to Gary Kurutz and his very patient staff in the California History Room of the California State Library. It is THE place to start any research into California history.

And thanks especially to my editor at Arcadia Publishing, John Poultney. Looking over the shoulders of authors cannot be an easy job. Thank you for having faith in me.

The history community in Sacramento is relatively small, but it is full of very talented people who care deeply about maintaining a connection with the past. There is no better place in California to study history. I am honored to be a part of it.

INTRODUCTION

In December of 1849, Peter Burnett became the first United States Governor of California. His inaugural address ran in the *Daily Alta California*, the first daily newspaper in California, on December 29, 1849. In it, Burnett went on at some length about the potential dangers to a state built upon a single commodity, in this case, gold. He noted that in order to succeed, California would have to look beyond mineral wealth. "If she had only her gold mines the danger would be imminent, but she has still greater and more commanding interests than this . . . I mean her agricultural and commercial advantages," said Governor Burnett. Nine months later, on September 16, 1850, a week after California was admitted to the Union, E. C. Kemble and J. E. Durivage, editors of the *Daily Alta California*, ran an editorial in their usual florid style extolling the virtues of California agriculture. They stated that while gold and mining were important and would never fail, "the army of industry and perseverance now located on this western shore, the bone and muscle, the sinew and thews that have and are wrenching the bountiful gifts of Pluto from the heavy earth, can turn its attention to the cultivation of the soil and feed half of the United States, with our productions." They went on to call for a geological survey of California.

On November 5, 1850, the *Daily Alta California* printed an editorial calling for a state fair to be held at some point in the near future. The editors had been paying attention to what was happening and saw the state's great potential. According to them, fairs were common in the eastern portion of the country and were seen as a way to develop the resources, both agricultural and mechanical, of an area. Kemble and Durivage had much more to say on the subject. In October of 1851, C. A. Shelton secured the second-story hall of the Verandah Hotel at Washington and Kearny Streets in San Francisco for an "Exhibition of California Curiosities." The point of the exhibit was to highlight the potential for agriculture in California and to show some of the more impressive examples of what had been grown that year. Reporters from the *Daily Alta* attended the show and while finding it interesting, they noted "that it must be but a meagre display of the resources of California."

In 1849, James Lloyd LaFayette Franklin Warren had come to California from Massachusetts, where he ran a successful seed store in Boston. He set up a store at Mormon Island and later opened the New England Seed Store in Sacramento on J Street between Front and Second Streets. He also opened a store in San Francisco. Warren, like the editors of the *Daily Alta* and Governor Burnett, recognized that the future of California lay not in mining but in agriculture, and he began to devote considerable time and energy to promoting it. In 1852, he put out a circular announcing an agricultural fair and calling for the creation of a state agricultural society. The fair was held in Sacramento starting on September 20, awarding "Large amounts . . . in the form of cups and medals, for the specimens exhibited," according to the *Daily Alta*. The next year, Warren and his sons put on another agricultural fair, this time at their store on Bush Street in San Francisco. The two fairs were big successes and set the stage for what was to come.

Finally, on May 13, 1854, the California State Legislature created the State Agricultural Society. An exhibition was authorized and funded with $5,000 to be awarded as premiums for the best examples of fruits, flowers, grains, and vegetables. The first official California State Fair was held in San Francisco, starting on October 4, 1854, at the Musical Hall on Bush Street near Montgomery Street. A plaque now marks the location. The stock show was held at Mission Delores. The fair was to be held in a different city each year. In 1855, it was held in Sacramento; in 1856, it went to San Jose; 1857 had it in Stockton; and in 1858, it went to Marysville. A new hall at Sixth and M Streets was constructed for the fair's return to Sacramento in 1859 and 1860. And after much debate, Sacramento was chosen in 1861 as the permanent home of the State Fair.

The State Fair grew quickly and by 1883 a new Exposition Hall was under construction in Capitol Park at Fifteenth and N Streets. It was supported by a special tax of $30,000 approved by Sacramento voters, 3,655 to 102. Containing 124,000 square feet, the building was the largest of its type in the United States at that time. It was to be ready in time for the 1883 fair, but a fatal accident, blamed on the carelessness of the victim, delayed the project. It was completed in January 1884. By 1904, the Agricultural Society decided to look for a larger site. Starting in 1905, land was purchased near Broadway and Stockton Boulevard; and in 1909, the first State Fair was held at this new site. This location was an almost immediate success, and the fair continued to grow. This period, particularly the 1950s and 1960s, is considered by many to be the golden age of the California State Fair. But it eventually outgrew this spot as well. In 1949, a tract of 1,000 acres on the north side of the American River was purchased for the fair. It took 19 years, but in 1968 the fair was moved again. Not everyone was enthusiastic about the new location. The architecture was very different from the last site, and there was a definite lack of trees, one thing that made a late August event in Sacramento bearable. Something that everybody did appreciate was the open space. It took a few years, but gradually people grew to enjoy Cal Expo. Cal Expo has now been the site of the State Fair for over 40 years and will continue to be for the foreseeable future.

While this book is a history of the California State Fair, it is by no means complete and definitive due to time and space considerations. Rather, the point is to focus on the fun things at the fair in the context of the important moments. And there were and are lots of fun things at the State Fair. The largest number of images by far date from the late 1940s to the early 1970s, and that is reflected in the length of the chapters. The story is told, for the most part, chronologically. Certainly, many thousands of images exist, and this story could be told in any number of ways. This is mine.

One

San Francisco to Sacramento

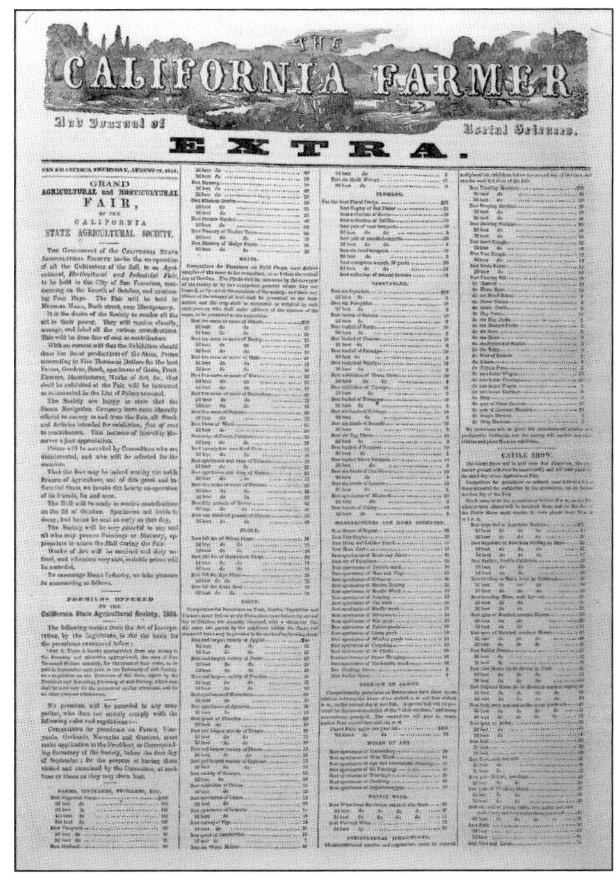

The first annual state agricultural exposition authorized by the California State Agricultural Society was held in San Francisco starting on October 4, 1854, at the Musical Hall on Bush Street near Montgomery Street. The stock show was held at Mission Delores. *The California Farmer and Journal of Useful Sciences* ran this as the front page of its August 17, 1854 extra edition. (California State Library, California Section.)

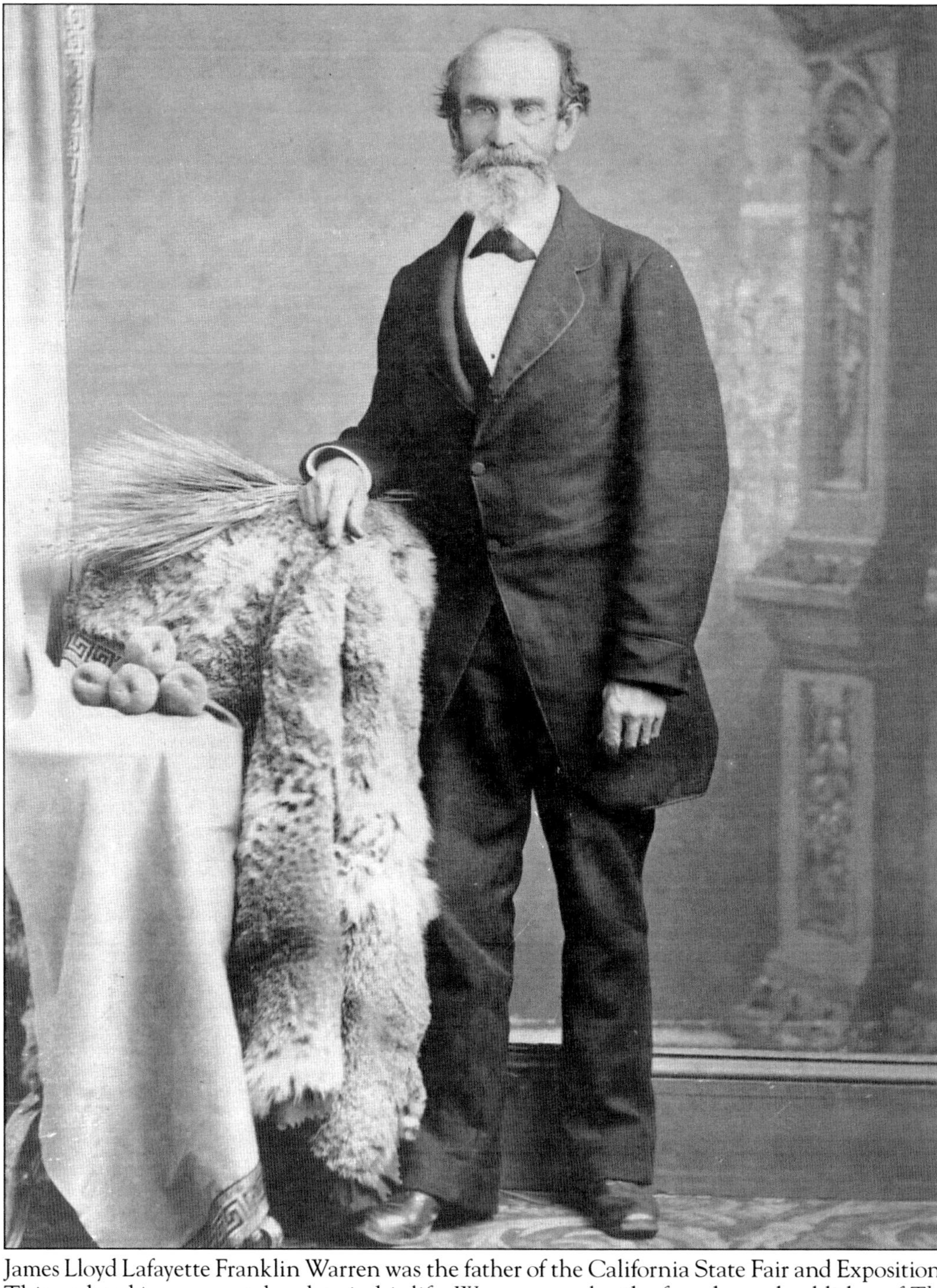

James Lloyd Lafayette Franklin Warren was the father of the California State Fair and Exposition. This undated image was taken late in his life. Warren was also the founder and publisher of *The California Farmer and Journal of Useful Sciences*, in which all things agricultural were discussed. In the first issue, January 5, 1854, he covered the convention held in San Francisco for the purpose of founding the state agricultural society. The convention came about as a result of both a petition he had circulated earlier and the success of his two prior agricultural expositions. (CSH.)

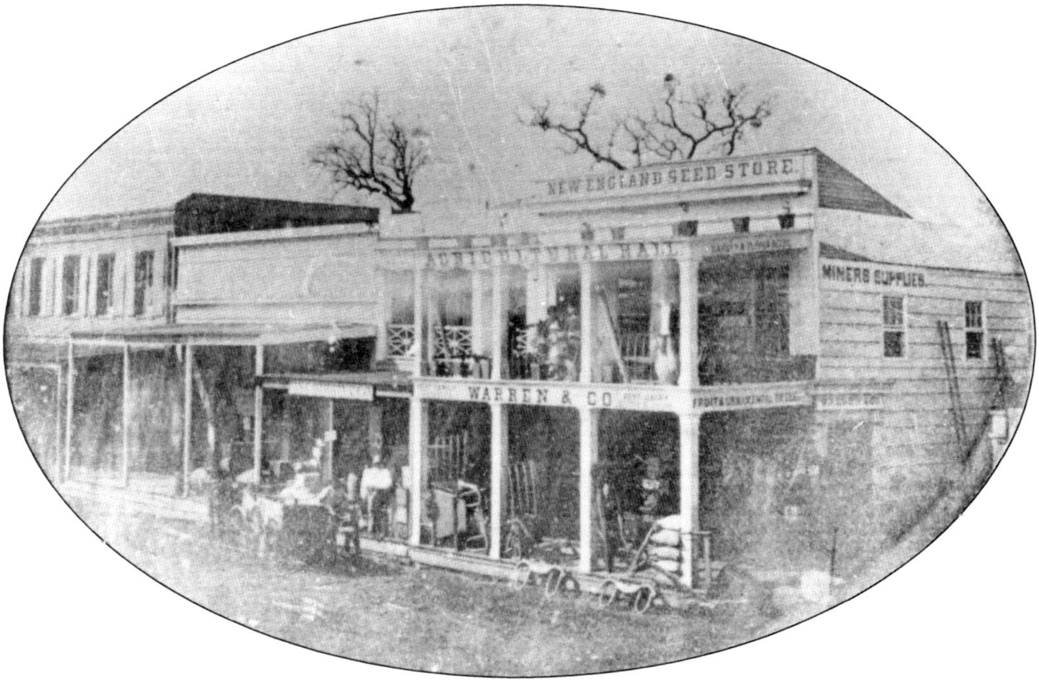

Pictured here is James L. L. F. Warren's New England Seed Store at 3 J Street in Sacramento. His first fair, in 1852, was held in the second floor Agricultural Hall. Among many other accomplishments, Warren is credited with bringing the camellia to Sacramento, where it continues to be a favorite with landscapers and homeowners. (CSH.)

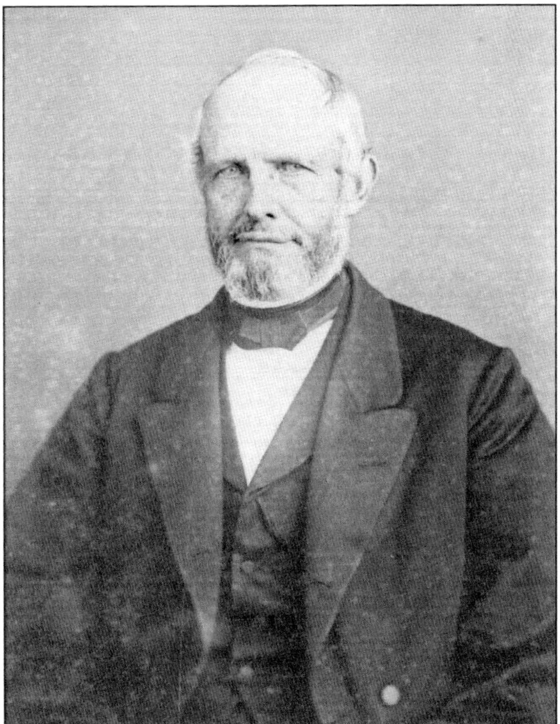

The first United States Governor of California, Peter Burnett, supported the growth of agriculture in California. He noted that, while the mineral wealth of California was impressive, it was the potential of agricultural and commercial endeavors that would make the state great. (CSH.)

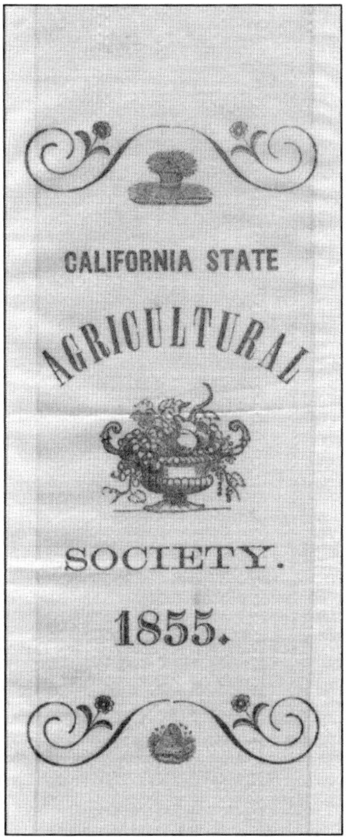

This ribbon is from the 1855 fair held in Sacramento. The ribbon is white silk and the design and lettering are blue. It is not known what it was awarded for, though perhaps it was given as a first prize or to an exhibitor. (CSH.).

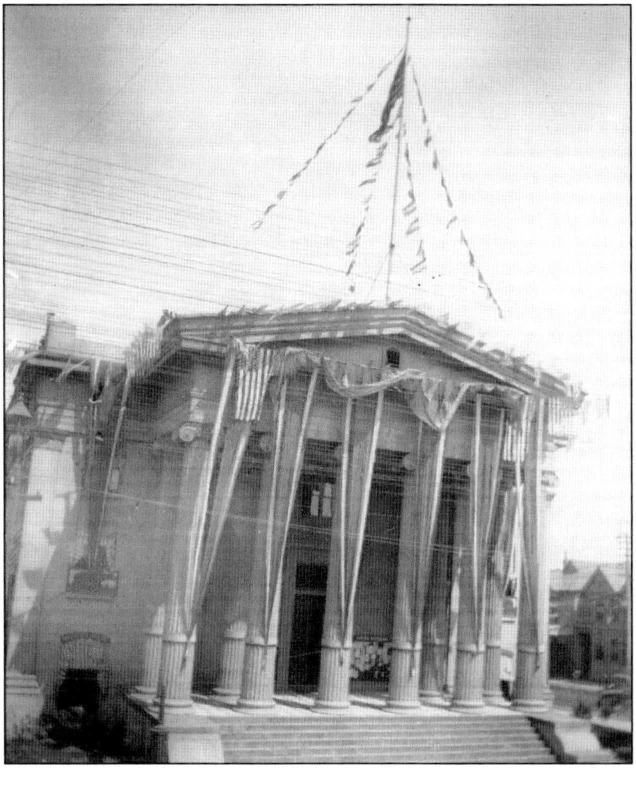

Pictured here is the first Sacramento County courthouse at Seventh & I Streets. The exhibits of the State Fair of 1855 were held in this building, which also housed state offices. While it may appear to be decorated for the fair, this photograph was taken during a celebration for the Fourth of July. (CSH.)

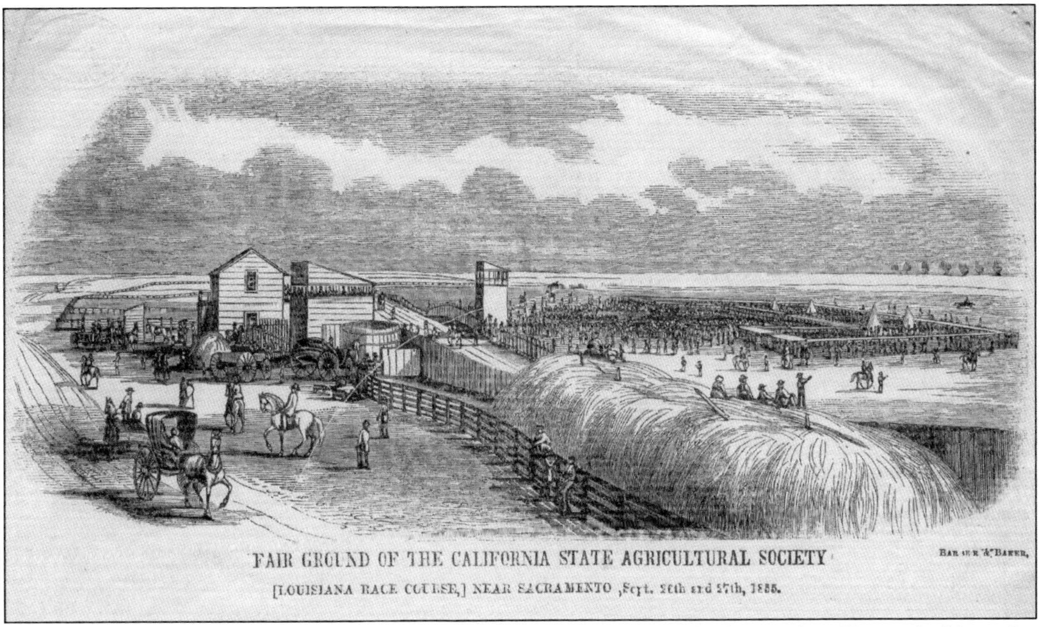

While the main exhibition was held in Sacramento, the stock show of 1855 was held at the Louisiana Race Course, near what is now the Curtis Park neighborhood south of downtown Sacramento. As depicted here, the venue was probably quite a busy place. Note the large pile of hay in the right foreground. (CSH.)

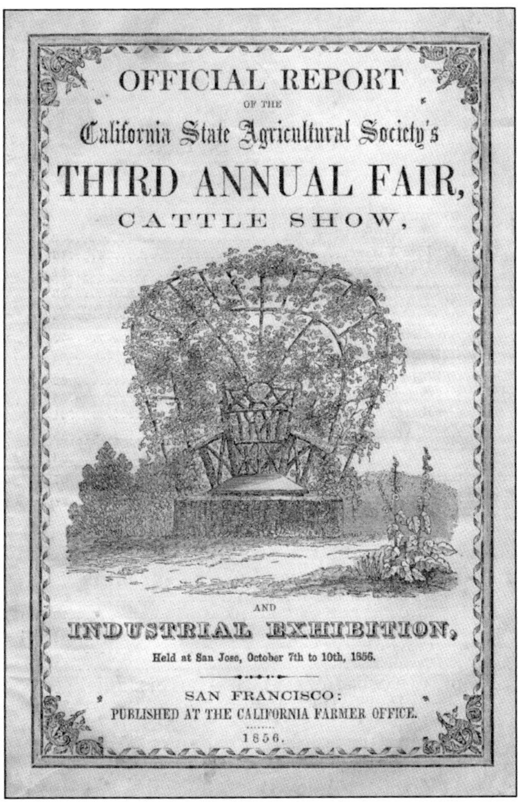
OFFICIAL REPORT
OF THE
California State Agricultural Society's
THIRD ANNUAL FAIR,
CATTLE SHOW,
AND
INDUSTRIAL EXHIBITION,
Held at San Jose, October 7th to 10th, 1856.
SAN FRANCISCO:
PUBLISHED AT THE CALIFORNIA FARMER OFFICE.
1856.

In 1856, the State Fair was held in San Jose. Shown here is the cover of the "Official Report" for 1856. It is one of the few pieces from the San Jose fair to survive. (CSH.)

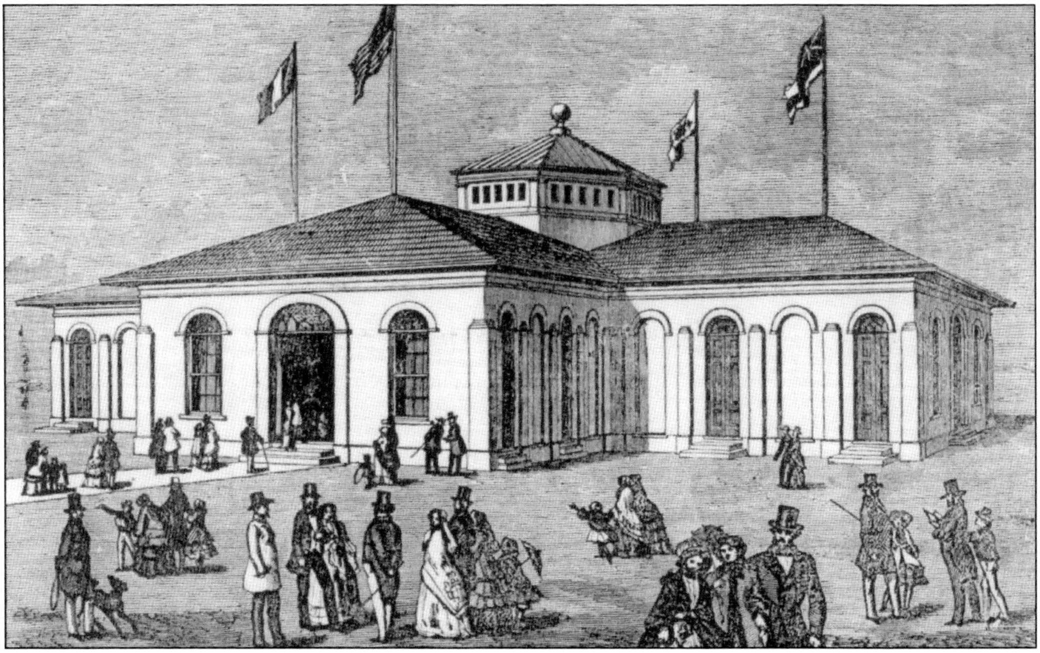

In the 1850s, the fair was held in a different venue each year to give as many people as possible an opportunity to attend. One possible reason for this is that transportation was difficult in this period. The fair was held in Marysville in 1858 at this exhibit hall, built specifically for the exposition. (California State Archives.)

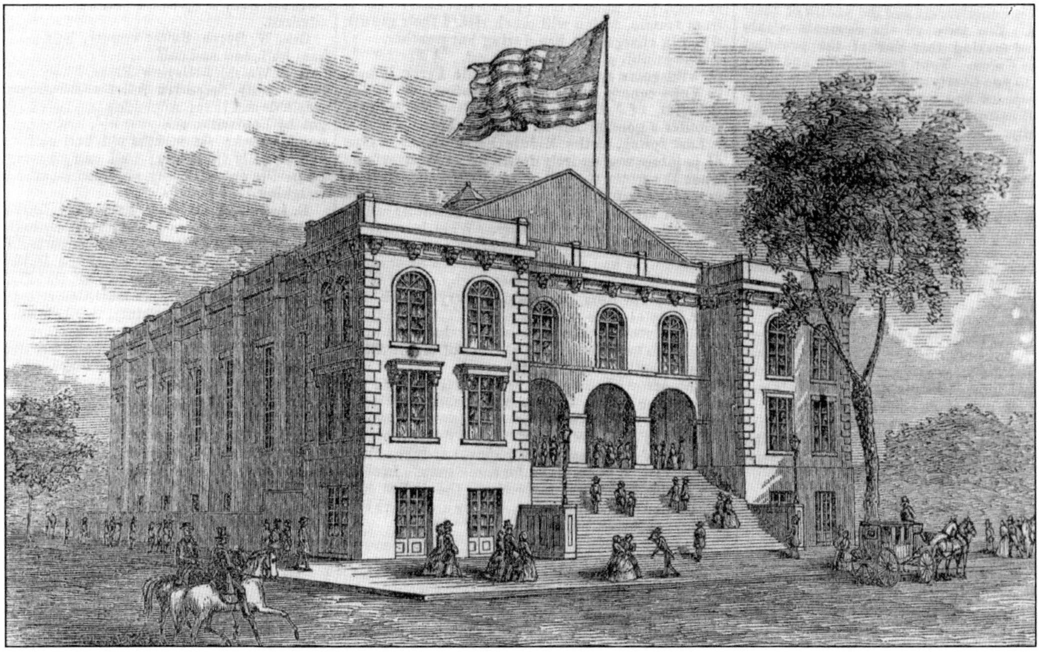

In 1859, the exposition came back to Sacramento and was held at the new Agricultural Hall designed by Miner Frederic Butler, the architect of the state capitol. Upon his death in 1871 at the young age of 46, the *Daily Alta California* referred to him as the "pioneer architect" of San Francisco. (CSH.)

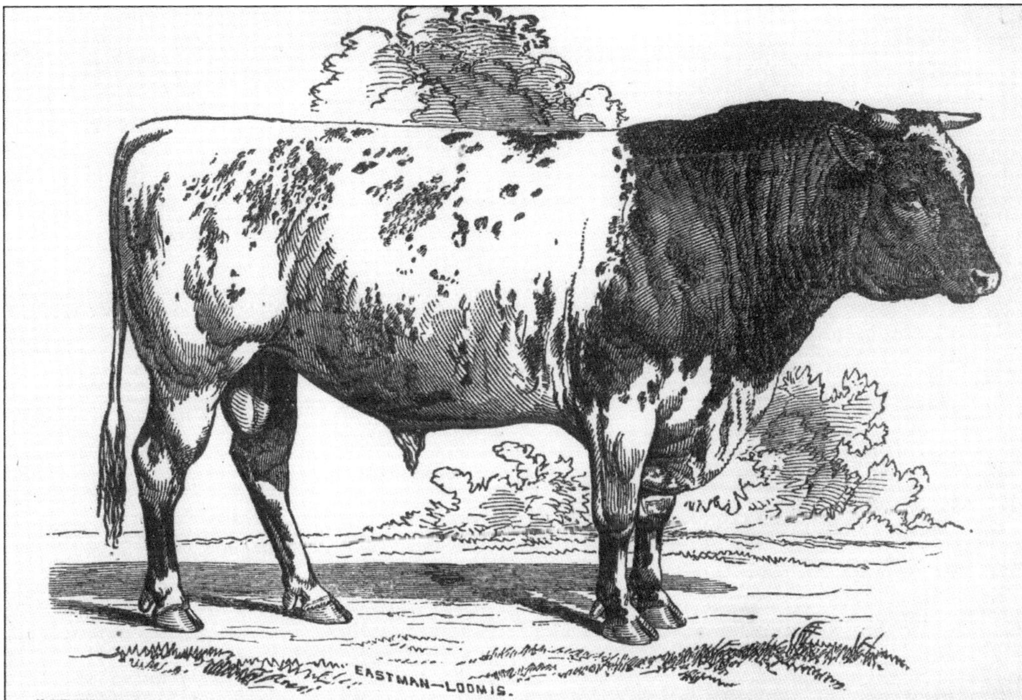

"GUELPH," owned by S. B. Emerson, of Mountain View, Santa Clara County. Winner of the first prize in his class; also, sweepstakes at California State Fair, at Sacramento, 1859. Roan Bull, calved in November 3d, 1856, bred by F. W. Stone, "Guelph," c. w. got by imperial "John O. Gaunt, 2d," (13,089), dam, "Young Velvet," (11,788); Gr. Gr. D. "Velvet," by "Cossack," (1,880); Gr. Gr. Gr. D. "Victoria," by "Eclipse," (1,949); Gr. Gr. Gr. Gr. D. "Miss Points, Jr." by "Northern Light," (1,060); Gr. Gr. Gr. Gr. Gr. D. "Miss Points," by "Aid-de-Camp," (722); Gr. Gr. Gr. Gr. Gr. Gr. D. by "Charles," (127); Gr. Gr. Gr. Gr. Gr. Gr. Gr. D. by "Prince," (521); Gr. Gr. Gr. Gr. Gr. Gr. Gr. Gr. D. by "Koswick," (1,266.)

This is an image of Guelph, awarded the prize for best bull in the 1859 fair. This is what hundreds of stockmen were trying to accomplish, to win a grand prize at the State Fair. Guelph's lineage is detailed back eight generations. Besides winning the premium of about $40, the owner, S. B. Emerson, could probably be assured of making a fair amount of income from stud fees. (CSH.)

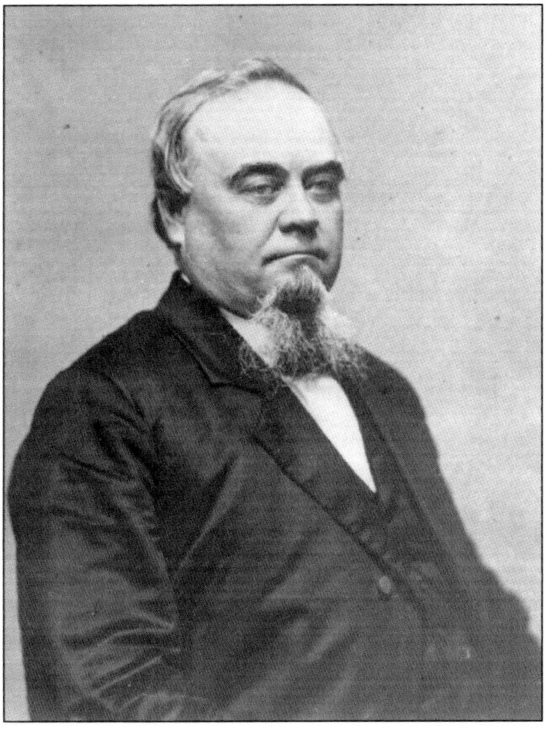

In 1861, the fair was permanently located in Sacramento. One of the main proponents of this was Sacramento judge E. B. Crocker. During the 1859 meeting of the California State Agricultural Society, which lasted at least three days, he argued passionately that the fair should be held in one location, Sacramento. The 1859 and 1860 fairs were held in Sacramento as well. (CSH.)

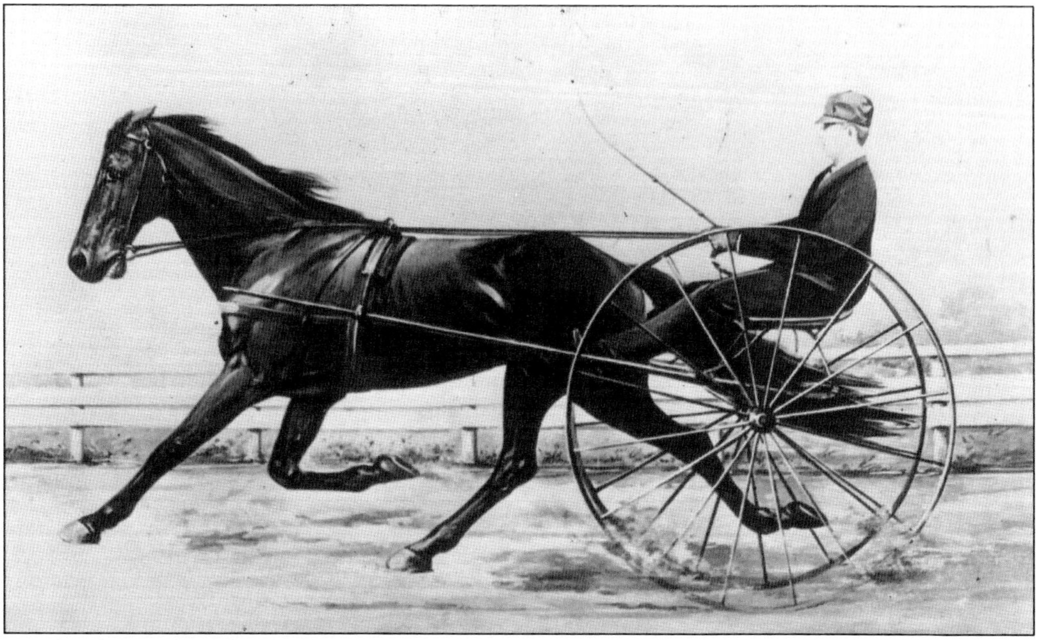

Besides thoroughbred racing, the State Fair also featured harness racing from a very early period. This 1877 image of a trotter, sulky, and jockey is by Eadweard Muybridge. Muybridge is best known for his "The Horse in Motion" photographs that showed that a horse's hooves do leave the ground when galloping. Some believe the images were taken at the Agricultural Park in Sacramento. (CSH.)

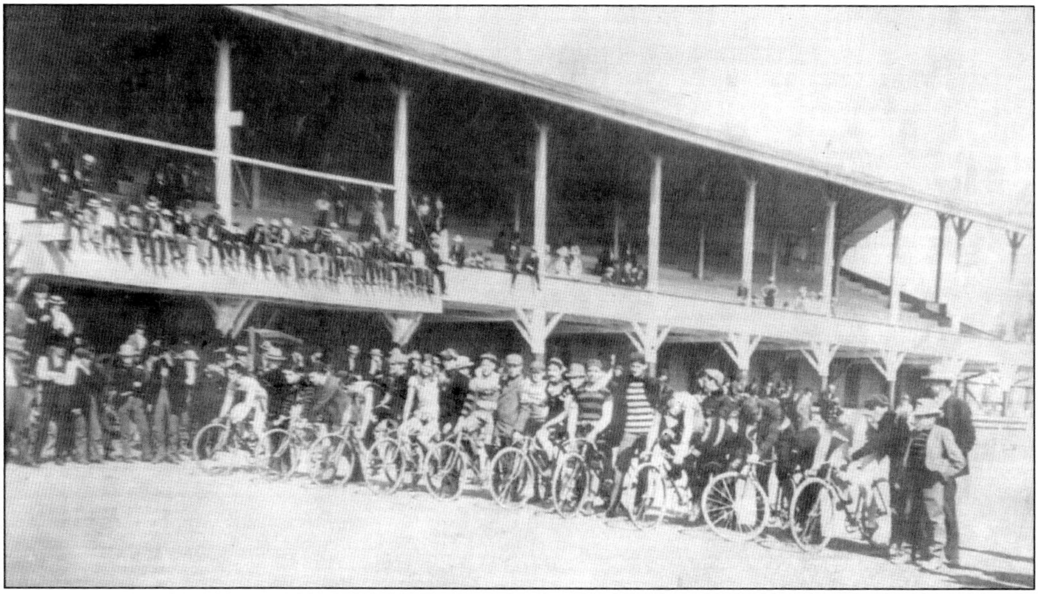

This image of the grandstand at the California State Agricultural Park racetrack is from 1900. The track was used for many events, including this tryout to join the Sacramento Wheelmen, Sacramento's premier bicycling club. The land was purchased by a committee led by Dr. J. F. Morse in 1861. It was used by the Society until 1909, when the fair was moved to Broadway and Stockton Boulevard. (CSH.)

The State Fair made a point of bringing spectacle to its annual run. One way to do that was to display the latest technology or things that most people had not seen. This c. 1895 photograph shows a balloon rising above the grandstand at Agricultural Park. It is probably safe to assume that most of those attending had never before seen a hot air balloon. (CSH.)

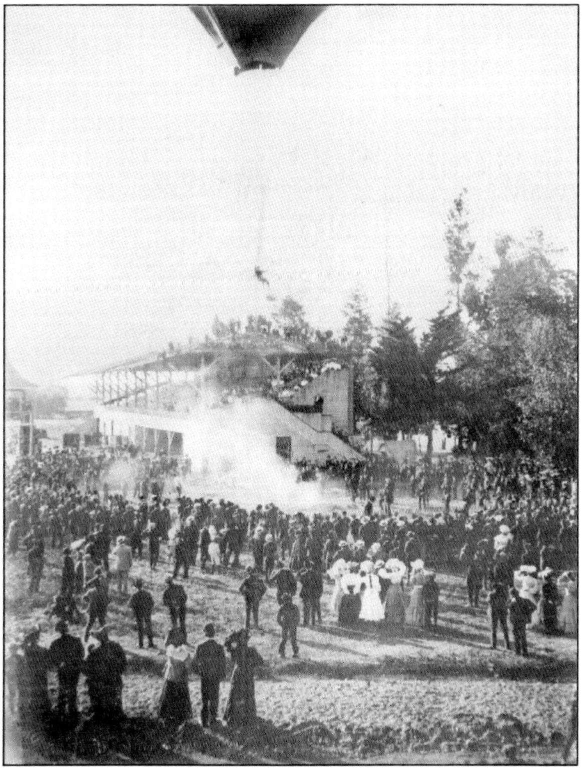

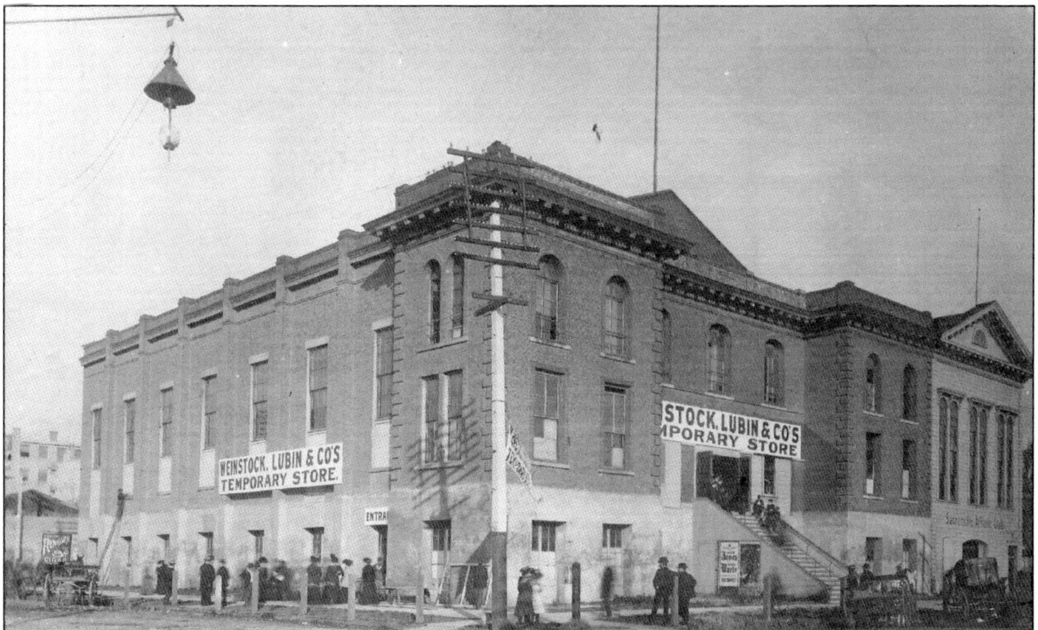

The Agricultural Hall at Sixth and M Streets was used for the exhibitions of the State Fair until 1884. It was sold at auction in November 1883 to Ben F. Crocker for $15,000. In 1903, it was used by Weinstocks Lubin as a temporary store after a fire destroyed their original store. (CSH.)

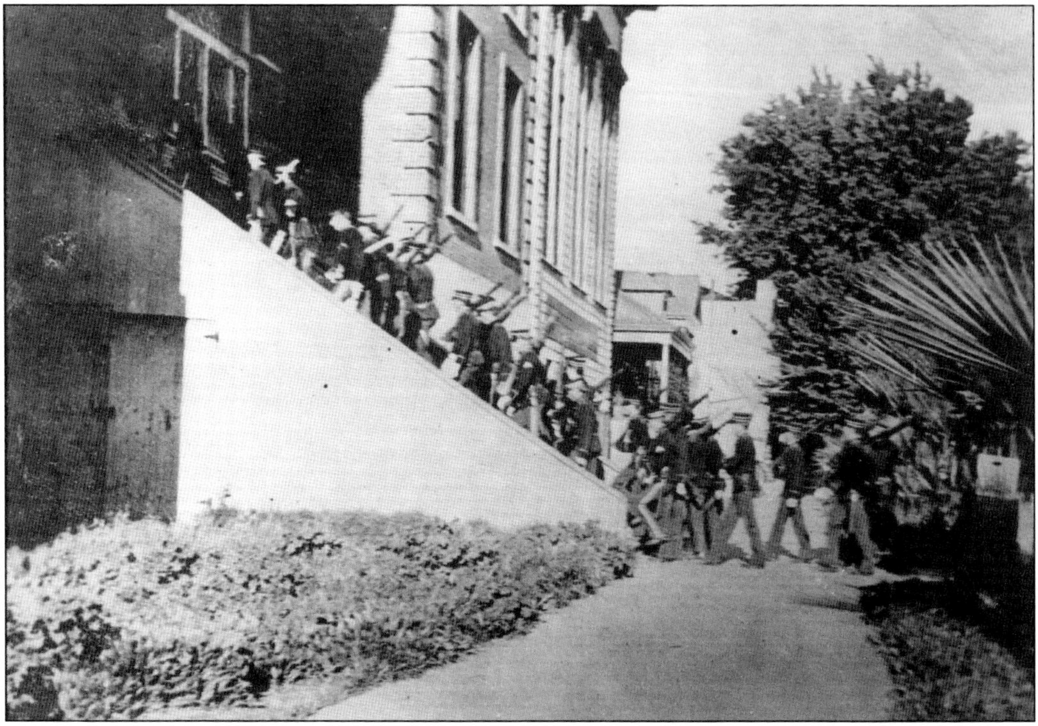

After being used by Weinstocks Lubin, the Agricultural Hall was an armory for the national guard until 1912. Soldiers are seen here entering the building in this *c.* 1907 photograph. (CSH.)

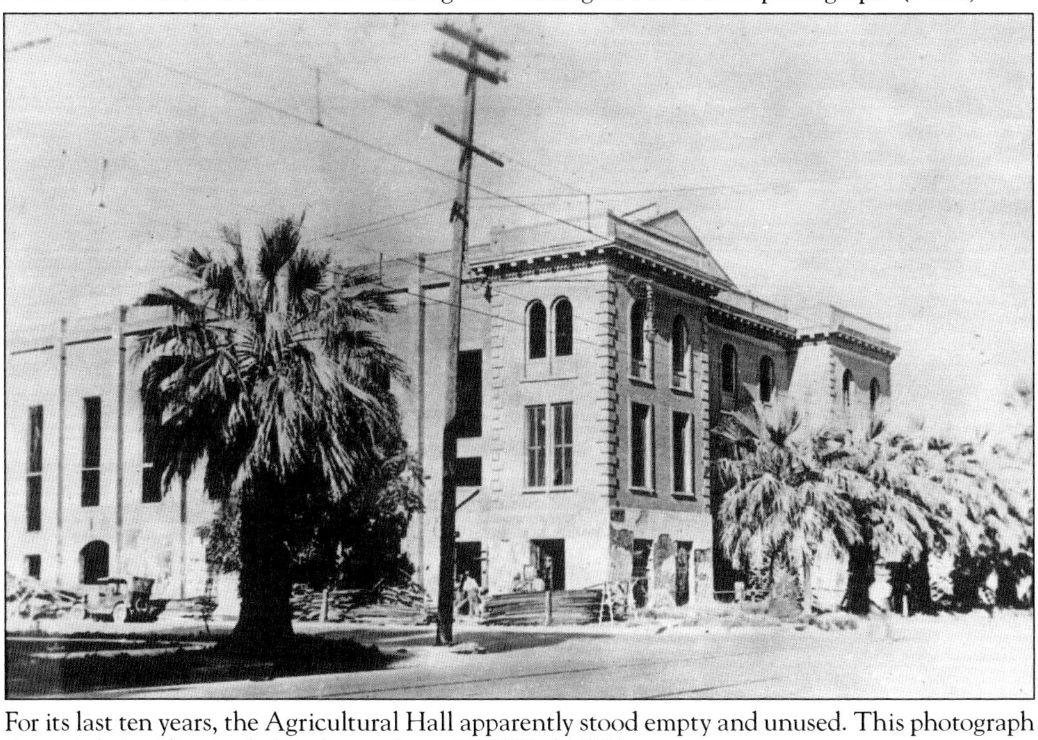

For its last ten years, the Agricultural Hall apparently stood empty and unused. This photograph shows it being dismantled and torn down in 1922. (CSH.)

Two

CAPITOL PARK

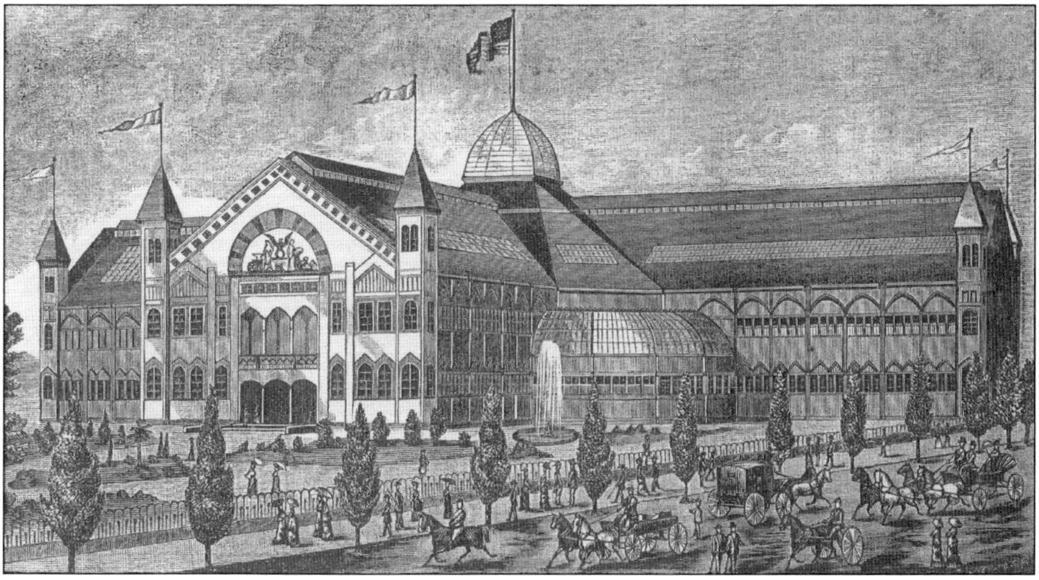

By the 1880s, the State Fair had grown so large that expansion became necessary and a new exposition building was erected in Capitol Park at Fifteenth and N Streets. In an overwhelming vote in 1883, Sacramento agreed to put up $30,000 for the construction of the pavilion, the largest of its kind in the United States. A fatal construction accident delayed completion until January 22, 1884. (CSH.)

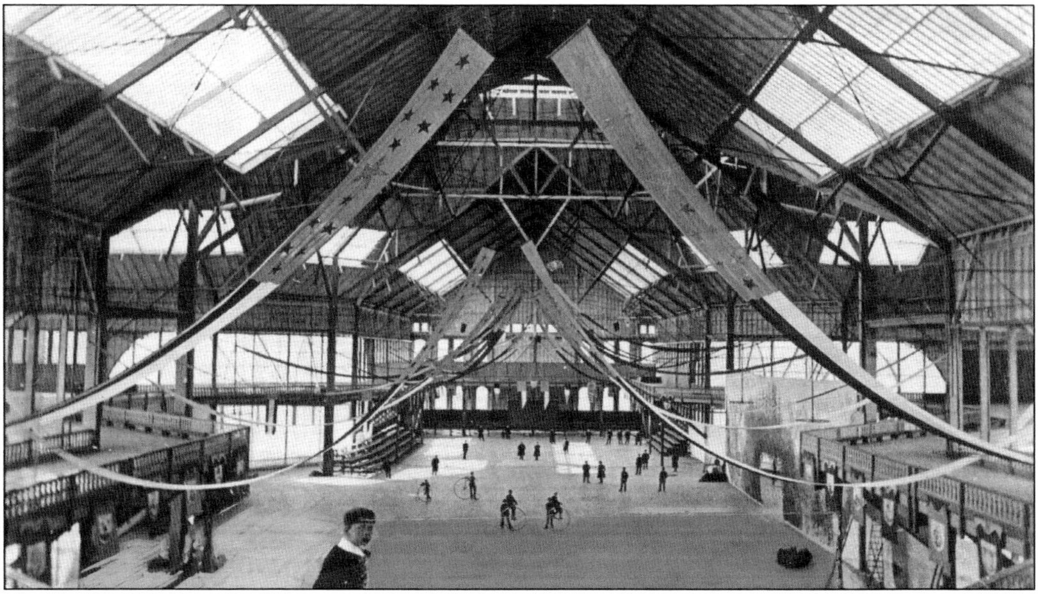

The size of the interior of the new Agricultural Hall is obvious in this undated photograph taken during a bicycling event. This view appears to be looking from the back of the building toward the front. (CSH.)

Louis F. Bruener, one of the sons of Bruener's Furniture founder John Bruener, is seen in this c. 1890 photograph in front of the Agricultural Hall. The image clearly shows the south side of the main entrance. The buggy is decorated for a parade. Bruener's companion is unidentified. (CSH.)

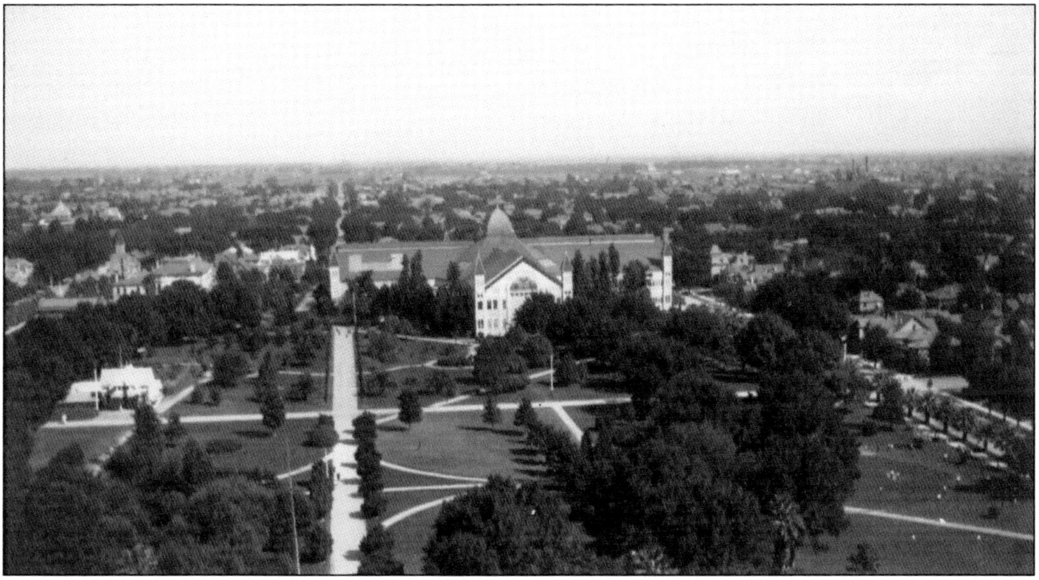

Taken from the top of the state capitol building around 1905, this photograph shows just how much of Capitol Park the pavilion took up at N Street, to the right, and Fifteenth Street, behind the building. A picnic or baseball game is seen in the lower right corner. (CSH.)

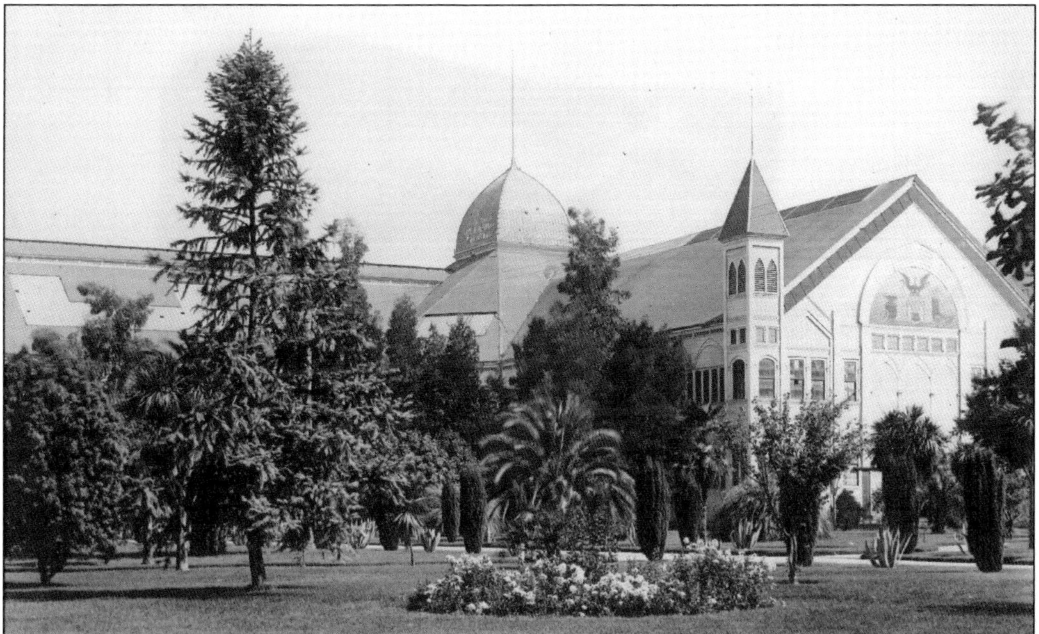

The pavilion was an imposing structure when seen from the ground. This photograph shows some of the architectural details and landscaping. It was probably taken about 1909 or shortly thereafter, as a couple of small windows look to be broken. (CSH.)

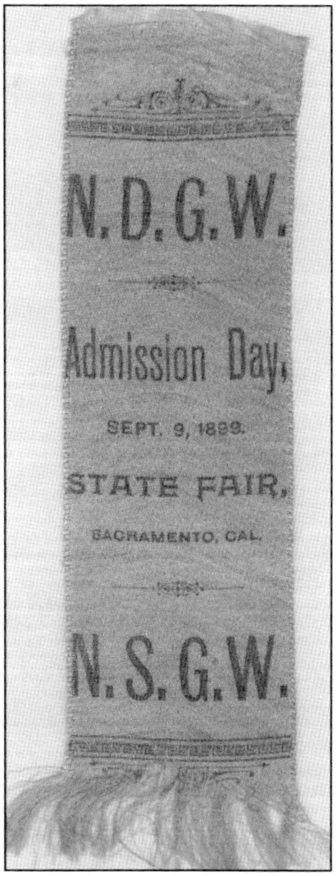

The Native Sons and Native Daughters of the Golden West were always enthusiastic supporters of the fair. They oversaw the annual Admission Day festivities held at the State Fair. This ribbon from 1899 commemorates the event. The Sons and Daughters also put on the Grand Electrical Carnival of Lights of 1895 to celebrate Sacramento as the first U.S. city to receive hydroelectric power. (Sacramento Room, Sacramento Public Library.)

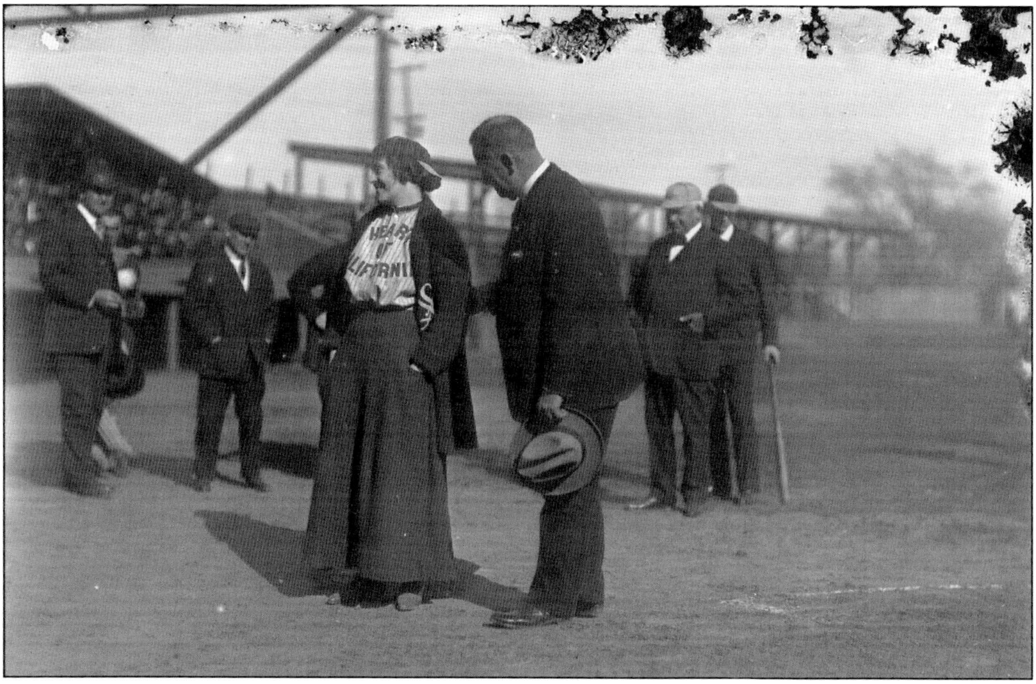

The racetrack at Agricultural Park was also used for baseball games from time to time. This glassplate negative from the 1890s shows such an event. Clearly visible are the extra bleacher seats on the north end of the grandstand. (CSH.)

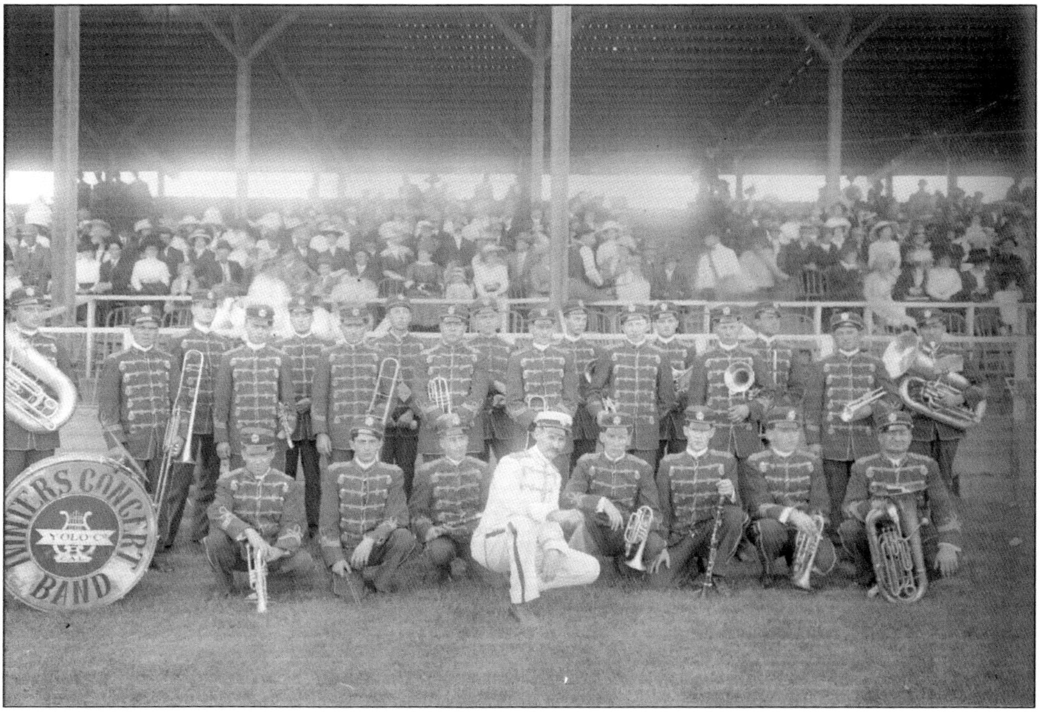

This undated glassplate negative, also probably from the mid 1890s, captures the Winters Concert Band, from Yolo County, in front of the grandstand at Agricultural Park. The conductor may be impatient with the process as he is waving his baton in his hand. (CSH.)

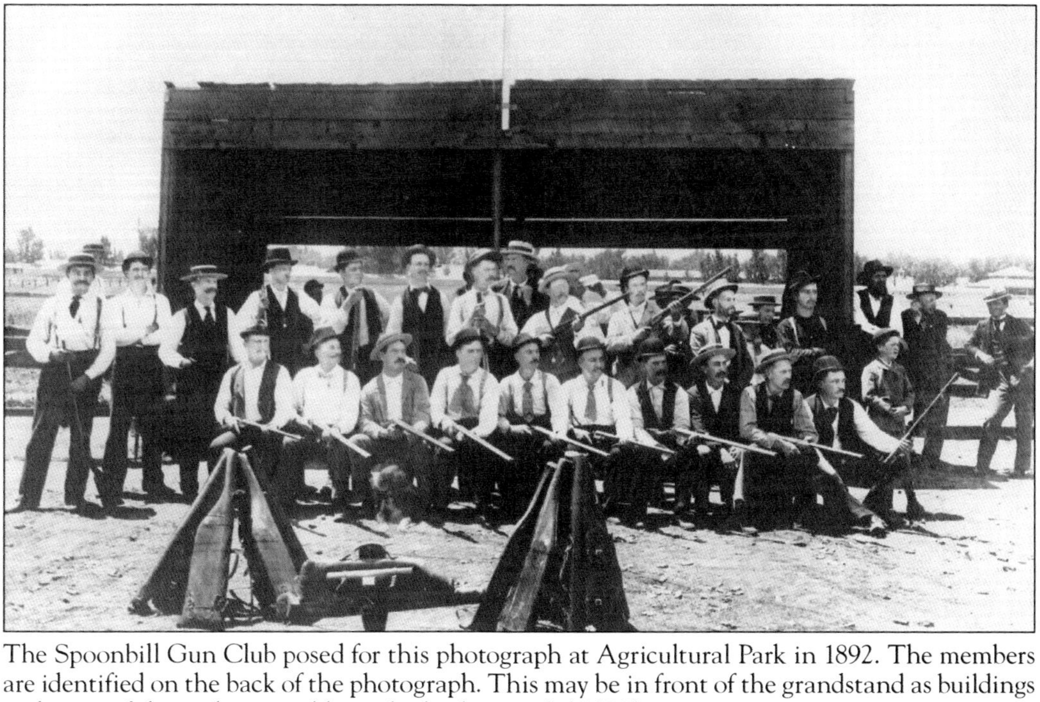

The Spoonbill Gun Club posed for this photograph at Agricultural Park in 1892. The members are identified on the back of the photograph. This may be in front of the grandstand as buildings and tents of the park are visible in the background. (CSH.)

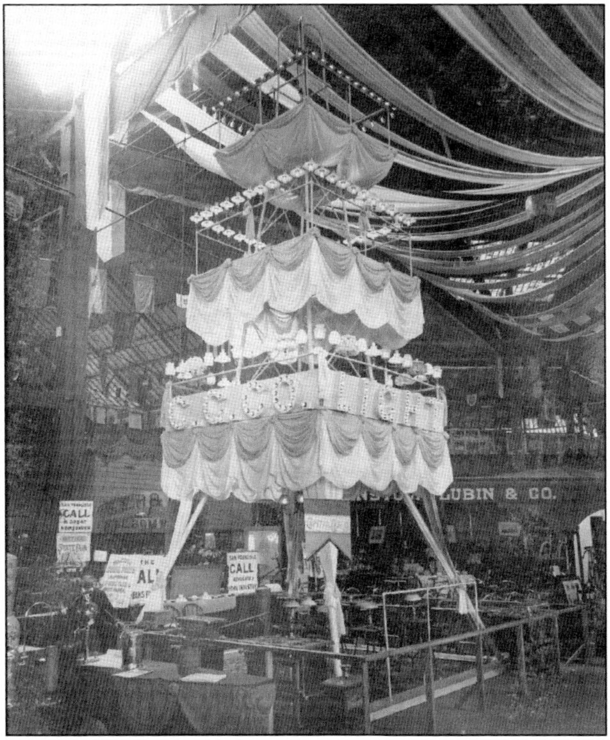

The size of the new hall made it possible to install larger and more grandiose exhibits. Sacramento was increasing its industrial ability, as this "Display of Light, Heat, and Power" by the Capital Gas Company in 1895 shows. They provided electric arc lights, incandescent lights, and Welsbach gas lamps, plain and ornamental. The exhibit was awarded the Agricultural Society Special Medal and Diploma. (Sacramento Room, Sacramento Public Library.)

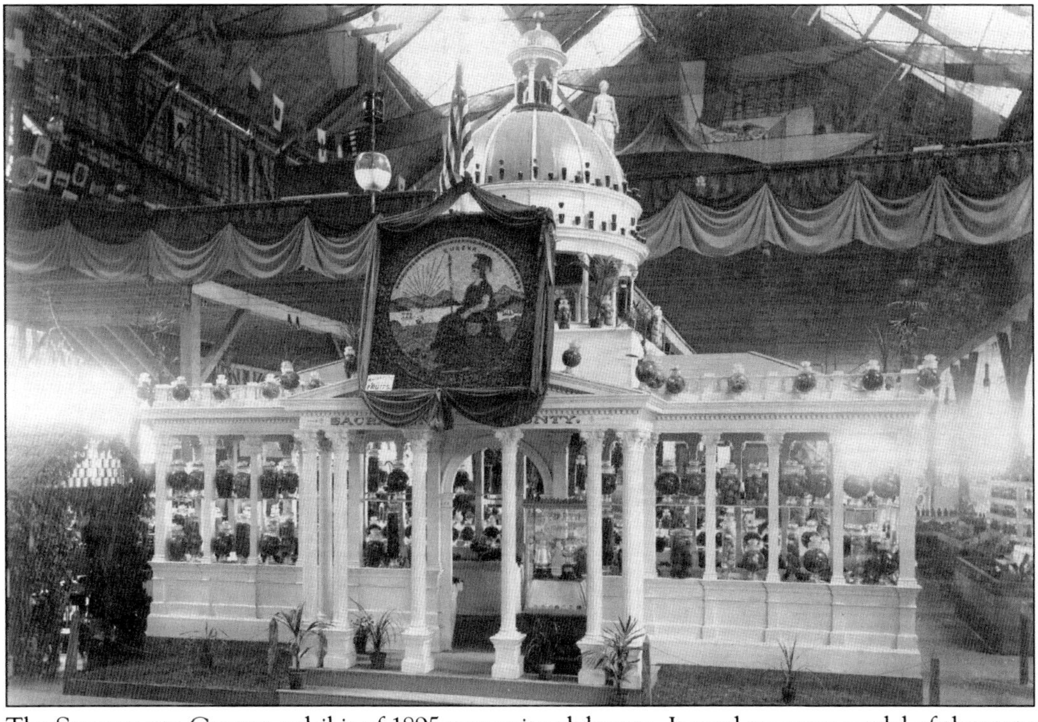

The Sacramento County exhibit of 1895 was quite elaborate. It used an open model of the state capitol filled with examples of the agricultural products of the county. (Sacramento Room, Sacramento Public Library.)

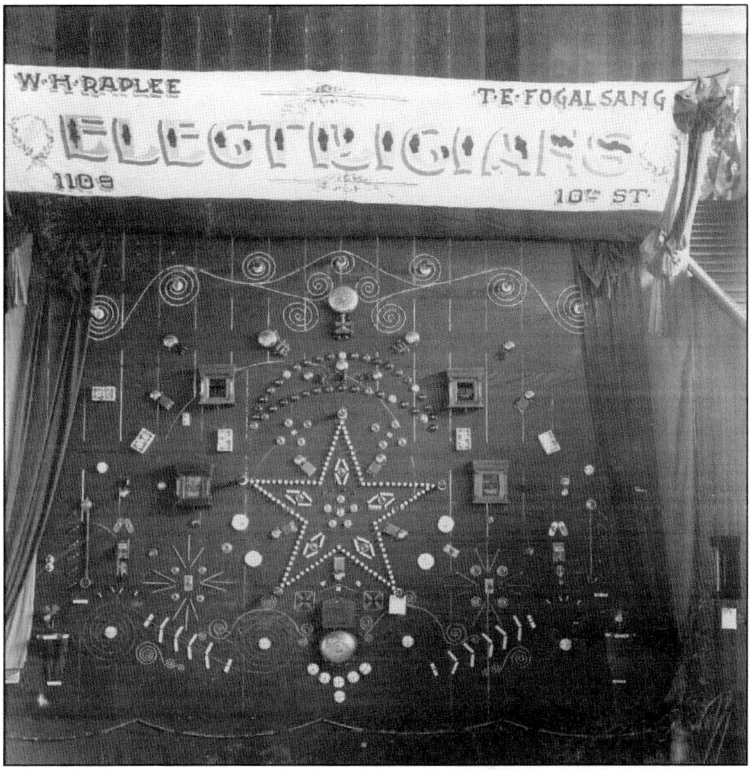

As the caption for this photograph of Fogalsang and Raplee, Electricians, states, 1895 was a big year in Sacramento: "July 13, just weeks before the fair's opening, the nation's first hydroelectric alternating-current power was sent via uninsulated copper wire a distance of 22 miles." As this exhibit demonstrated, Fogalsang and Raplee was ready to supply the electrical needs of Sacramento residents. (Sacramento Room, Sacramento Public Library.)

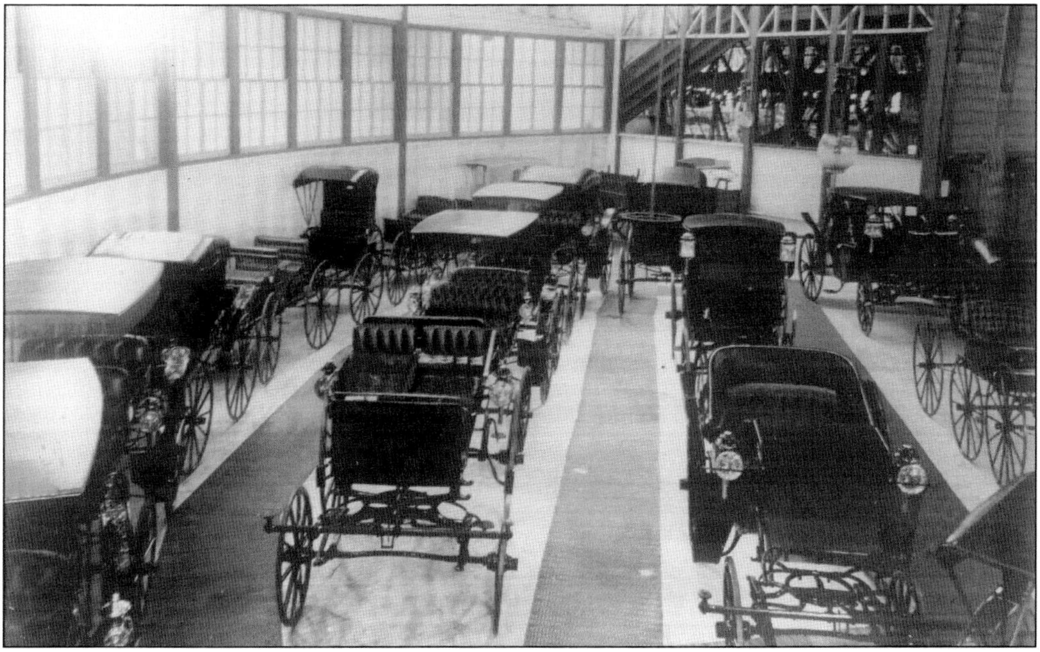

Another large exhibit in 1895 was by Schaw, Ingram, Batcher and Company. The company retailed Studebaker wagons, buggies, and carts; Remington bicycles, Oliver plows, McCormick mowers, and many other quality items in Sacramento. This exhibit was located in the area where the wings of the hall intersected. (CSH.)

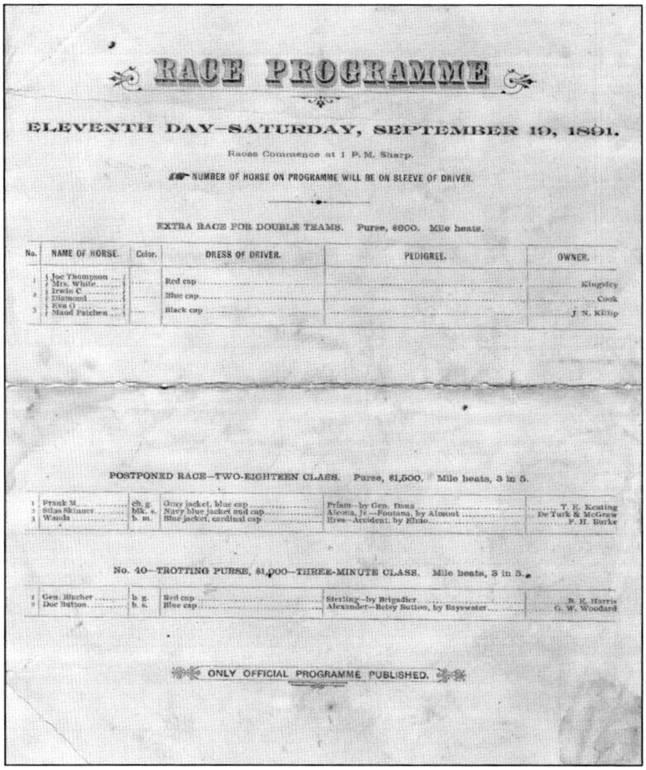

RACE PROGRAMME

ELEVENTH DAY—SATURDAY, SEPTEMBER 19, 1891.

Races Commence at 1 P. M. Sharp.

NUMBER OF HORSE ON PROGRAMME WILL BE ON SLEEVE OF DRIVER.

EXTRA RACE FOR DOUBLE TEAMS. Purse, $600. Mile heats.

No.	NAME OF HORSE.	Color.	DRESS OF DRIVER.	PEDIGREE.	OWNER.
1	Joe Thompson / Mrs. White		Red cap		Kingsley
2	Irwin C. / Diamond		Blue cap		Cook
3	Eva O / Maud Patchen		Black cap		J. N. Killip

POSTPONED RACE—TWO-EIGHTEEN CLASS. Purse, $1,500. Mile heats, 3 in 5.

No.	NAME OF HORSE.	Color.	DRESS OF DRIVER.	PEDIGREE.	OWNER.
1	Frank M.	ch. g.	Gray jacket, blue cap	Priam—by Gen. Dana	T. E. Keating
2	Silas Skinner	blk. s.	Navy blue jacket and cap	Alcona, Jr.—Fontana, by Almont	De Turk & McGraw
3	Wanda	b. m.	Blue jacket, cardinal cap	Eros—Accident, by Elmo	F. H. Burke

No. 40—TROTTING PURSE, $1,000—THREE-MINUTE CLASS. Mile heats, 3 in 5.

No.	NAME OF HORSE.	Color.	DRESS OF DRIVER.	PEDIGREE.	OWNER.
1	Gen. Blucher	b. g.	Red cap	Sterling—by Brigadier	B. E. Harris
2	Doc Button	b. s.	Blue cap	Alexander—Betsy Button, by Bayswater	G. W. Woodard

ONLY OFFICIAL PROGRAMME PUBLISHED.

Horse racing has been a big part of the State Fair. Shown here is the race program for the eleventh day of racing, on September 19, 1891. The cover of the program features the logo of the California State Agricultural Society. (Sacramento Room, Sacramento Public Library.)

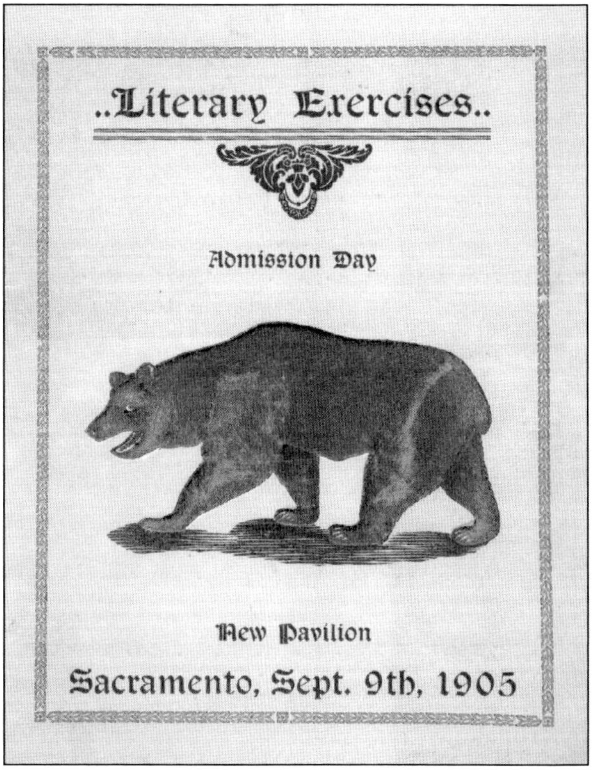

The Native Sons of the Golden West always held an event celebrating the date of California's admission to the Union, September 9, during the State Fair. In 1905, the event featured a series of readings by prominent citizens and officials about California and its significance to the United States. (Sacramento Room, Sacramento Public Library.)

Three

Broadway and Stockton Boulevard

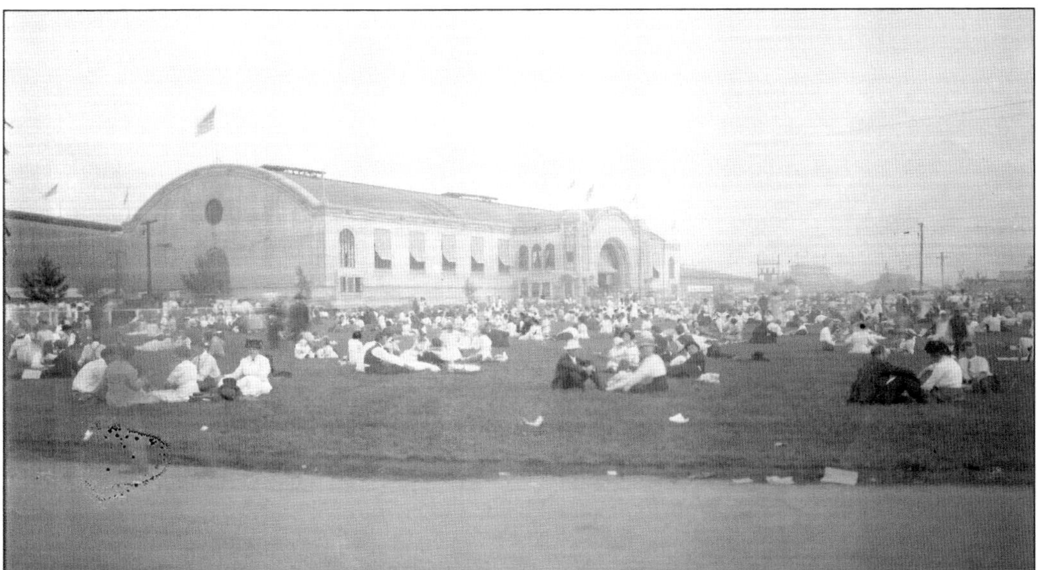

In 1904, the State Agricultural Society decided to move the site of the fair. In 1909, the fairgrounds were officially relocated to Broadway and Stockton Boulevard. This photograph shows the Horticultural Building with a large crowd on the lawn in front. Fire destroyed the building in 1916. This glass plate negative was taken around 1911, possibly as early as 1909, judging by the lack of trees. (CSH.)

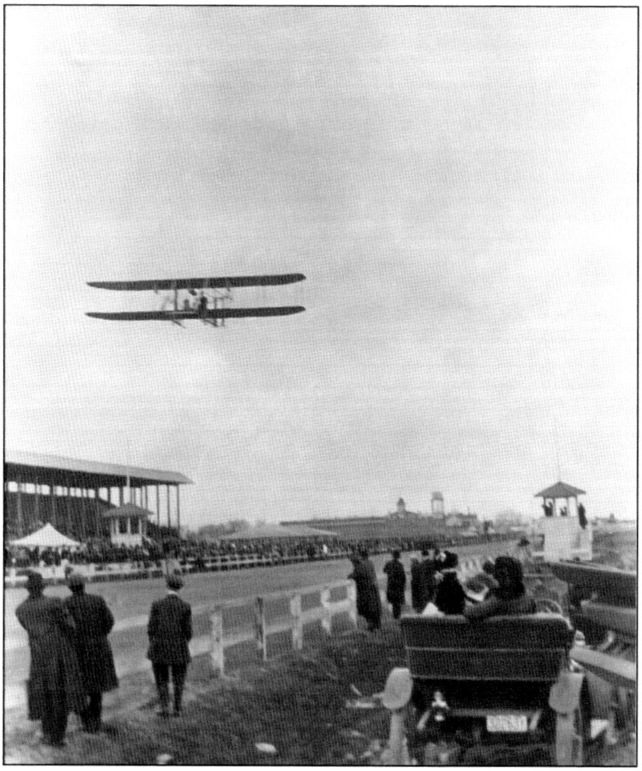

The fair always offers exciting events for fairgoers. The big feature in 1910 was a flight by aviator Charles K. Hamilton, who flew faster than a mile a minute, a world record at the time. He avoided death when the engine misfired, and he nearly hit some telegraph lines while trying to land. Hamilton was bruised during the landing but was able to walk away. (CSH.)

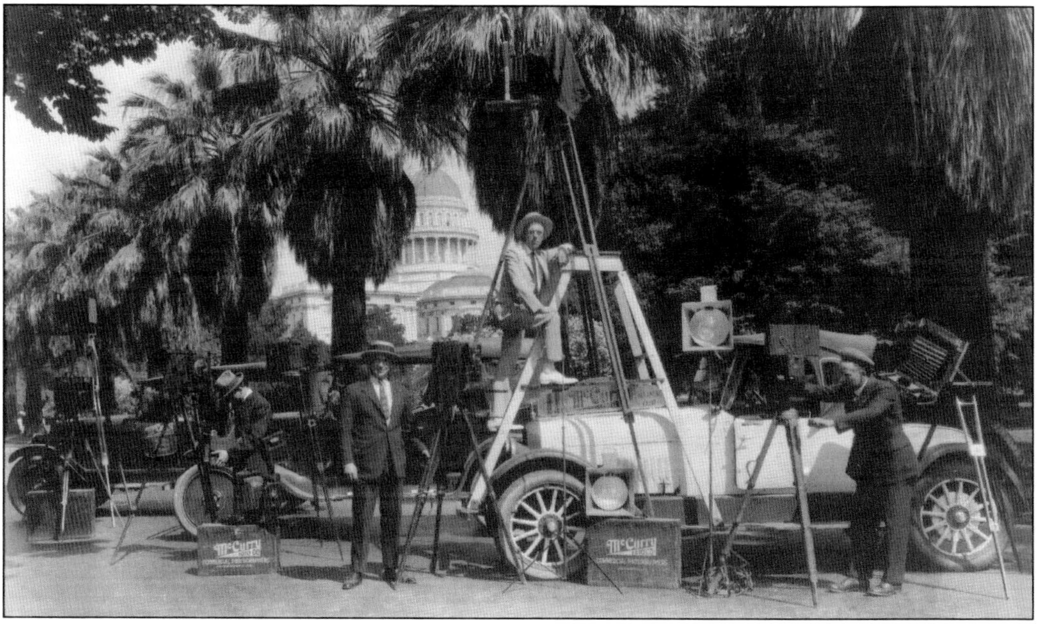

In 1909, Harold McCurry was named the official photographer of the California State Fair. McCurry was well acquainted with J. A. Filcher, the secretary of the state agricultural board, and had just completed work for the well-received San Luis Obispo and Monterey Counties exhibits at the St. Louis Exposition. The McCurrry Foto Company continued to work with the State Fair for decades. (CSH.)

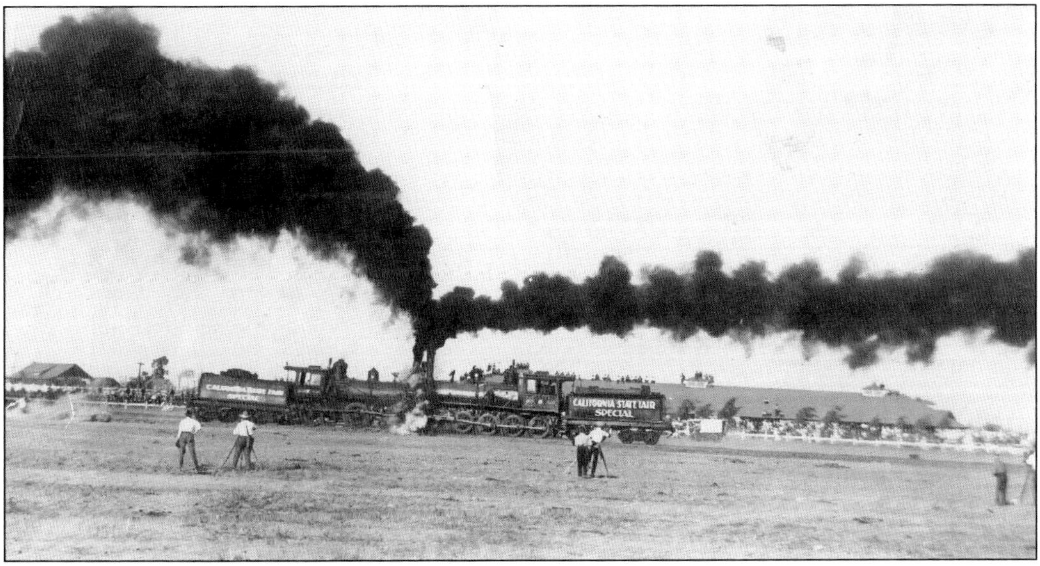

Starting in 1913, the State Fair began crashing trains head-on to amuse fairgoers. As official photographer, McCurry was required to get close for a good shot. This photograph shows just how close photographers were to the crash at the moment of impact. To the far left, one of the engineers is seen tumbling on the ground after jumping off the engine. (CSH.)

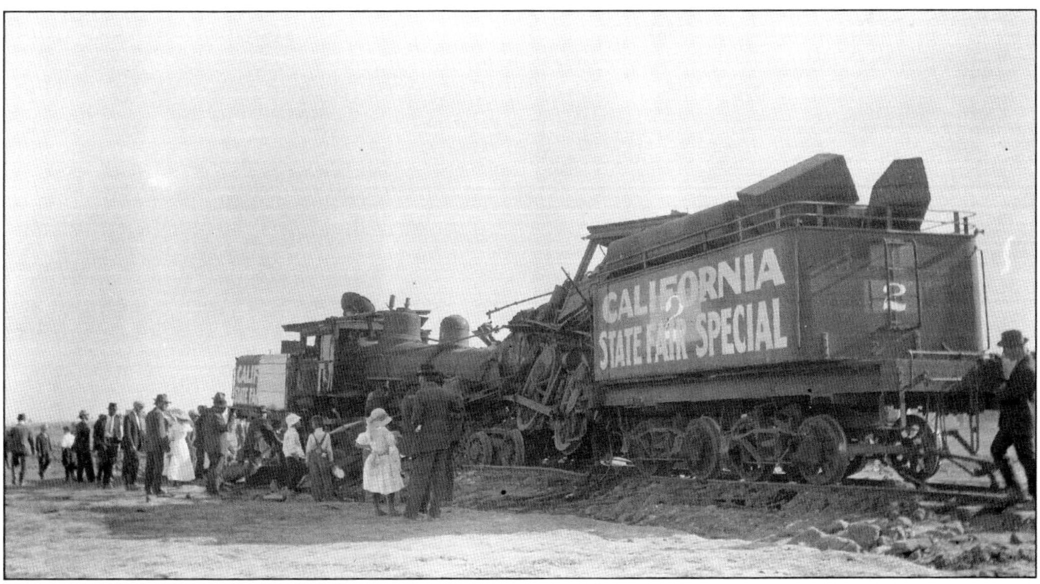

The aftermath of the train crash of September 5, 1916. Spectators were allowed to get in close to see firsthand how much damage two trains coming together at 25 miles per hour can cause. The practice was stopped after 1917, officially due to the shortage of metal caused by World War I. Another likely reason was that the Southern Pacific Railroad was running low on engines. (CSH.)

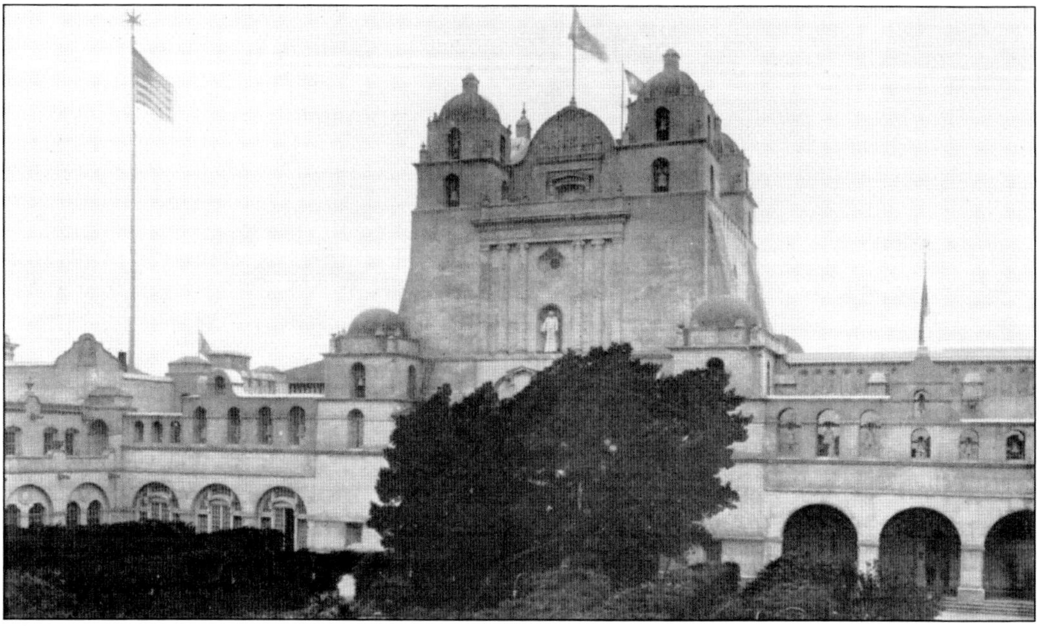

The State Fair was not held in 1915 due to the Panama Pacific International Exposition (PPIE) in San Francisco and the Panama-California Exposition in San Diego. Shown here is the California Building at the PPIE. This image and the one below are taken from the "Sacramento Valley Expositions Commissions Official Report," which covered both events. (Sacramento Room, Sacramento Public Library.)

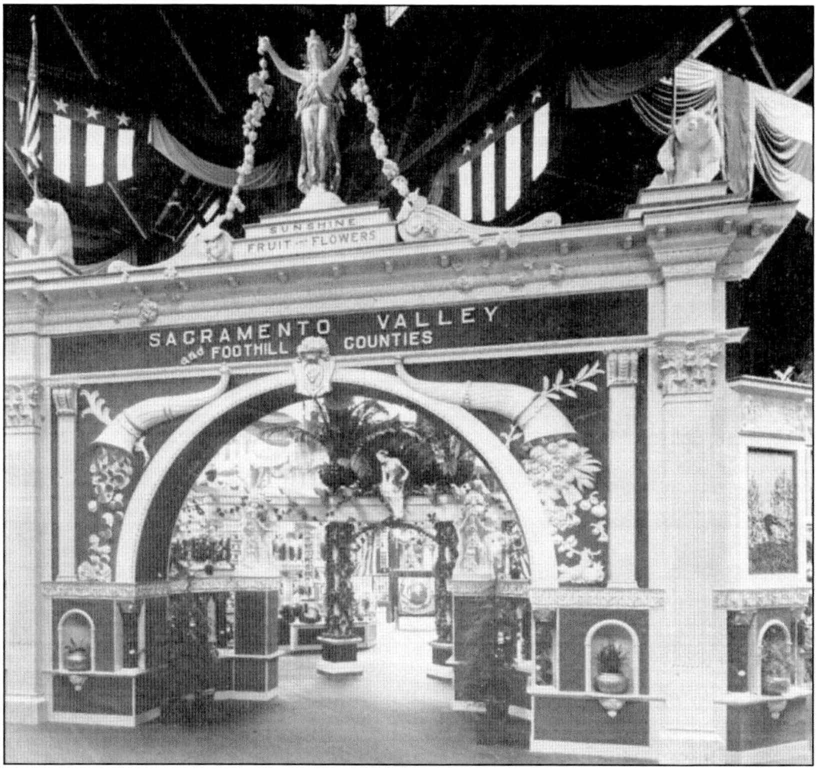

Seen here is the main arch entrance to the Sacramento Valley and Foothill Counties exhibit at the 1915 PPIE. The exhibit was quite elaborate and garnered a lot of attention. The exhibit was also set up at the Panama-California Exposition in San Diego that year. (Sacramento Room, Sacramento Public Library.)

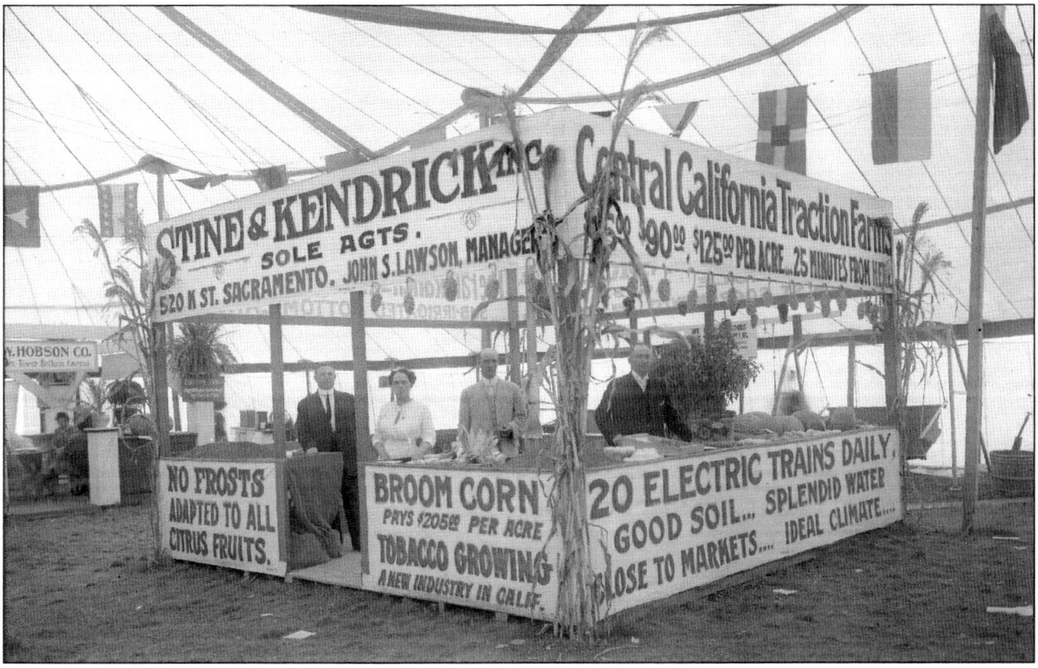

The Central California Traction Company's real estate agent, Stine & Kendrick, set up this booth in 1912 to sell land along the electric railroad's route to Stockton. The CCTC also developed the nearby Colonial Heights subdivision, whose growth, along with that of the Tahoe Park and Oak Park subdivisions, eventually led to the State Fair moving to its current site at Cal Expo. (CSH.)

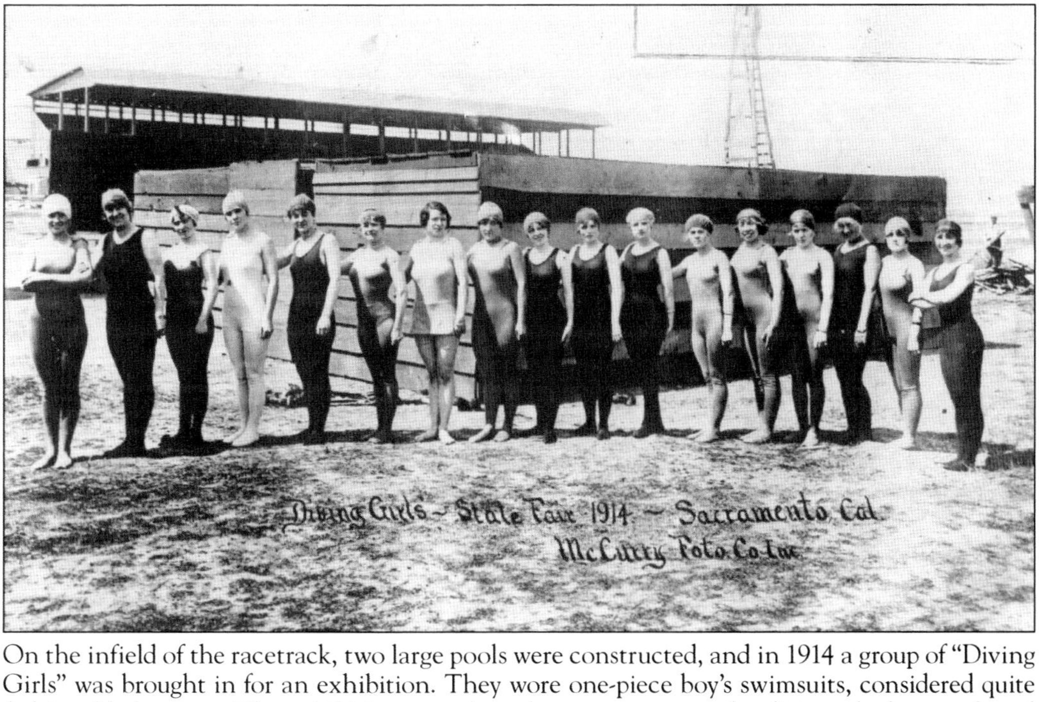

On the infield of the racetrack, two large pools were constructed, and in 1914 a group of "Diving Girls" was brought in for an exhibition. They wore one-piece boy's swimsuits, considered quite fashionable by some. The exhibition must have been a success as the diving platform and pool are seen in many later photographs, along with many different types of divers. (CSH.)

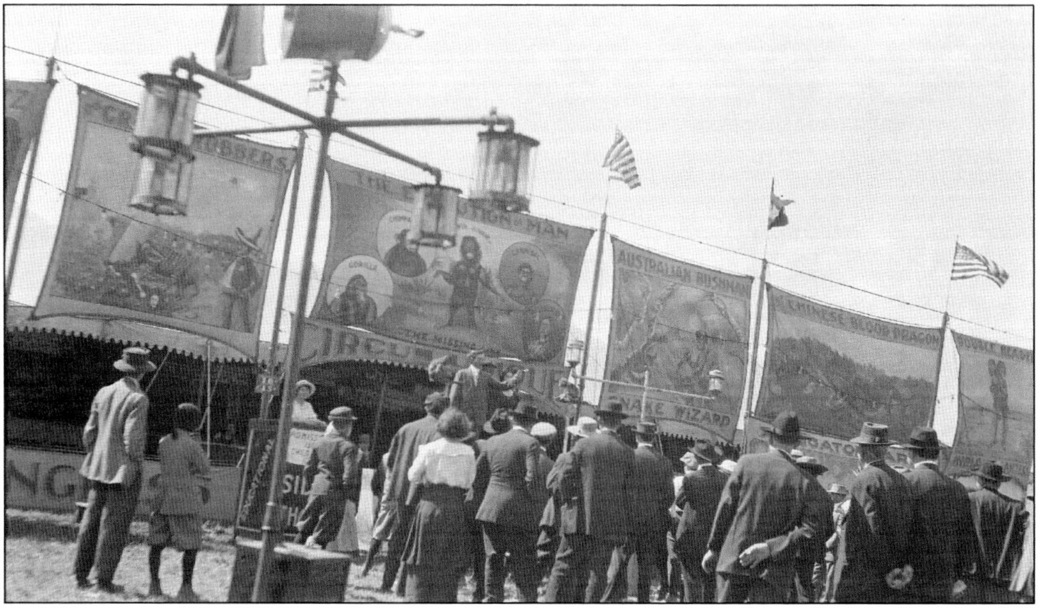

The following photographs were taken in 1916 by an unknown amateur photographer. These photographs were not official and offer a unique view of the fair. This image shows the ever popular midway sideshow. Note the banners for the Chinese Blood Dragon and the Double Headed Indian Giantess, sure to amaze and astound viewers of all ages. (CSH.)

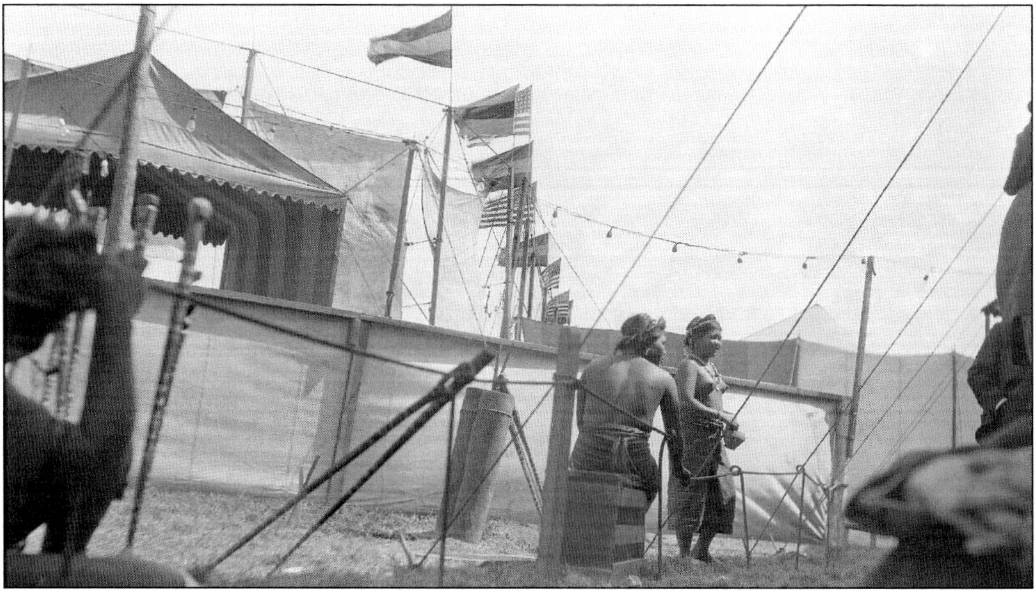

This photograph shows two indigenous Australians relaxing between performances. They were part of the Evolution of Man—Australian Bushman sideshow, advertised in the previous photograph. (CSH.)

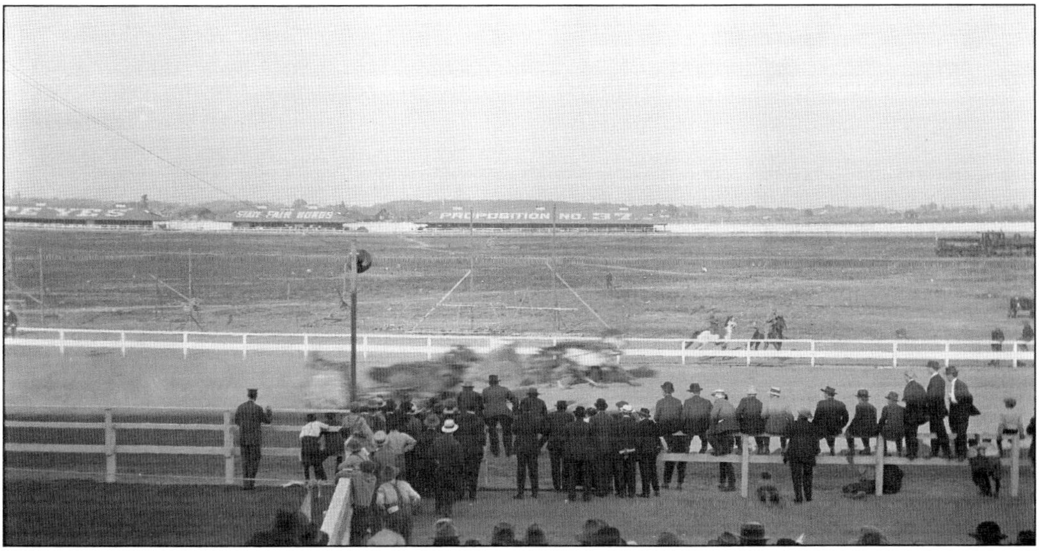

The exciting finish to a harness race in 1916 is seen here from the grandstand. This photograph captures the three buildings across the track infield painted with a political advertisement urging voters to "VOTE YES STATE FAIR BONDS PROPOSITION NO. 37." Also visible to the right is one of the locomotives seen in the image on page 29. (CSH.)

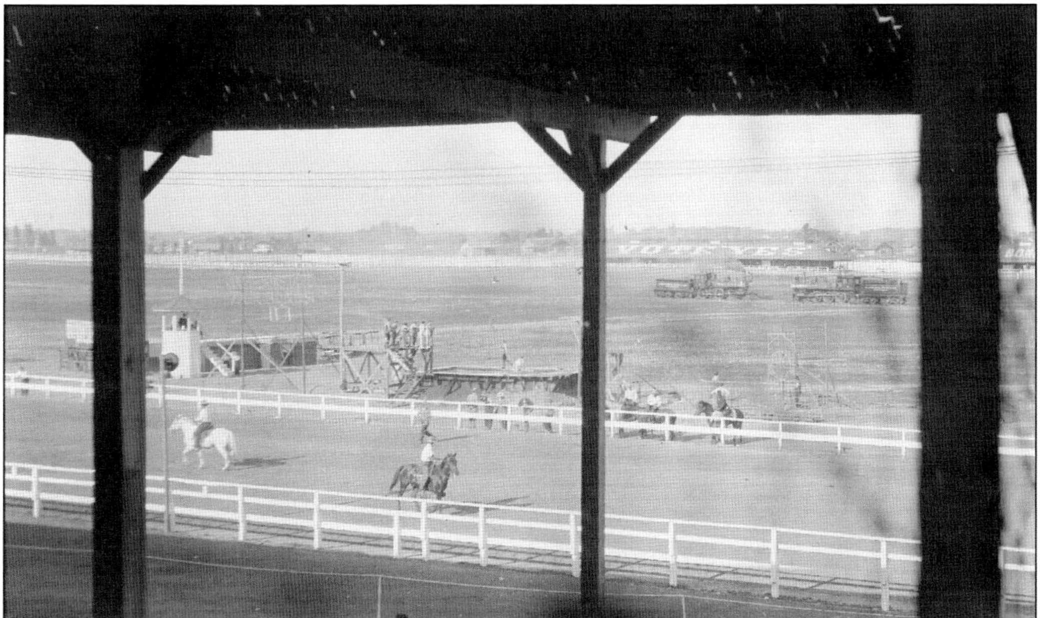

Also taken from the grandstand, this view shows the popular diving platform and pool, with several persons lined up to dive. In the background are the two trains that were crashed in 1916. Also visible is the framework for the fireworks display. The frame to the left of the diving platform spells out support for Proposition 37. (CSH.)

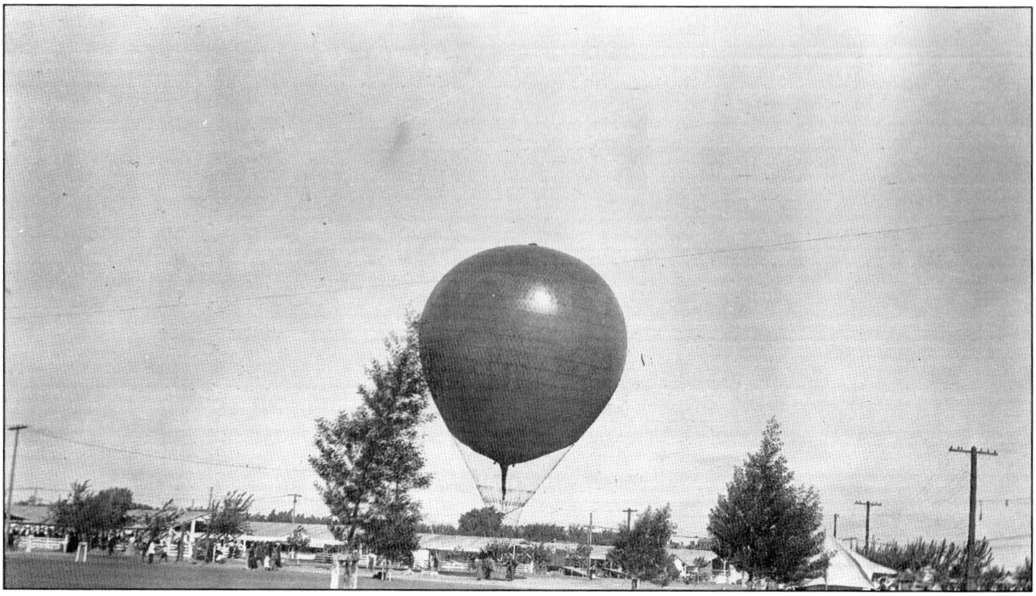

Balloons were popular attractions during the late 1800s and early 1900s. This appears to be a hydrogen balloon rather than a hot air balloon. It was launched from near the stables at the south end of the racetrack in 1916. Hydrogen is no longer used for balloons due to its flammability, as proven in the 1937 Hindenburg disaster. (CSH.)

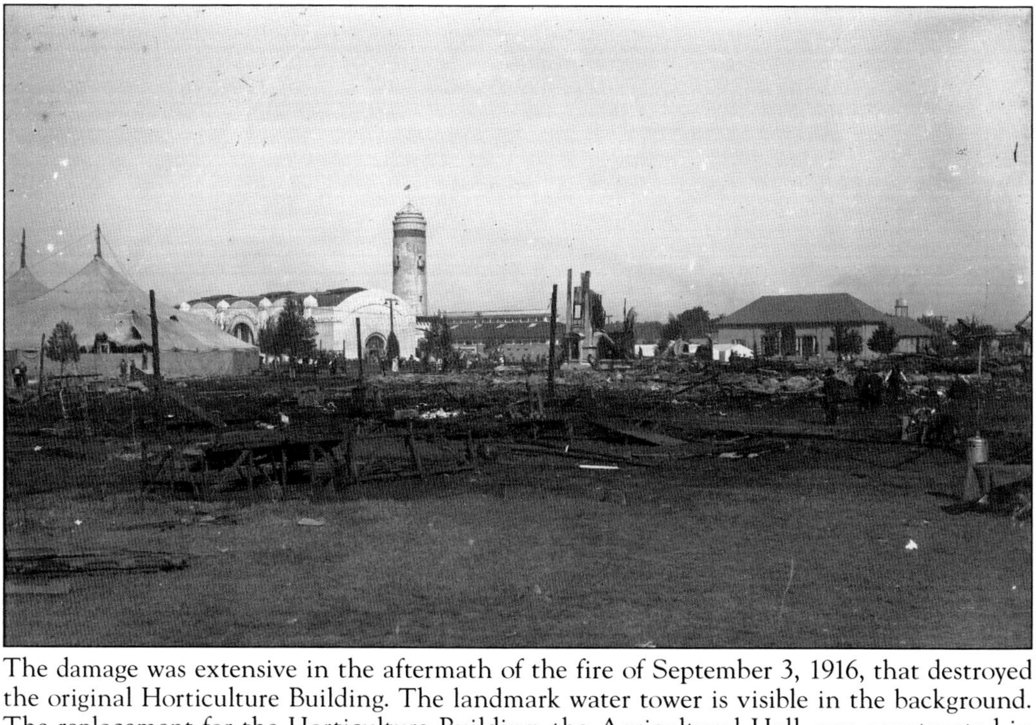

The damage was extensive in the aftermath of the fire of September 3, 1916, that destroyed the original Horticulture Building. The landmark water tower is visible in the background. The replacement for the Horticulture Building, the Agricultural Hall, was constructed in 1919. (CSH.)

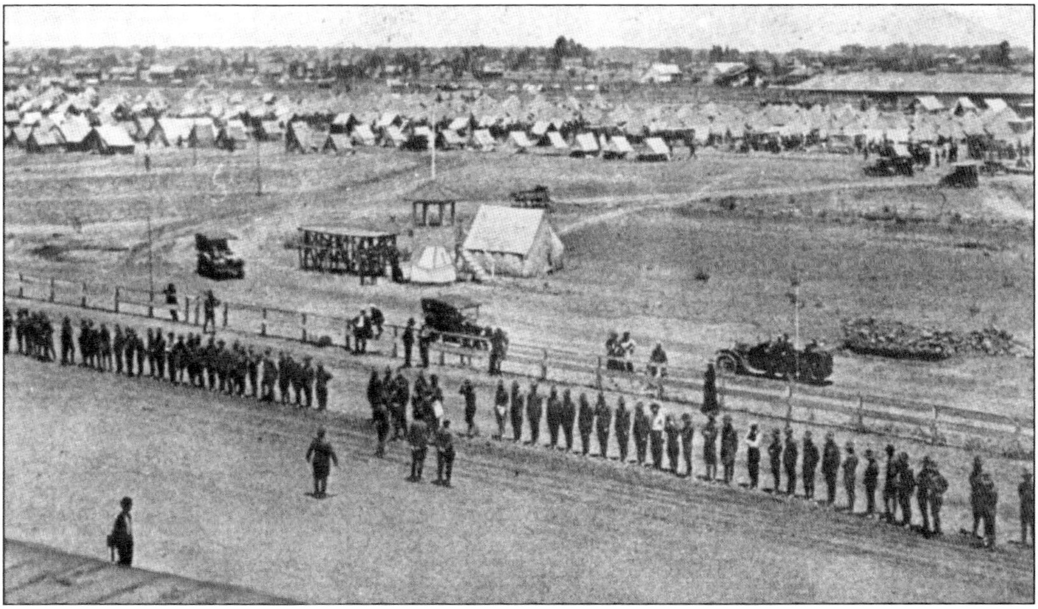

During World War I, the United States Army used the infield of the State Fair racetrack as a temporary camp, as this c. 1918 image shows. The fair did not take place from 1942 through 1946, as the Army again used the grounds as a camp during World War II. (CSH.)

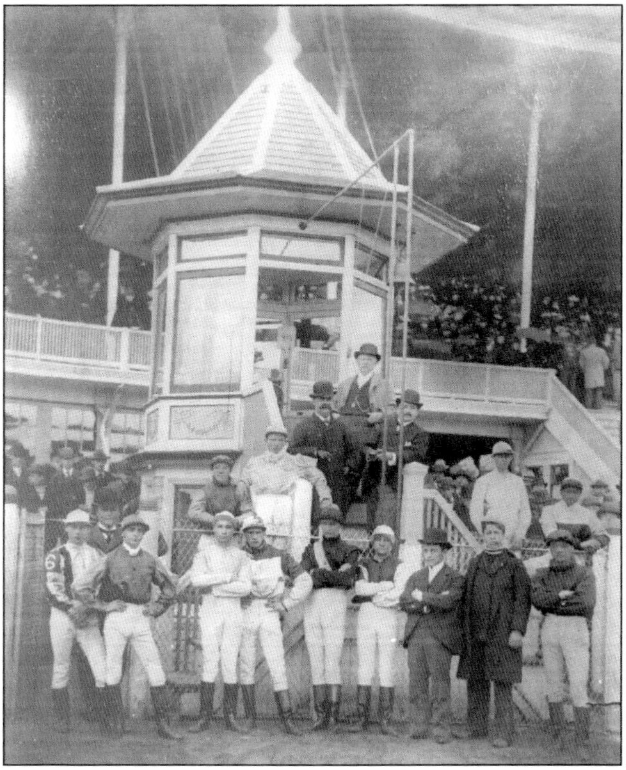

This c. 1910 image shows a group of jockeys and officials gathered together at the grandstand. Behind the wire fence, at the far right, is Jerry Chon, one of the few African Americans to ride the state fair circuit during this period. Also shown, second from the top to the right and holding a stopwatch, is David Ahern, the Sacramento County sheriff. (CSH.)

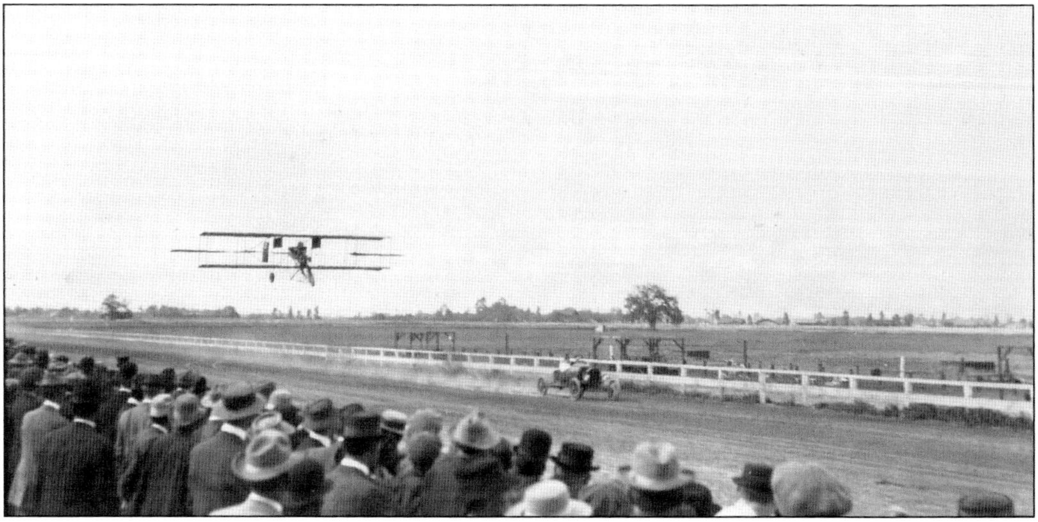

In 1912, aviator Charles Hamilton was back at the State Fair. This time, he participated in a race with Frank Ruhstaller, the well-known Sacramento brewer. This photograph captures the action as they approach the finish line. Ruhstaller appears to be leading. (CSH.)

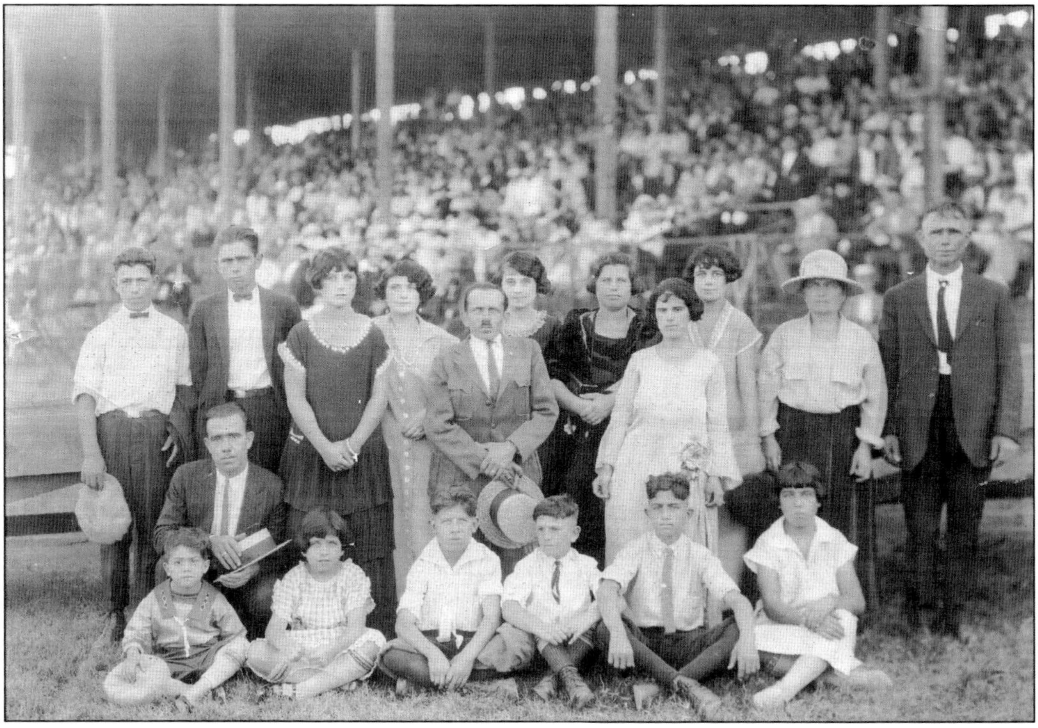

As part of the publicity for the State Fair of 1924, the Domingo family was recognized as the largest family in California, with 18 members. Governor Richardson presented them with a new car. It is believed that family members still visit the State Fair; but, with 16 children, it would be hard to imagine that none of the descendants attends. (CSH.)

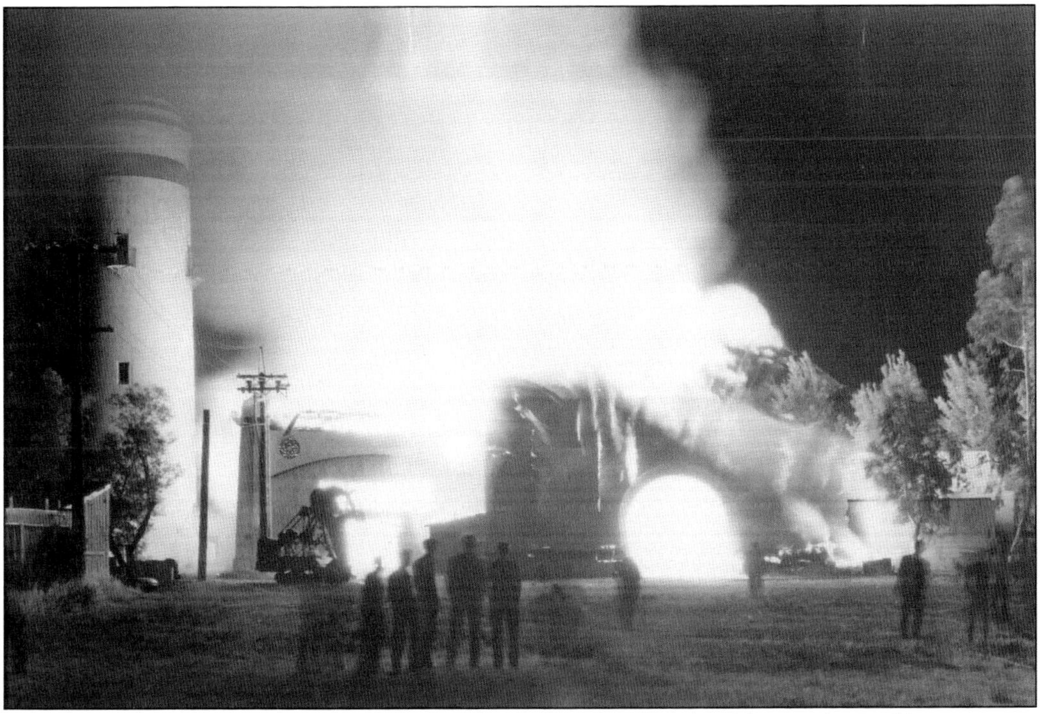

On the night of May 22, 1931, fire destroyed the Education and Public Works Building, as seen in this dramatic shot. Coincidentally, this building was due to be demolished and replaced with a larger one in time for the 1932 fair. This was not the first time fire hit the fairgrounds. In 1916, fire had destroyed the original Horticultural Hall. (Sacramento Room, Sacramento Public Library.)

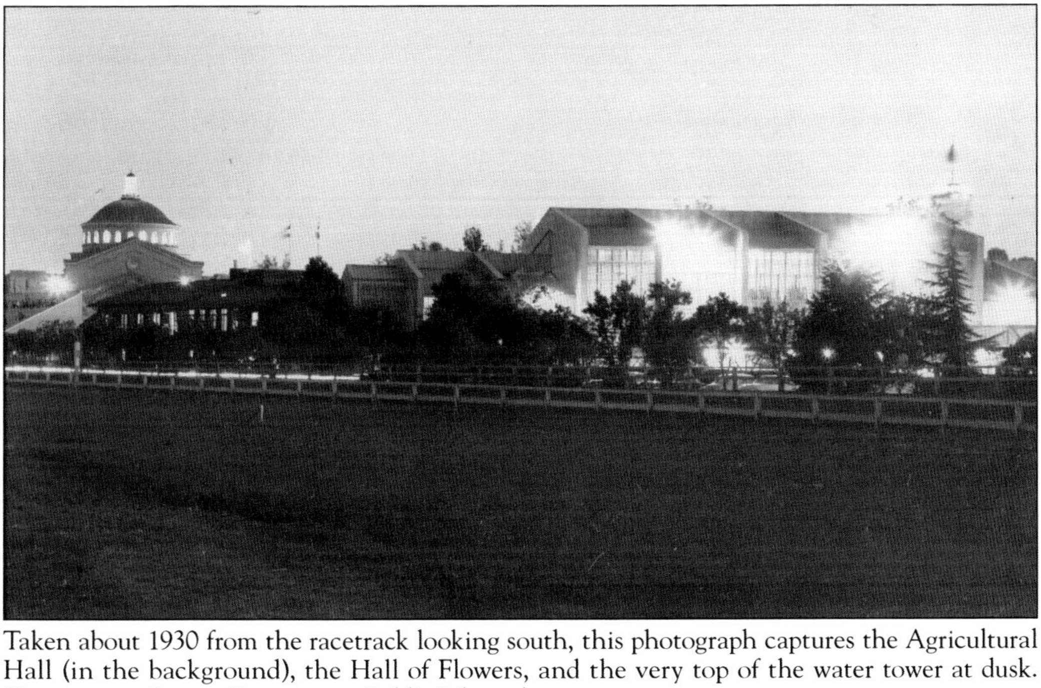

Taken about 1930 from the racetrack looking south, this photograph captures the Agricultural Hall (in the background), the Hall of Flowers, and the very top of the water tower at dusk. (Sacramento Room, Sacramento Public Library.)

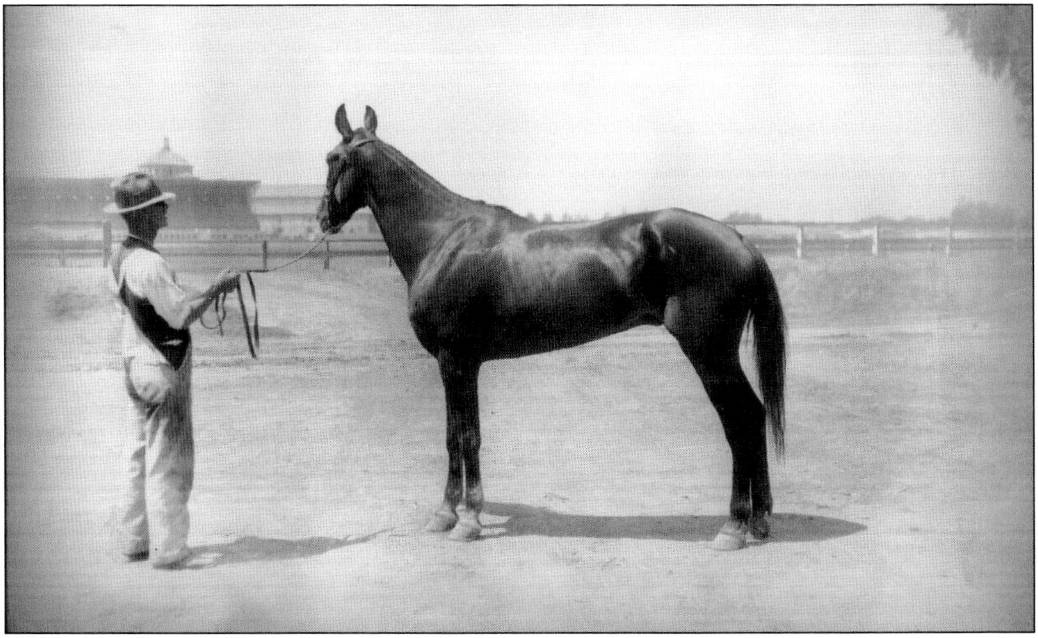

During August 1929, McCurry's took this photograph of a beautiful horse named Red Mack. The man holding the reins is unidentified. This is at the stables on the far side of the racetrack. The grandstand and top of the Agricultural Hall are visible in the distance. (CSH.)

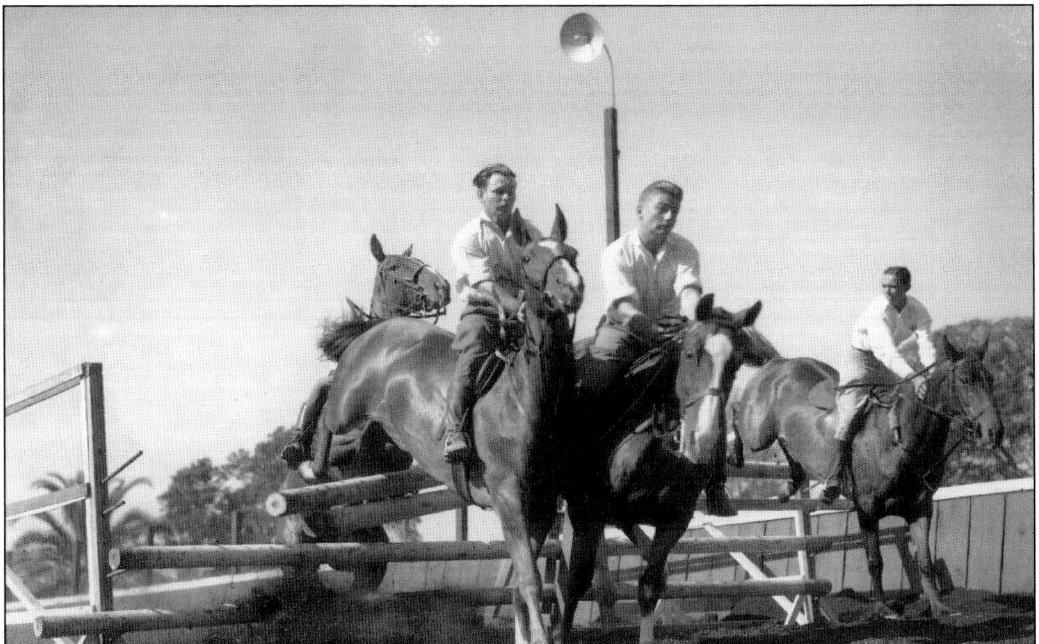

Harness and thoroughbred were not the only type of horse racing that took place at the fair. As this 1934 McCurry photograph shows, steeplechases were also popular. Here, three riders and their mounts clear, in a manner of speaking, a four-bar jump. A fourth horse is seen behind them starting its jump. (CSH.)

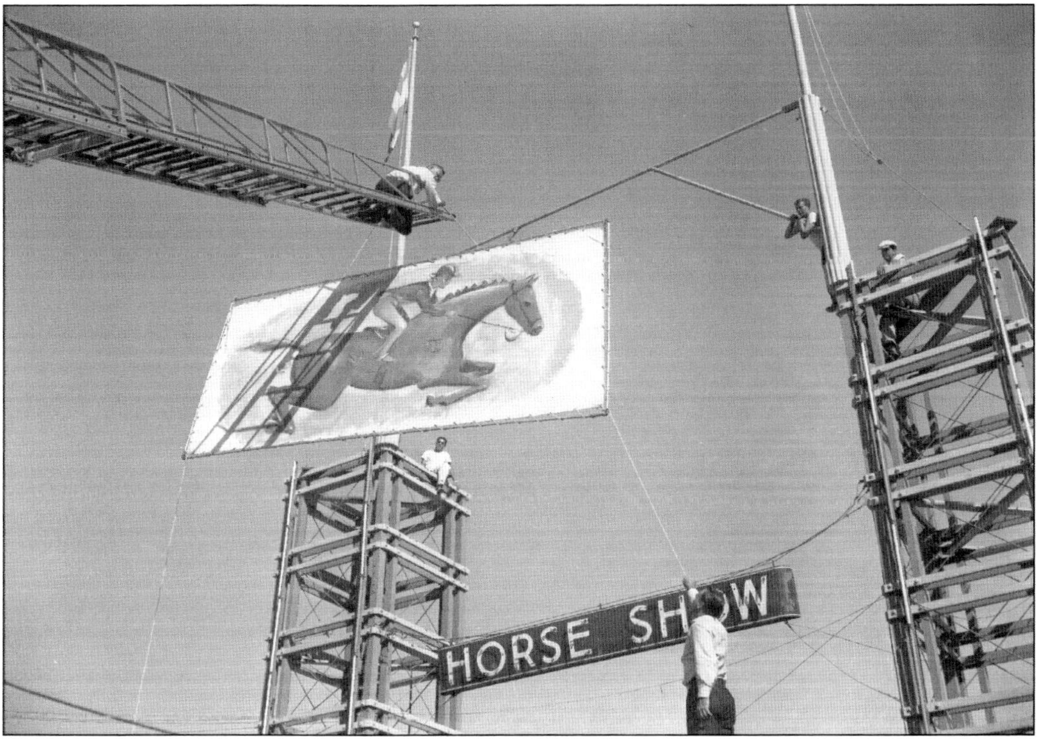

This 1952 photograph shows part of what goes into putting on the fair. Five unidentified workers use a crane to install the sign for the horse show. (CSH.)

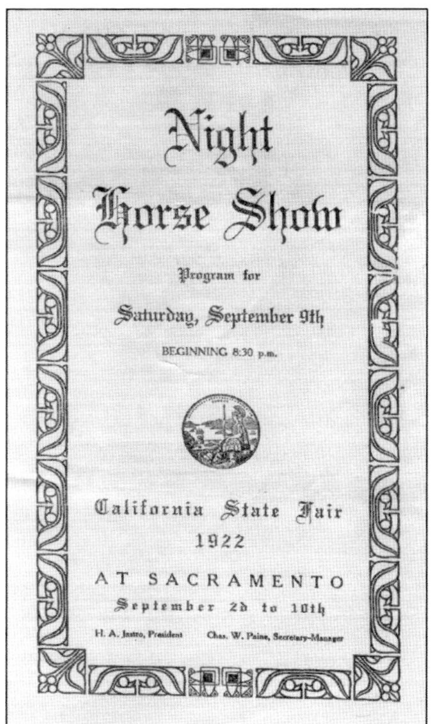
Night
Horse Show
Program for
Saturday, September 9th
BEGINNING 8:30 p.m.
California State Fair
1922
AT SACRAMENTO
September 2d to 10th
H. A. Jastro, President Chas. W. Paine, Secretary-Manager

In 1922, the State Fair held a nighttime horse show. This must have been a special event to celebrate Admission Day (September 9). The program is quite elaborate. The horse show was usually held during daylight hours, so this may have been an exhibition rather than a competition. (Sacramento Room, Sacramento Public Library.)

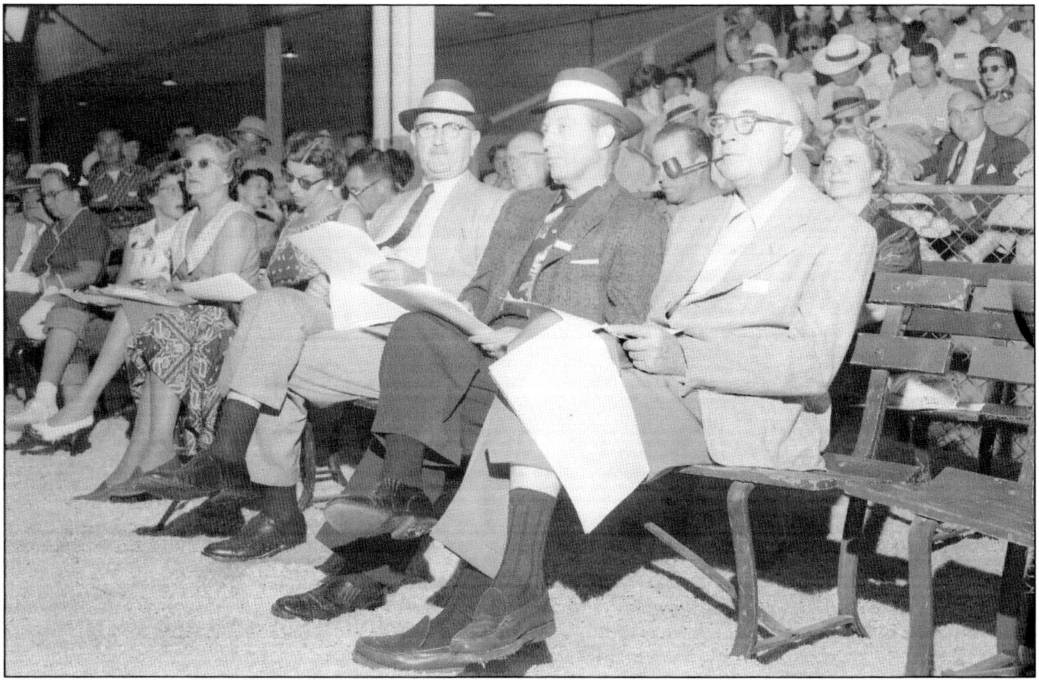

Horse racing attracts people of every type. And everybody believes he or she knows how to pick a winner. In this photograph are fans of the sport who lead a more sedate and relaxed lifestyle, but they certainly want their picks to win. (CSH.)

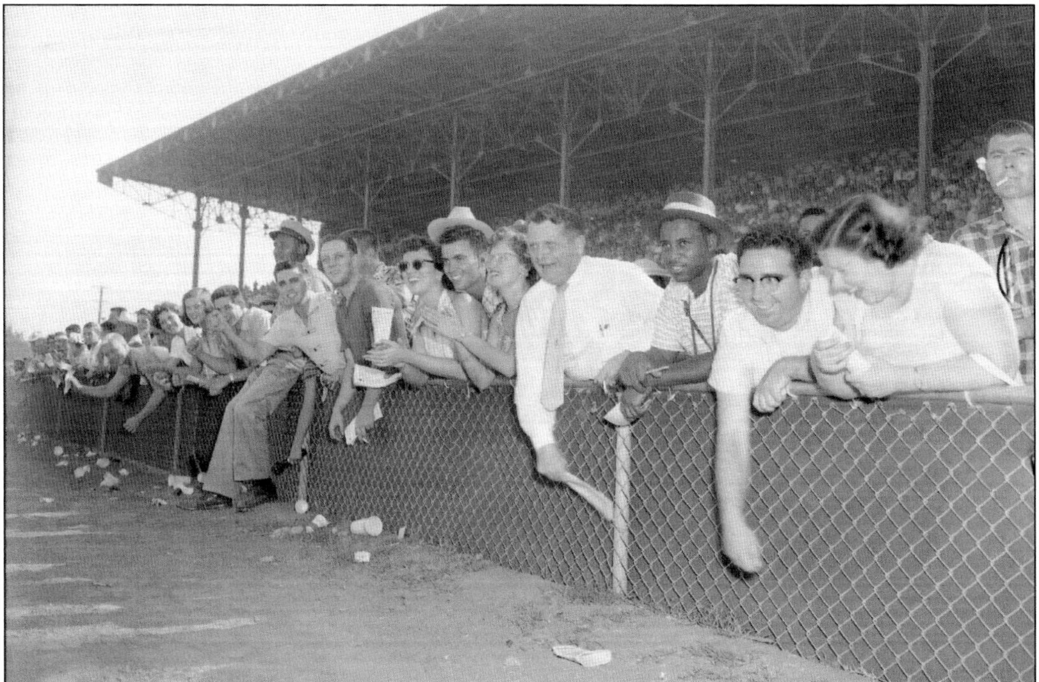

This photograph shows fans who are ready to give their all for their picks. They apparently really do want and need to have their horses win. (CSH.)

Of course, actually knowing how to pick a winner is more important than cheering them on, fun as that may be. This photograph shows that it comes down not to whom you know, but rather to what they think they know. (CSH.)

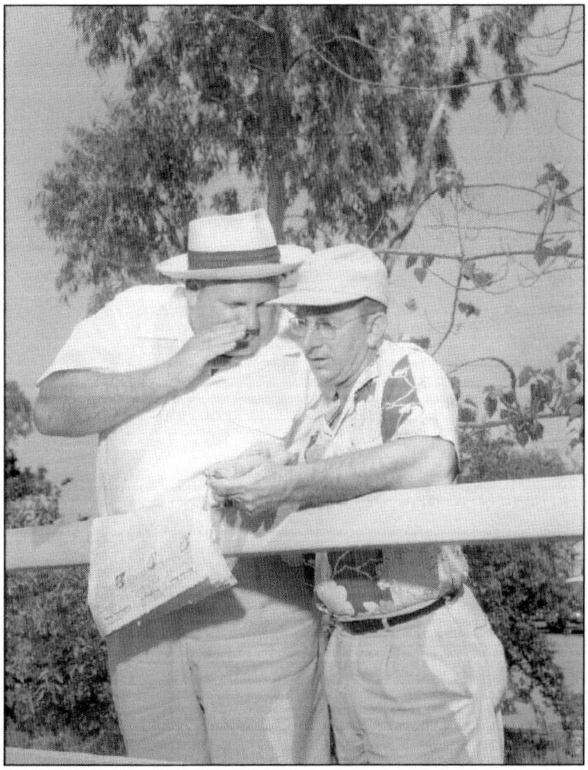

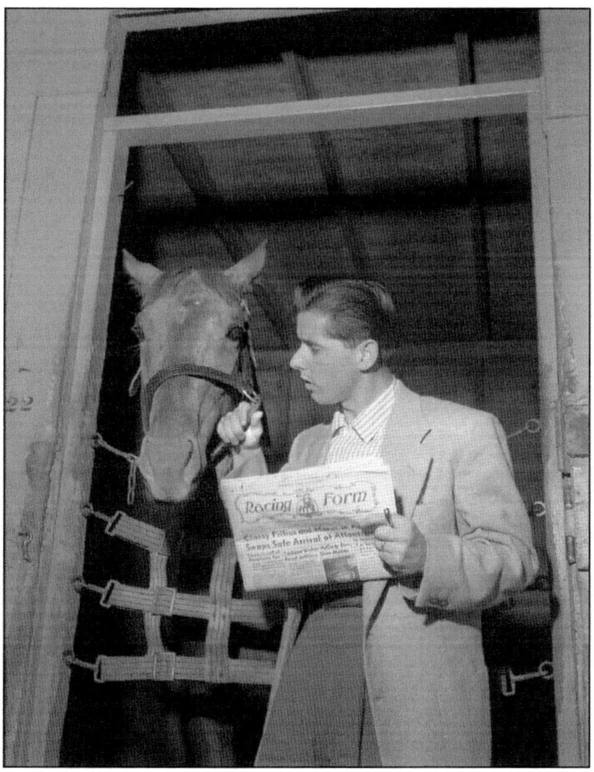

But the best way to know how a race will turn out is to consult a primary source. This must be the origin of the expression "straight from the horse's mouth." Of course, deciphering any answer you may receive is the key. (CSH.)

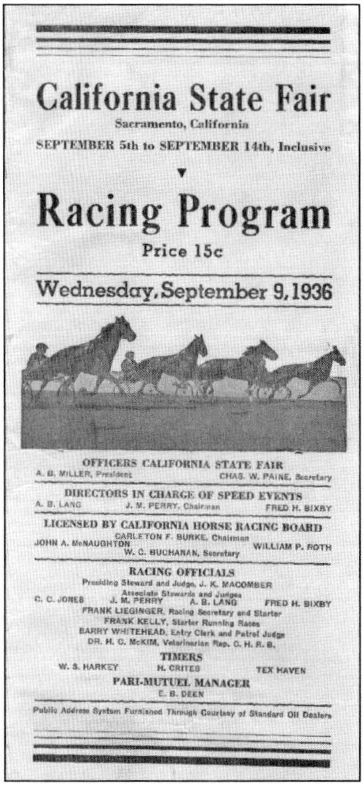

California State Fair
Sacramento, California
SEPTEMBER 5th to SEPTEMBER 14th, Inclusive

Racing Program
Price 15c

Wednesday, September 9, 1936

OFFICERS CALIFORNIA STATE FAIR
A. B. MILLER, President — CHAS. W. PAINE, Secretary

DIRECTORS IN CHARGE OF SPEED EVENTS
A. B. LANG — J. M. PERRY, Chairman — FRED H. BIXBY

LICENSED BY CALIFORNIA HORSE RACING BOARD
CARLETON F. BURKE, Chairman
JOHN A. McNAUGHTON — WILLIAM P. ROTH
W. C. BUCHANAN, Secretary

RACING OFFICIALS
Presiding Steward and Judge, J. K. MACOMBER
Associate Stewards and Judges
C. C. JONES — J. M. PERRY — A. B. LANG — FRED H. BIXBY
FRANK LIEGINGER, Racing Secretary and Starter
FRANK KELLY, Starter Running Races
BARRY WHITEHEAD, Entry Clerk and Patrol Judge
DR. H. C. McKIM, Veterinarian Rep. C. H. R. B.

TIMERS
W. S. HARKEY — H. CRITES — TEX HAVEN

PARI-MUTUEL MANAGER
E. B. DEEN

Public Address System Furnished Through Courtesy of Standard Oil Dealers

The "Racing Program" for September 9, 1936, Admission Day. When all else fails, racing fans can turn to the program to pick the winners. It will not actually state the winners, but the program does list all horses, jockeys, and odds for the races. The rest is up to chance. (Sacramento Room, Sacramento Public Library.)

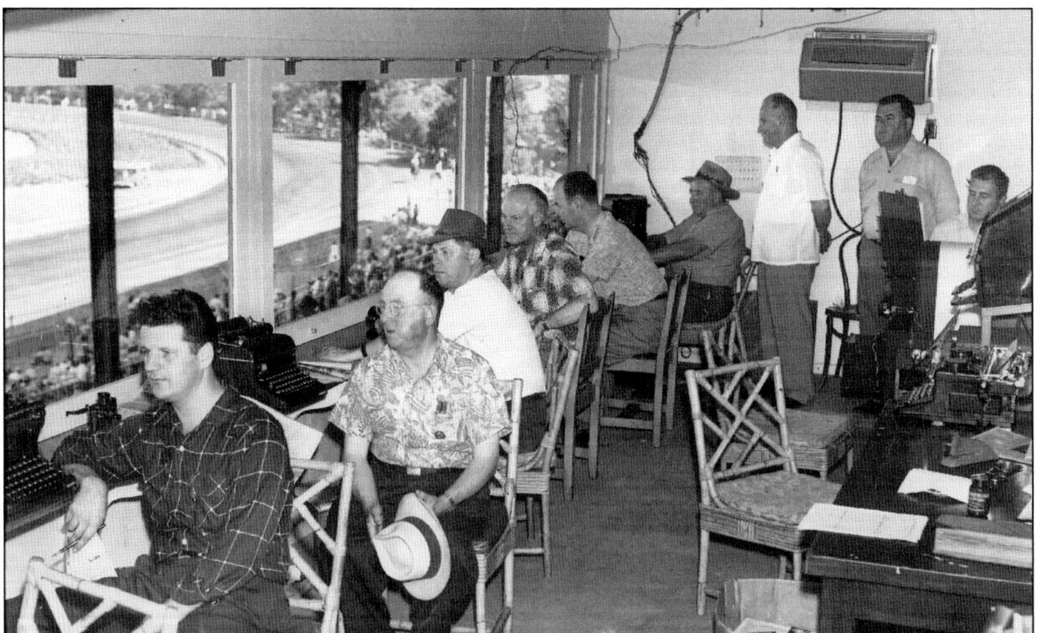

Naturally, the press always seems to have the best view. In this c. 1950 image, members of the press corps watch a race from the grandstand press box. It appears the race is coming to a conclusion. Note the many typewriters and the teletype machines visible to the far right. (CSH.)

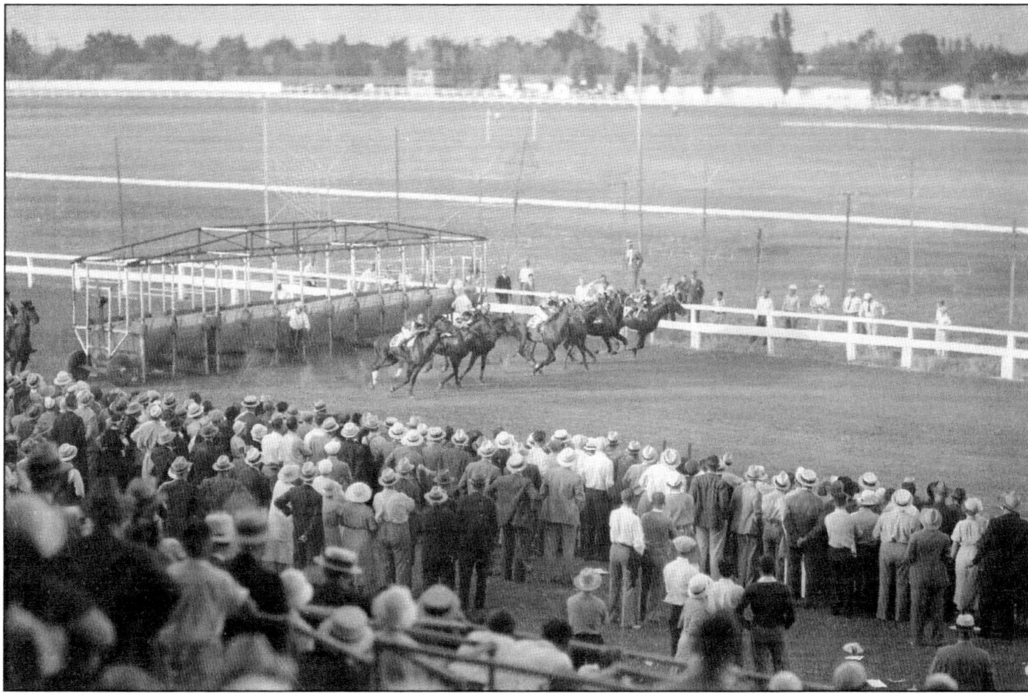

"AND THEY'RE OFF!" This is the second most important moment in a race fan's life. From a race during the 1932 run of the State Fair, this photograph captures the start from high in the grandstand. (CSH.)

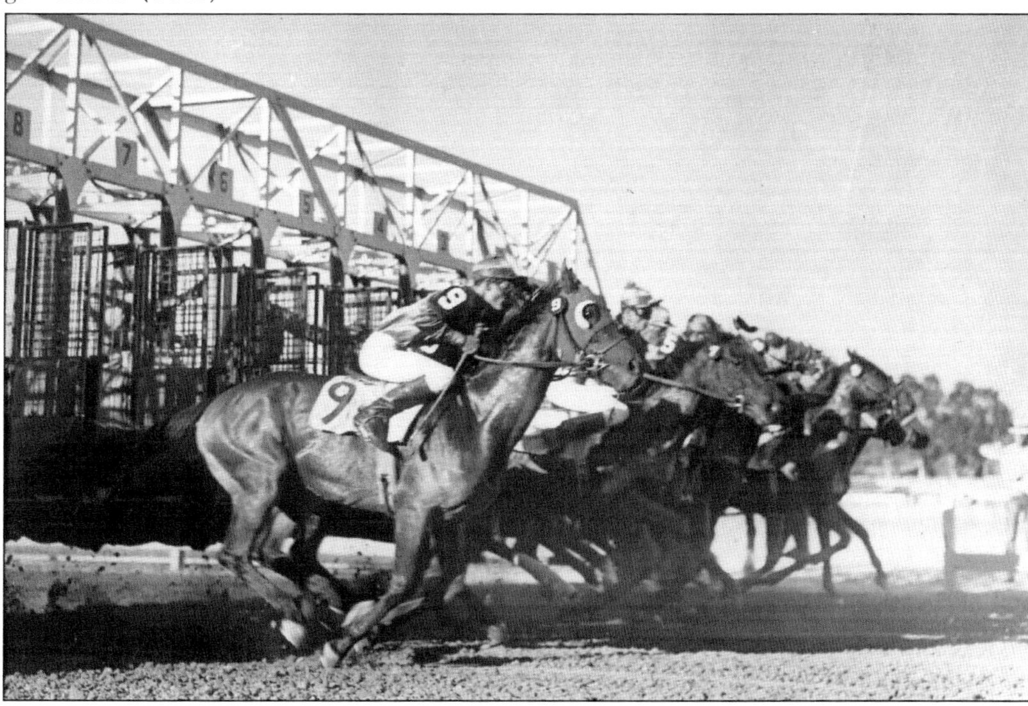

This undated photograph, probably from the mid 1950s, shows the field bursting out of the starting gate from the best possible vantage point, right next to the gate. (CSH.)

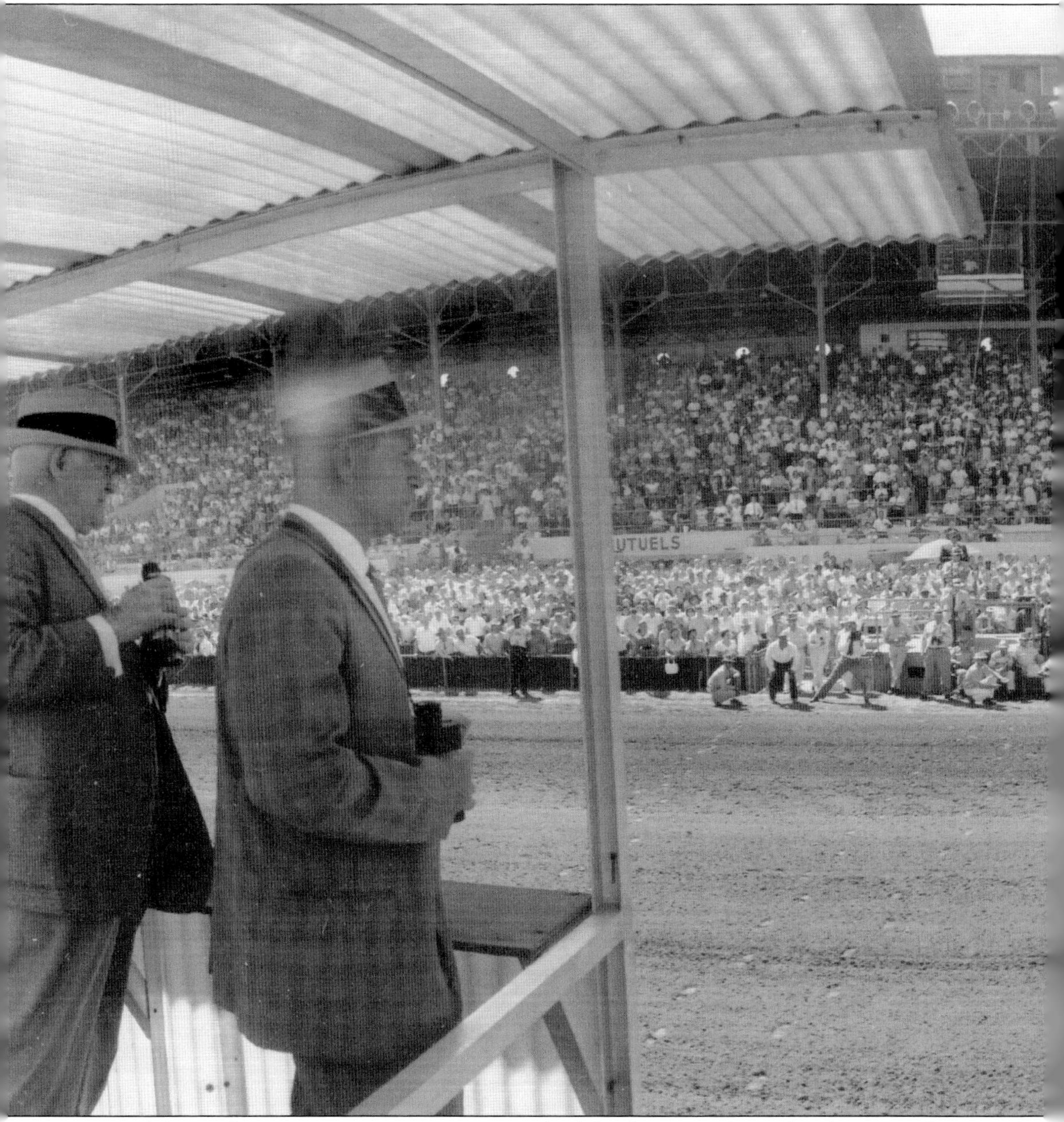

And this is the most important moment in the life of a racing fan. This dramatic photograph from the 1960 State Fair shows just how exciting horse racing can be. The field of nine horses is tightly bunched together, only about one second from the finish. It appears that the horse second

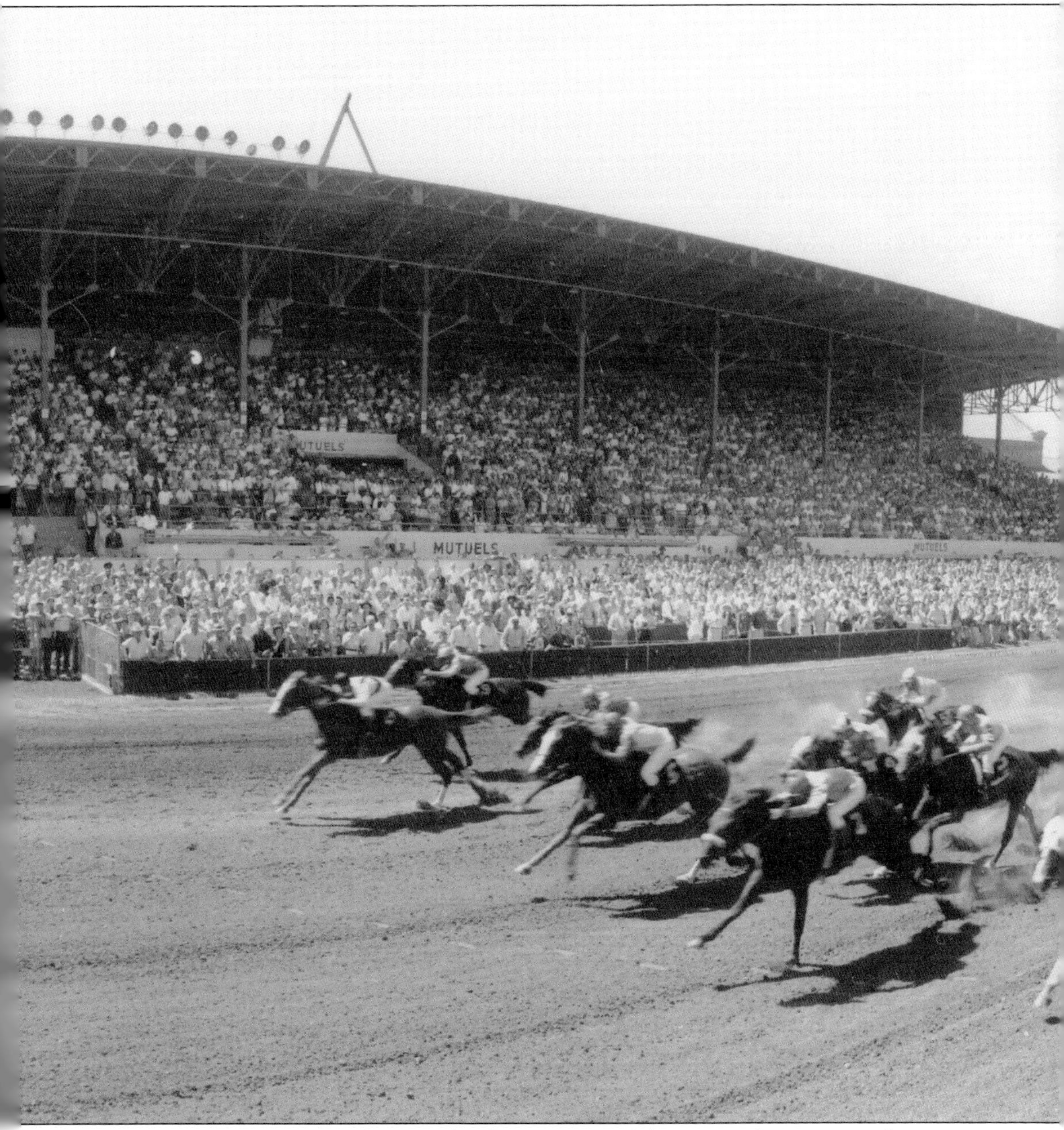

from the top is going to win. Unfortunately, the outcome of this particular race is unknown. Nearly the entire grandstand is visible, and it was clearly a full house on this day. Also visible to the left are the officials overseeing the race from the finish line. (CSH.)

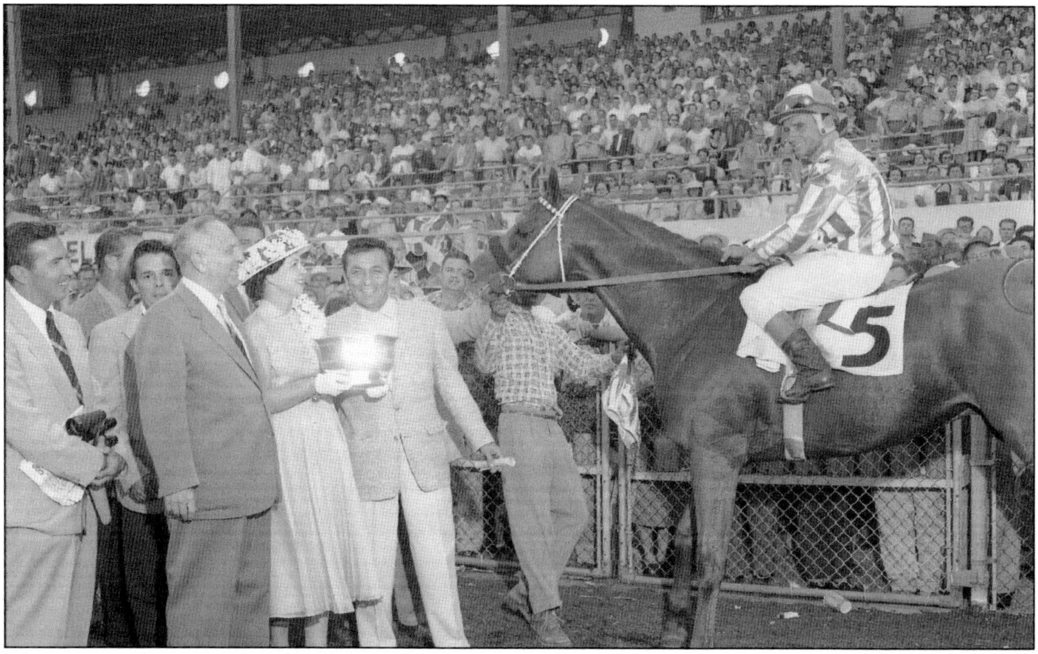

This September 7, 1956, photograph shows the result of the Governor's Handicap. From left to right are Gov. and Mrs. Goodwin Knight, horse owner Dick Griegoria, winning horse Arrogate, and jockey Ralph Neves. Neves and Arrogate set a track record at a mile and one sixteenth of 1:42, beating the previous mark by four-tenths of a second, and winning $11,700. (CSH.)

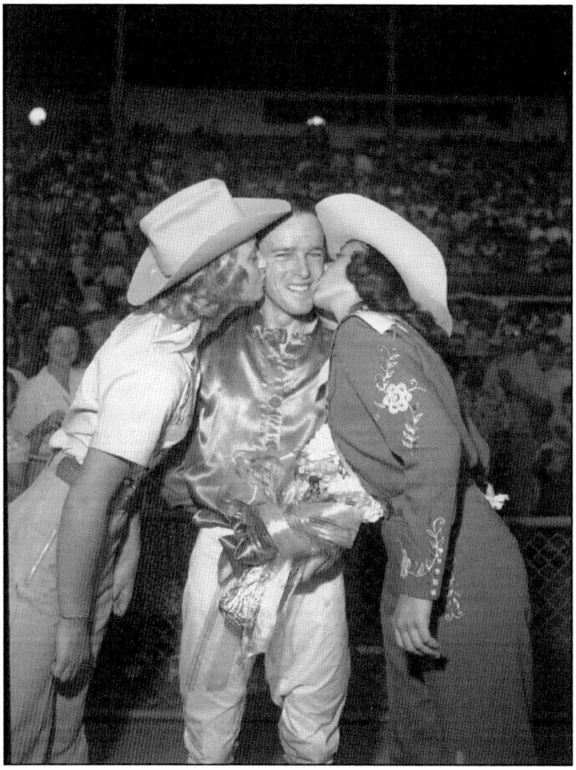

For the winning jockey, there are other benefits besides receiving a portion of the purse. The jockey and the women giving him his reward are unidentified in this photograph from 1952. (CSH.)

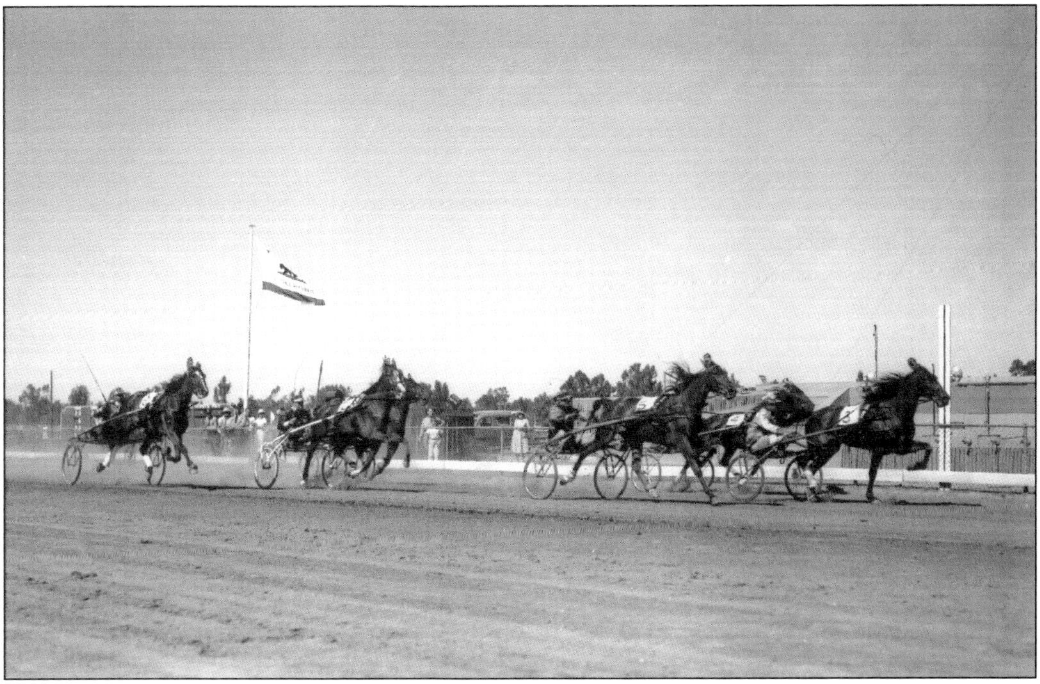

Along with thoroughbred racing, harness racing is a big part of the State Fair. This c. 1955 image shows the field on the final home stretch coming to the finish line. This photograph captures the speed that a trotter can attain. (CSH.)

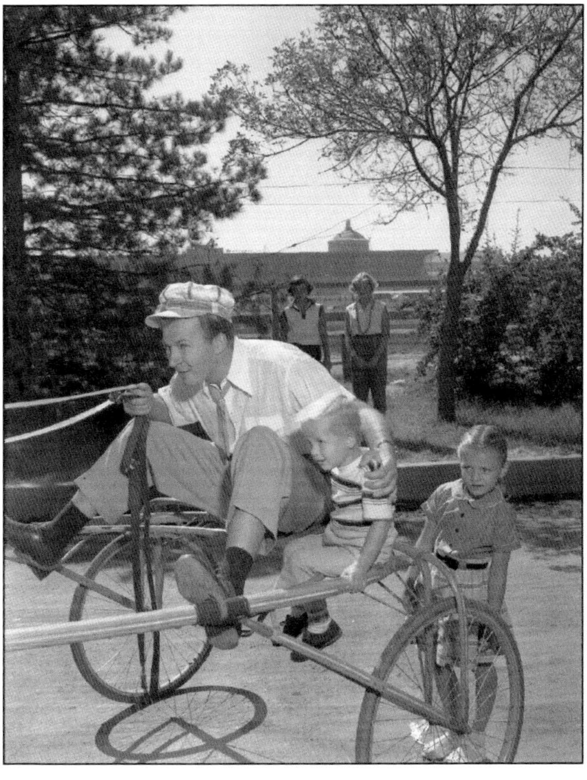

Harness racing is also popular with kids. Here an unidentified harness jockey shows the finer points of riding a sulky to two children during the 1954 fair. (CSH.)

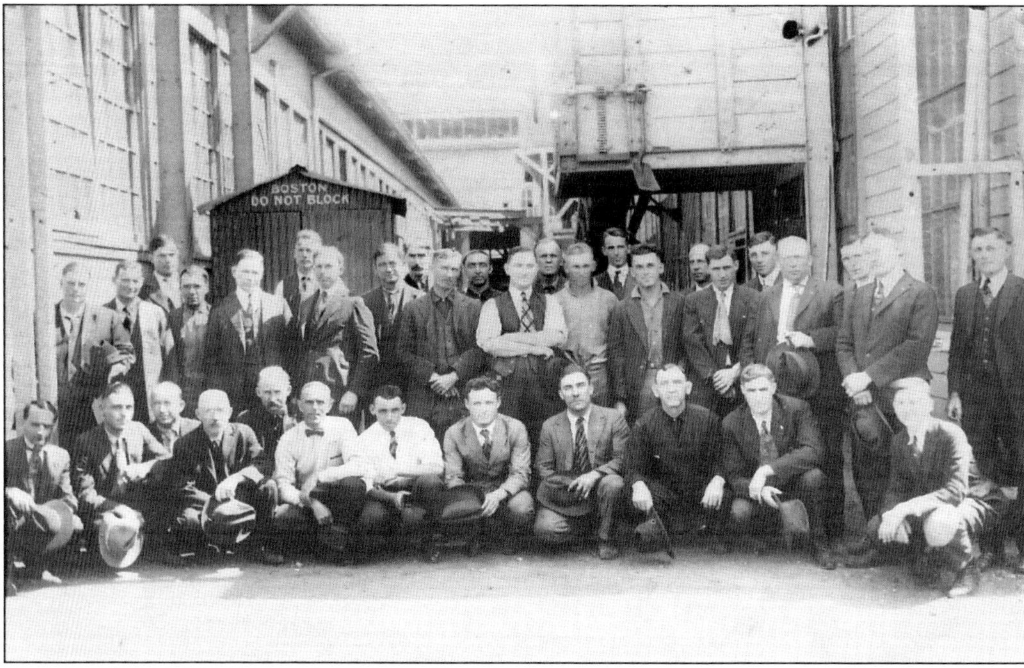

In 1930, the Southern Pacific Shopmen tug-of-war team beat the Stockton City Firemen at the State Fair. They won in two straight contests. This photograph from 1928 shows the team, including George Tetlow, fifth from the right in the front row. (CSH.)

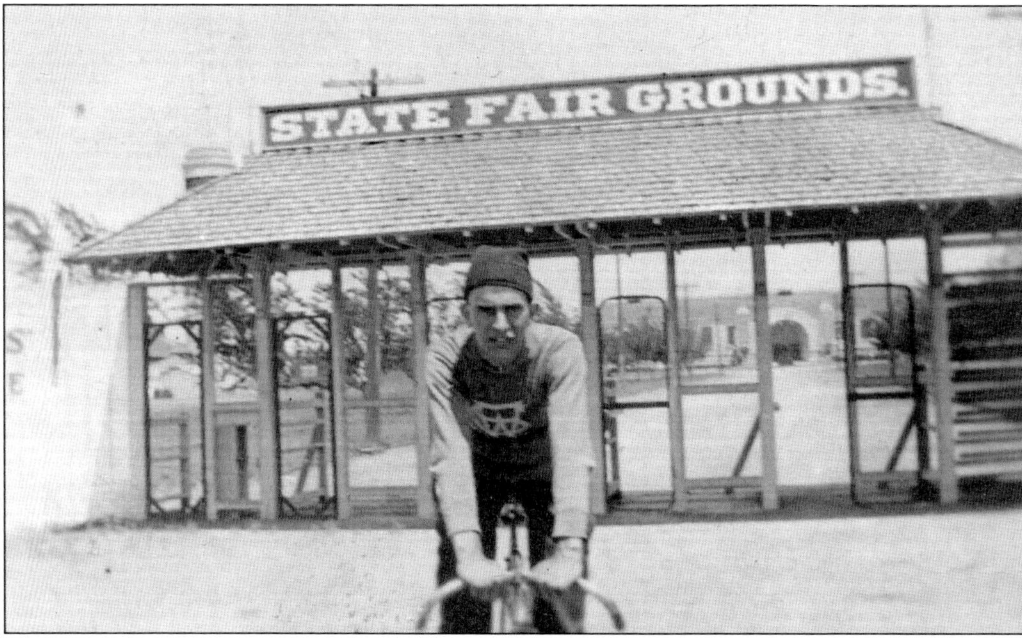

In 1916, Eugene Hepting and his friend, Hobert "Hobe" Henley, members of the Sacramento Wheelmen, rode from the state fairgrounds to Stockton in about three hours. Before starting, Hepting, an amateur photographer, took this photograph of his friend at the gate to the fairgrounds. This is probably the gate near the stock pens. Photographs that show the gate from this period are rare. (CSH.)

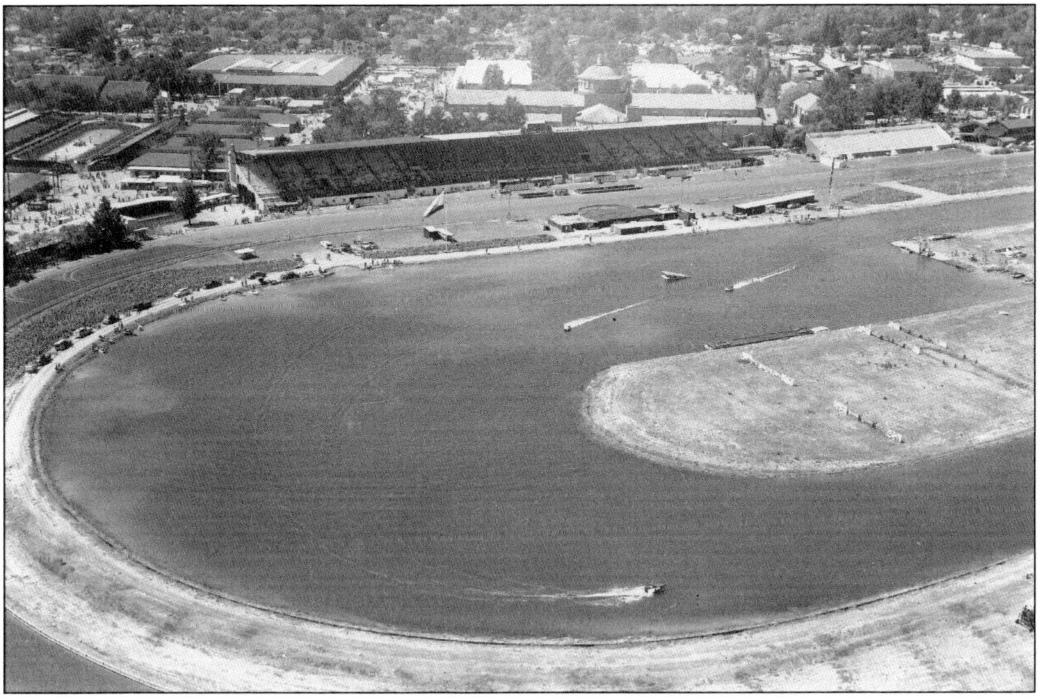

A lake was added to the infield of the racetrack for the 1947 State Fair. By 1950, it was enlarged to nearly the size of the track, with a large island in the middle. This photograph was taken in 1954 during a speedboat race. Note the ramp in the center right of the photo, which was used by water-skiers. (CSH.)

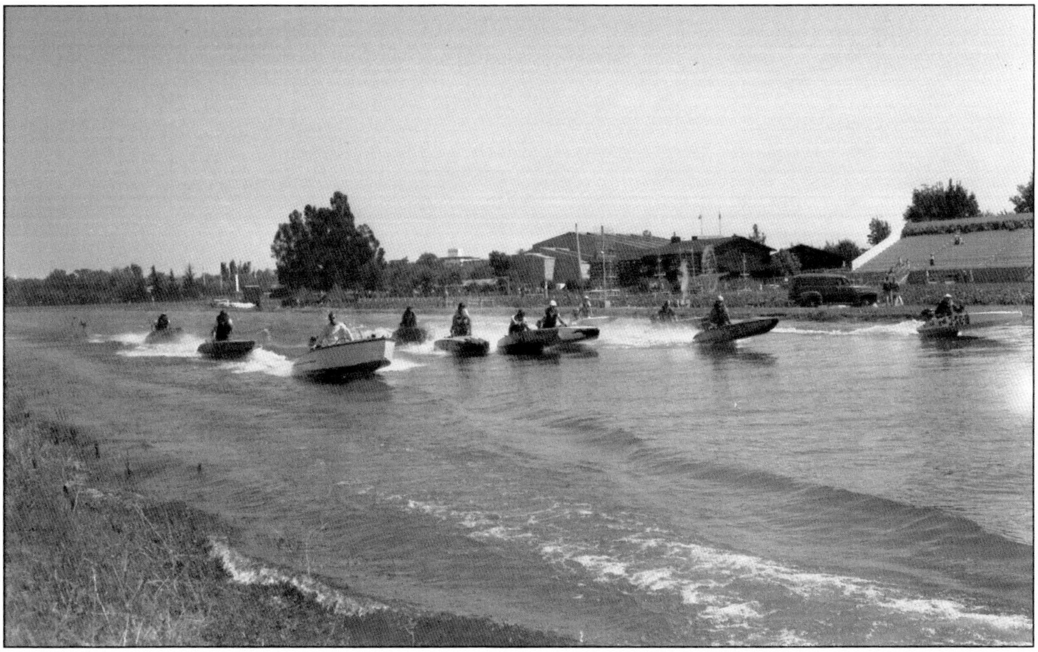

A boat race takes place on the lake in 1954. The boats pictured here were probably not the fastest, and this may have been an amateur race. (CSH.)

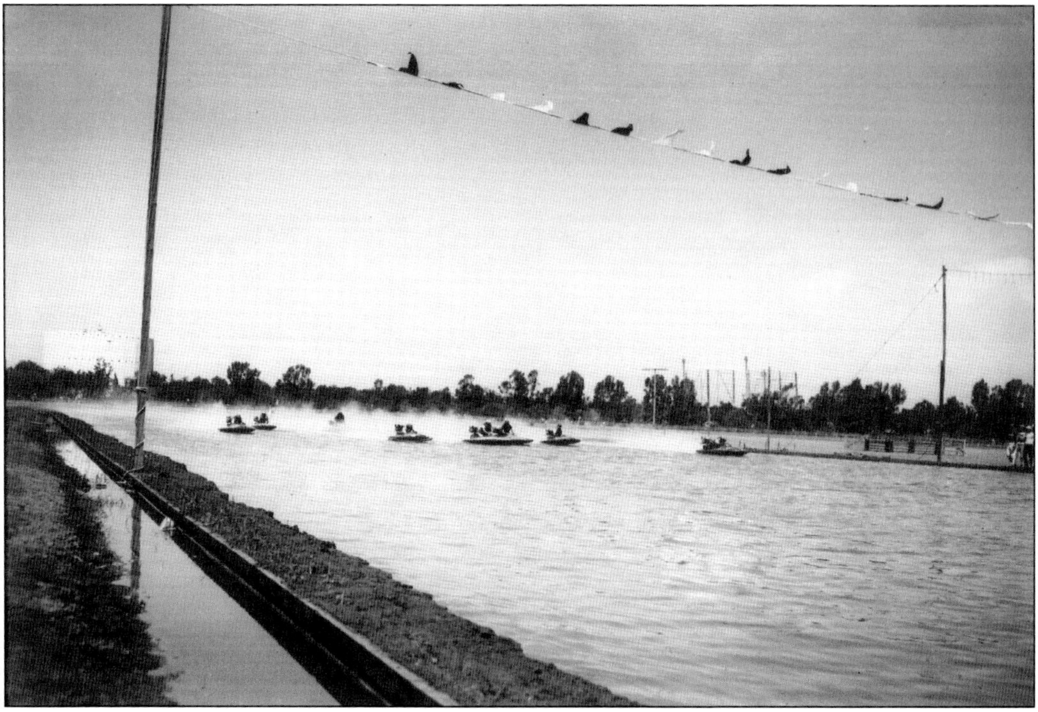

A race comes to an exciting finish in 1950. The boats here are early types of hydroplanes that could hit some impressive speeds. Visible in the background to the left is the large water tank that supplied water to the fair and the surrounding neighborhoods. It holds three million gallons. (CSH.)

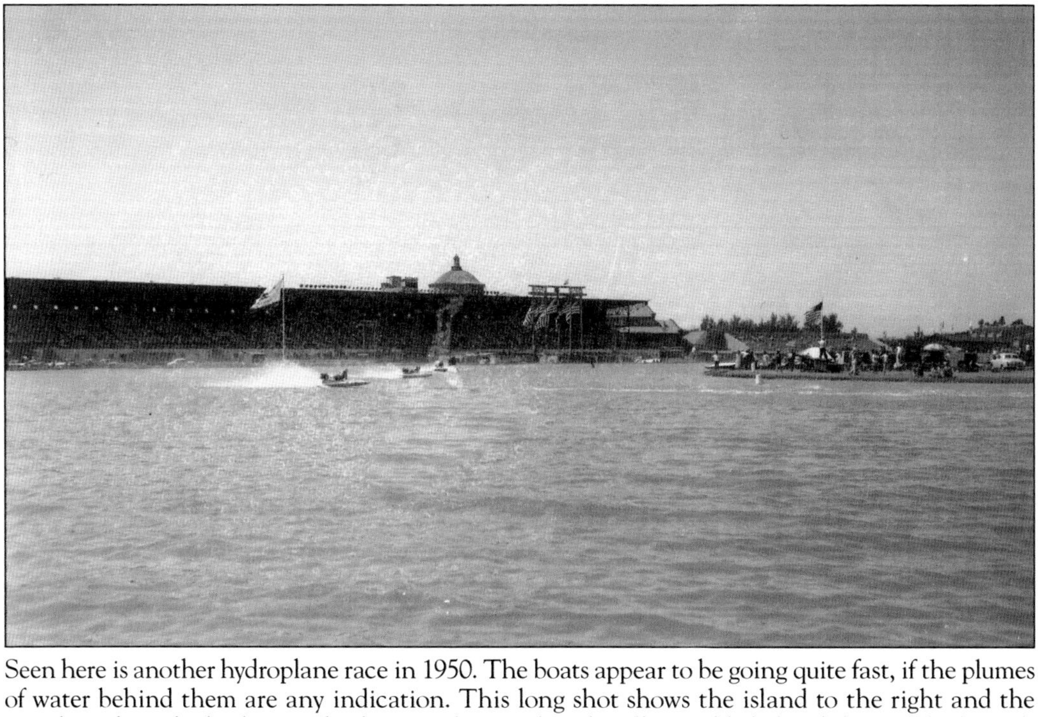

Seen here is another hydroplane race in 1950. The boats appear to be going quite fast, if the plumes of water behind them are any indication. This long shot shows the island to the right and the grandstands in the background. The top of Agricultural Hall is visible behind the stands. (CSH.)

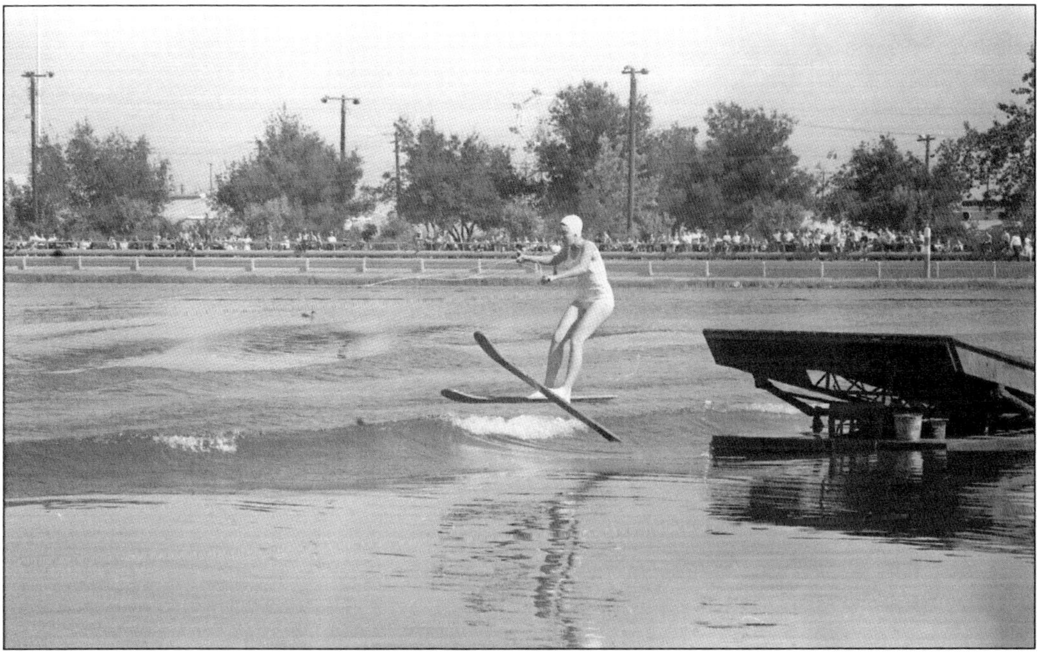

A unidentified water-skier is captured in mid-jump in 1961. There were many water-skiing events in this period, some professional and others, like the cowboy water-ski contest, not quite so professional. The event was very popular, as shown by the large crowd watching from the south end of the race track. (CSH.)

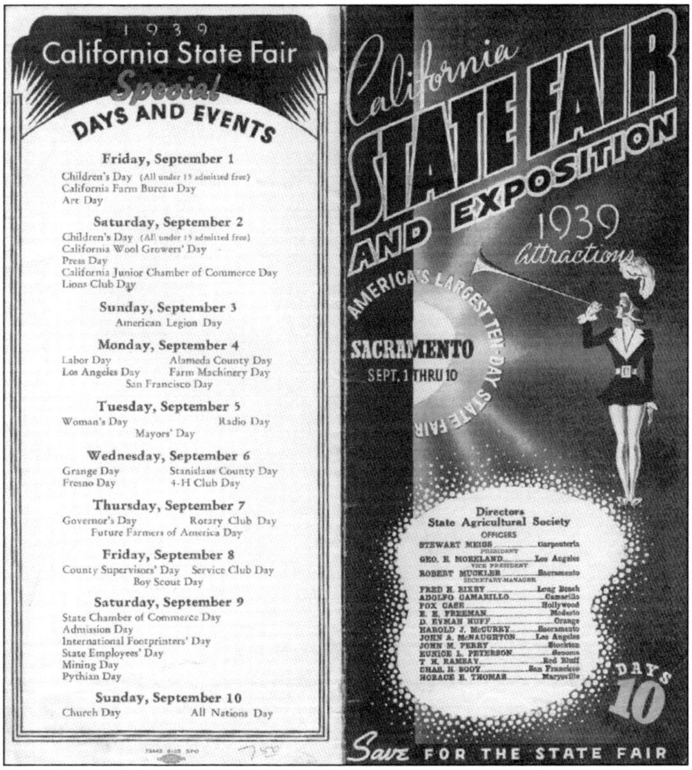

This 1939 pamphlet was unusual for the State Fair in that is was done in black and white, rather than color. This may have been done as a cost-cutting measure. And it was not boasting to call it "America's Largest Ten-Day State Fair." Officials could easily expect well over half a million visitors during the run. (Sacramento Room, Sacramento Public Library.)

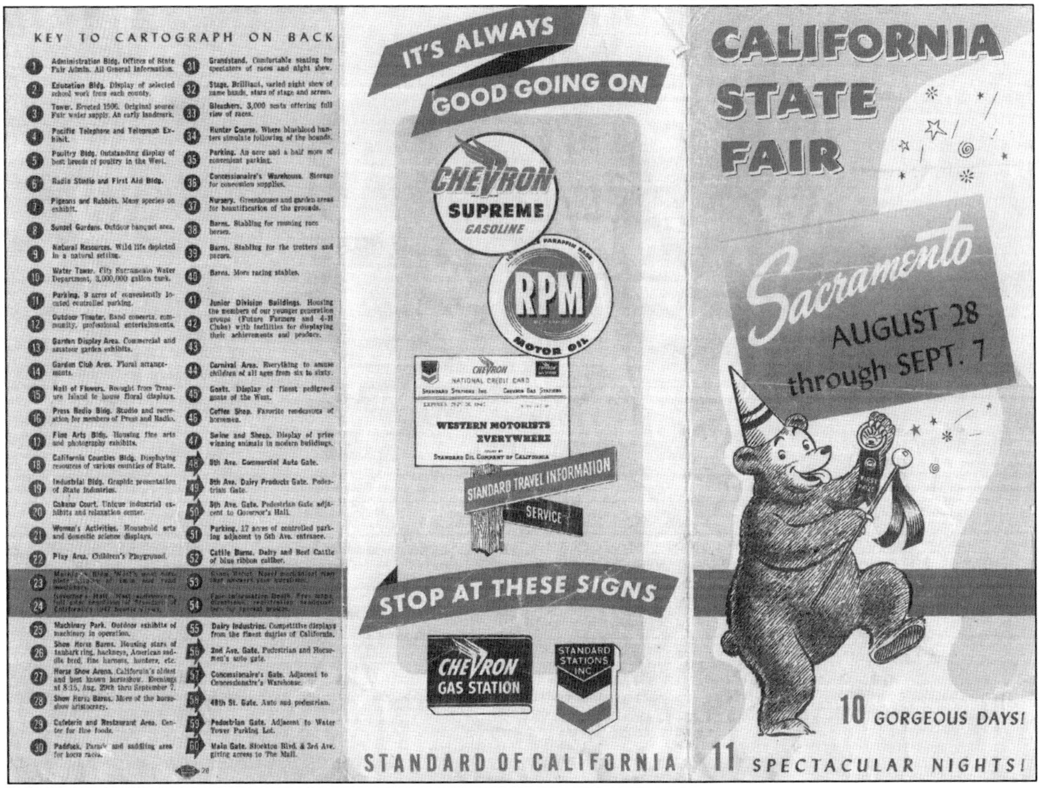

Shown here is the 1947 pamphlet. Due to World War II, the fair had last been held in 1941, and the State Fair board wanted everyone to attend. This pamphlet was likely sent outside of the Sacramento area as it was sponsored by Standard Oil of California, which wanted travelers to keep an eye open for its stations on the way to the fair. (Sacramento Room, Sacramento Public Library.)

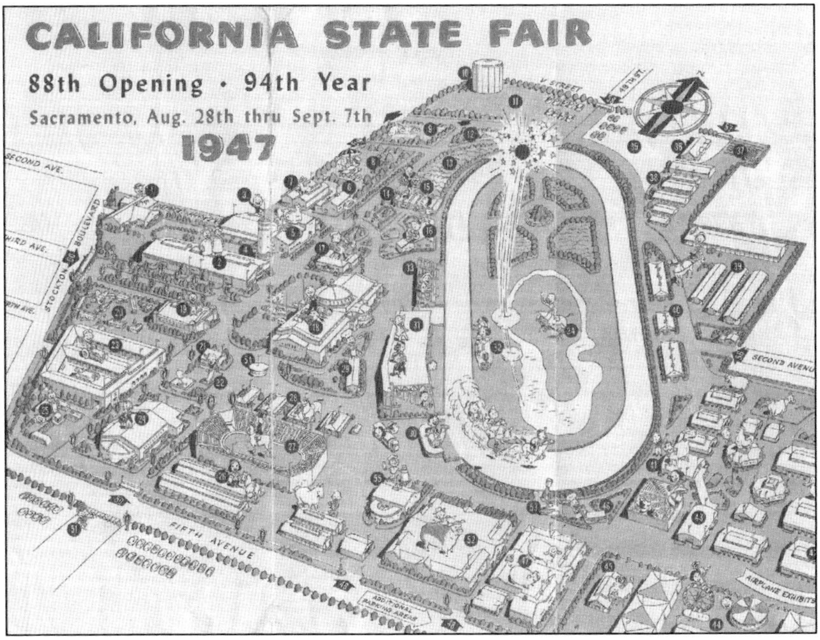

Of note on the inside of the 1947 pamphlet are the new lake in the middle of the track and the stage in front of the grandstand. The stage was used for night shows for name bands and "stars of stage and screen." (Sacramento Room, Sacramento Public Library.)

This letter went out in 1948 to businesses throughout California urging them to exhibit at the next State Fair. The message at the beginning of the letter echoes the original message in the 1854 act that created the fair: to educate the public about agriculture and industry in California. It was also an attempt to boost revenues that were put back into the fair to make it even larger. (Sacramento Room, Sacramento Public Library.)

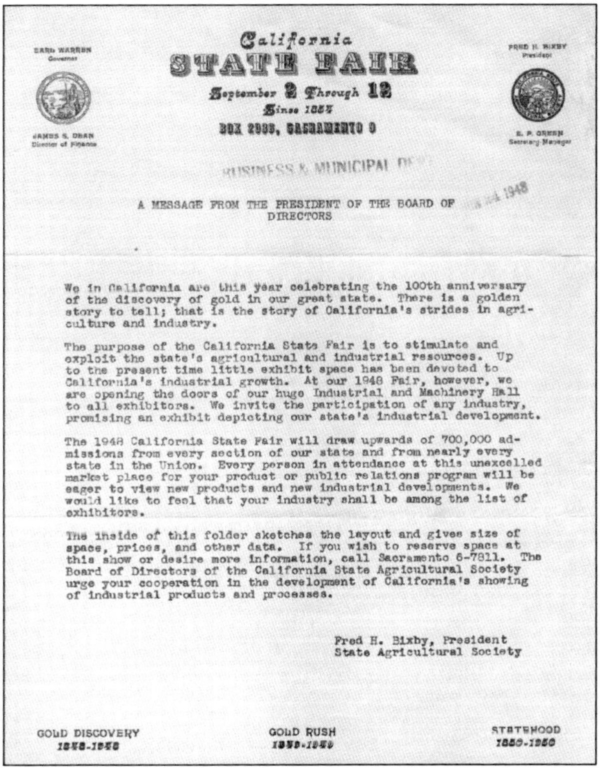

EARL WARREN
Governor

JAMES S. DEAN
Director of Finance

California
STATE FAIR
September 2 Through 12
Since 1854
BOX 2036, SACRAMENTO 9

FRED H. BIXBY
President

E. P. GREEN
Secretary-Manager

BUSINESS & MUNICIPAL D...

...1948

A MESSAGE FROM THE PRESIDENT OF THE BOARD OF DIRECTORS

We in California are this year celebrating the 100th anniversary of the discovery of gold in our great state. There is a golden story to tell; that is the story of California's strides in agriculture and industry.

The purpose of the California State Fair is to stimulate and exploit the state's agricultural and industrial resources. Up to the present time little exhibit space has been devoted to California's industrial growth. At our 1948 Fair, however, we are opening the doors of our huge Industrial and Machinery Hall to all exhibitors. We invite the participation of any industry, promising an exhibit depicting our state's industrial development.

The 1948 California State Fair will draw upwards of 700,000 admissions from every section of our state and from nearly every state in the Union. Every person in attendance at this unexcelled market place for your product or public relations program will be eager to view new products and new industrial developments. We would like to feel that your industry shall be among the list of exhibitors.

The inside of this folder sketches the layout and gives size of space, prices, and other data. If you wish to reserve space at this show or desire more information, call Sacramento 6-7811. The Board of Directors of the California State Agricultural Society urge your cooperation in the development of California's showing of industrial products and processes.

Fred H. Bixby, President
State Agricultural Society

GOLD DISCOVERY 1848-1948

GOLD RUSH 1849-1949

STATEHOOD 1850-1950

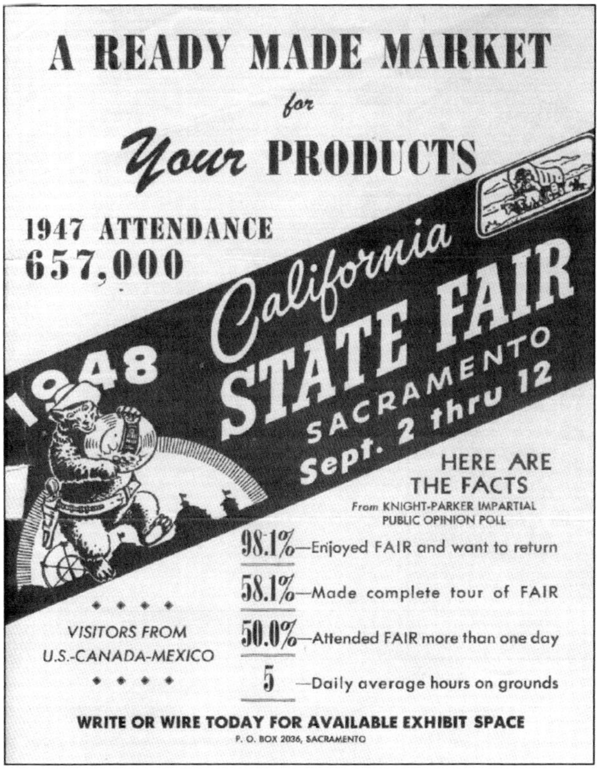

The reverse of the above letter trumpeted the benefits of exhibiting at the State Fair. It has some valid points, not the least of which is that close to three-quarters of a million people could potentially see a company's exhibit and products in ten days. In 1948, there was no other place to accomplish that. (Sacramento Room, Sacramento Public Library.)

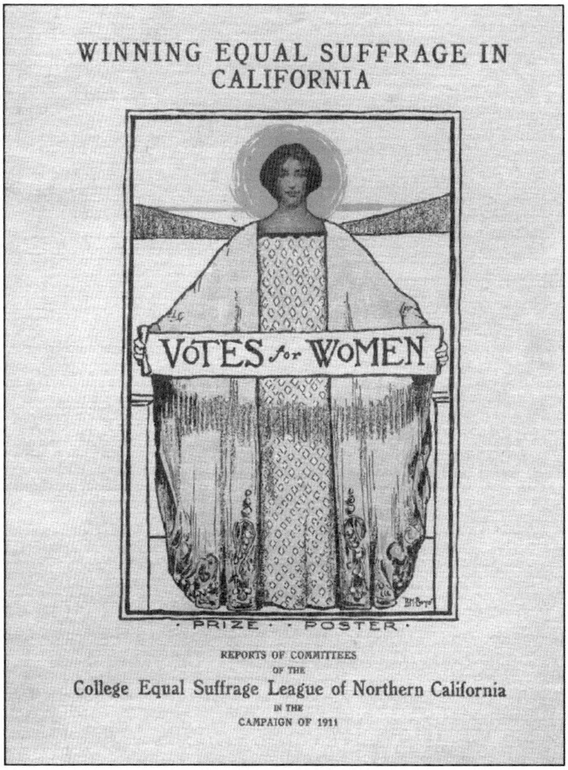

Lillian Cash Hough, the new leader of the College Equal Suffrage League of Northern California, went before the state agricultural board to lobby for a Women's Day at the 1911 fair as a show of support for the right to vote. The first Women's Day was held on August 26, 1911. In an October 1911 special election, California became the sixth state to grant the franchise to women. (CSH.)

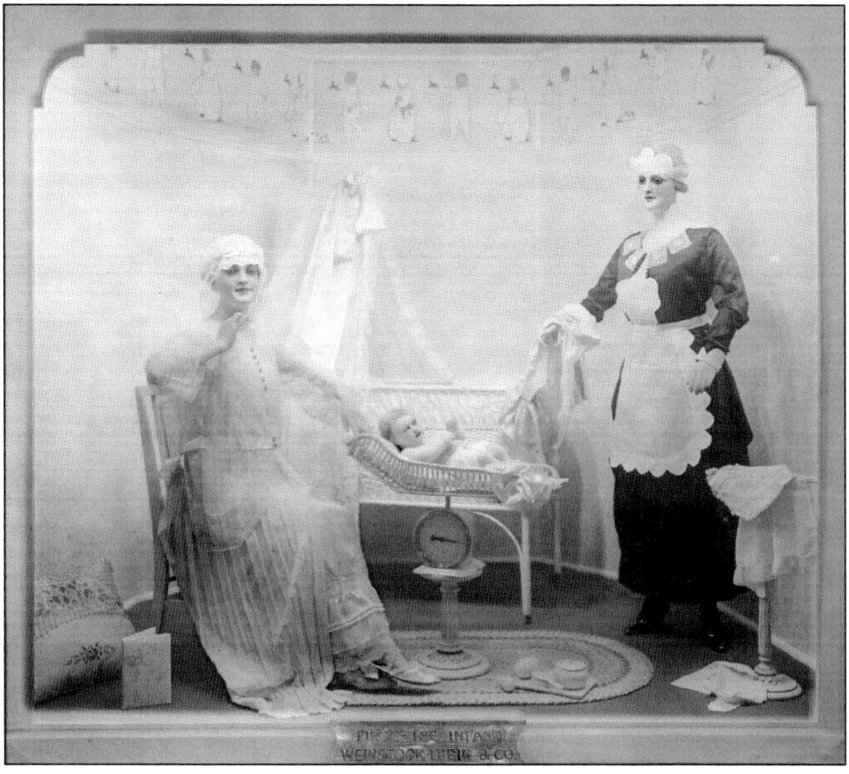

About 1923, Weinstock Lubin put up a display that chronicled the "Seven Ages of Women," designed by Charles W. Morton. The vignettes showed a woman's life from Infant (right) all the way up to Grandmother. The one thing that was not shown was a career or paying job of any sort. (CSH.)

The other "Seven Ages of Women" were School Girl, Graduate, Athlete, Bride, Mother, and Grandmother (right)—but no Career. While these vignettes were meant to be seen as a celebration of the lives of women, it is more likely they were used to highlight all the wonderful items that could be purchased at Weinstock Lubin. (CSH.)

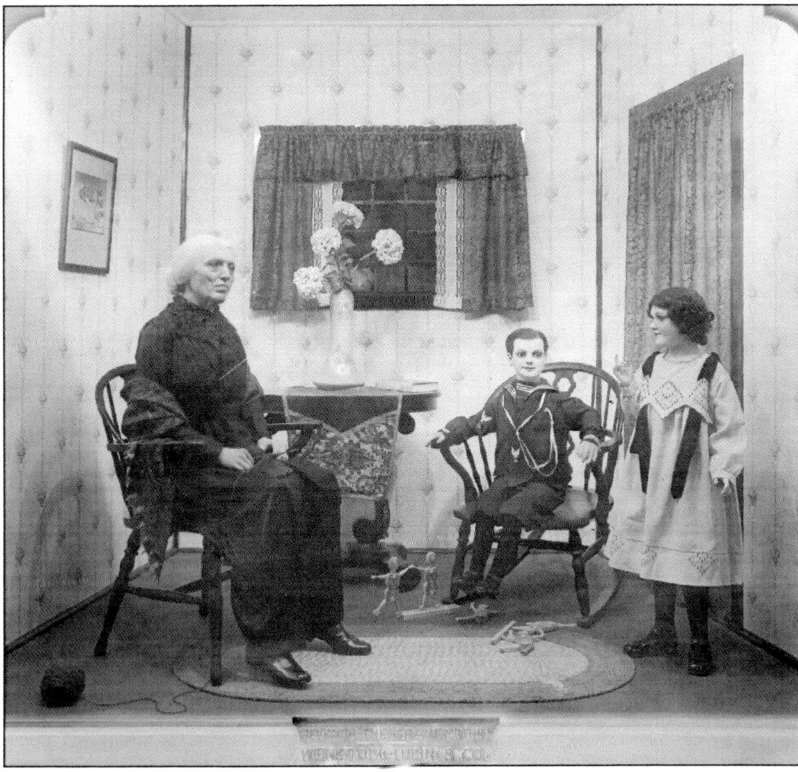

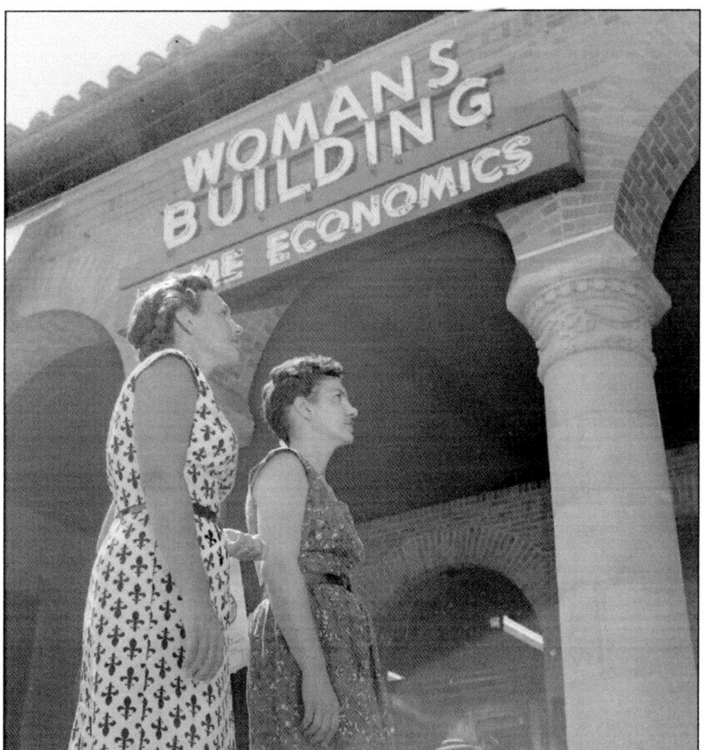

By the 1950s, women had their own building of exhibits. Mrs. Harry Huntington (left), of Santa Rosa, and Mrs. Fred Tremblay, of Folsom, stop at the entrance in 1957. The Woman's Building featured exhibits of foreign crafts, antique dolls, home cooking and preserves, needlecraft, party fashions, kitchen craft, and fashion shows twice a day. (CSH.)

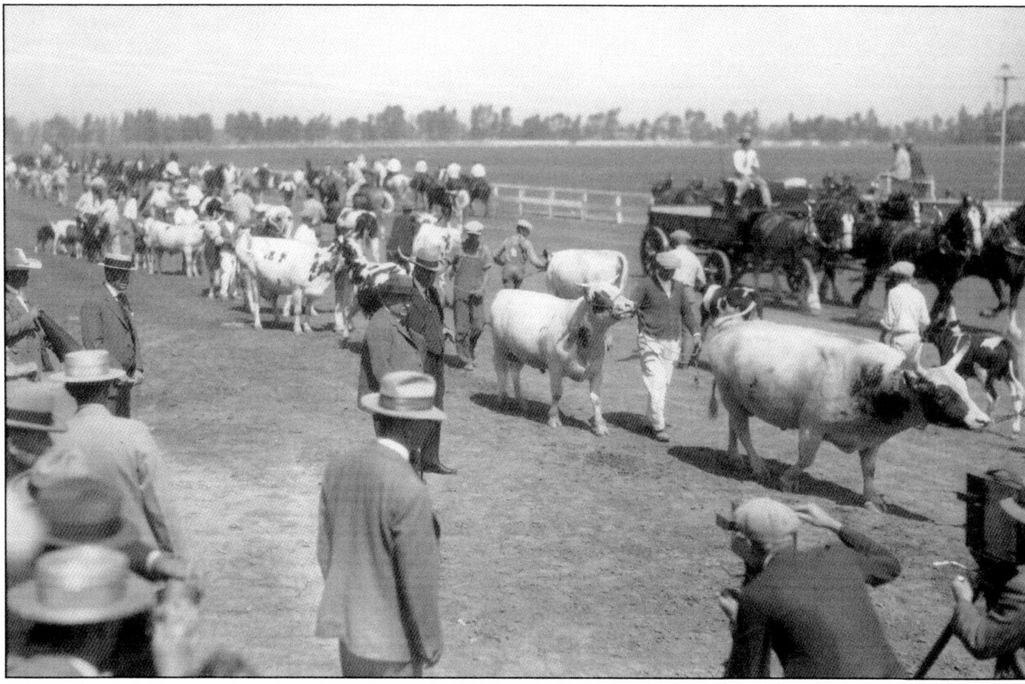

Seen here is the stock parade at the start of the 1932 State Fair. There are teams of Clydesdale horses, steers and cows of every type, calves, goats, and horses. In the right foreground are two cameras filming the whole thing. (CSH.)

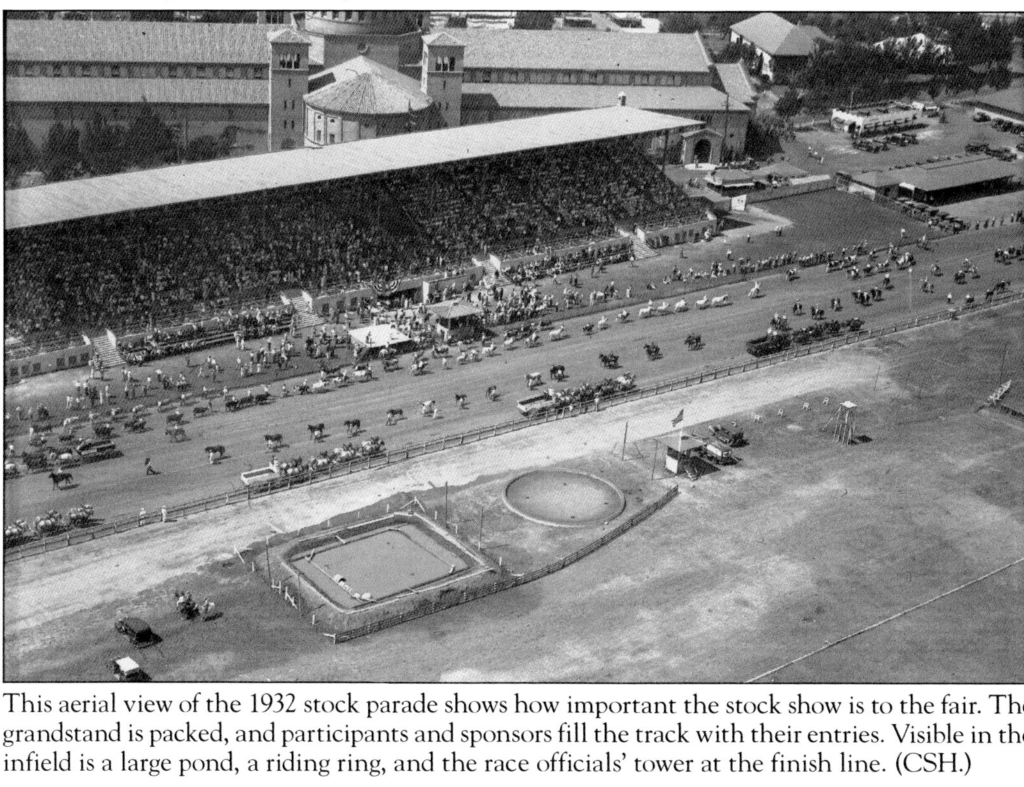

This aerial view of the 1932 stock parade shows how important the stock show is to the fair. The grandstand is packed, and participants and sponsors fill the track with their entries. Visible in the infield is a large pond, a riding ring, and the race officials' tower at the finish line. (CSH.)

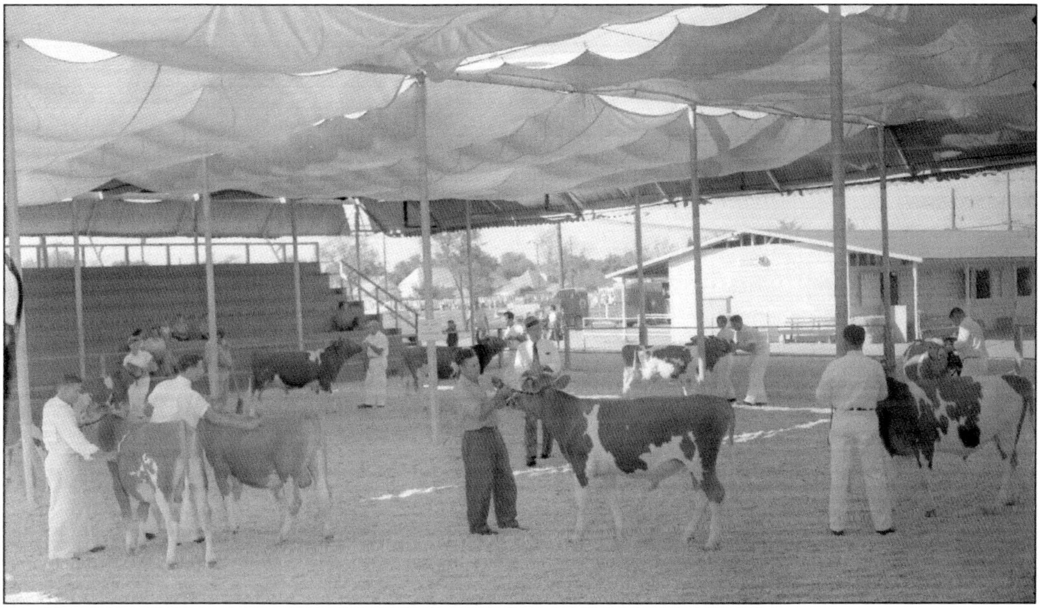

Seen here is part of the judging for the 1954 stock show. Contestants could, and probably did, spend hours getting their bulls ready for the judging ring. It should be noted that the bulls had to win smaller local contests in order to be eligible for the State Fair. What is seen here is a ring of champion bulls. (CSH.)

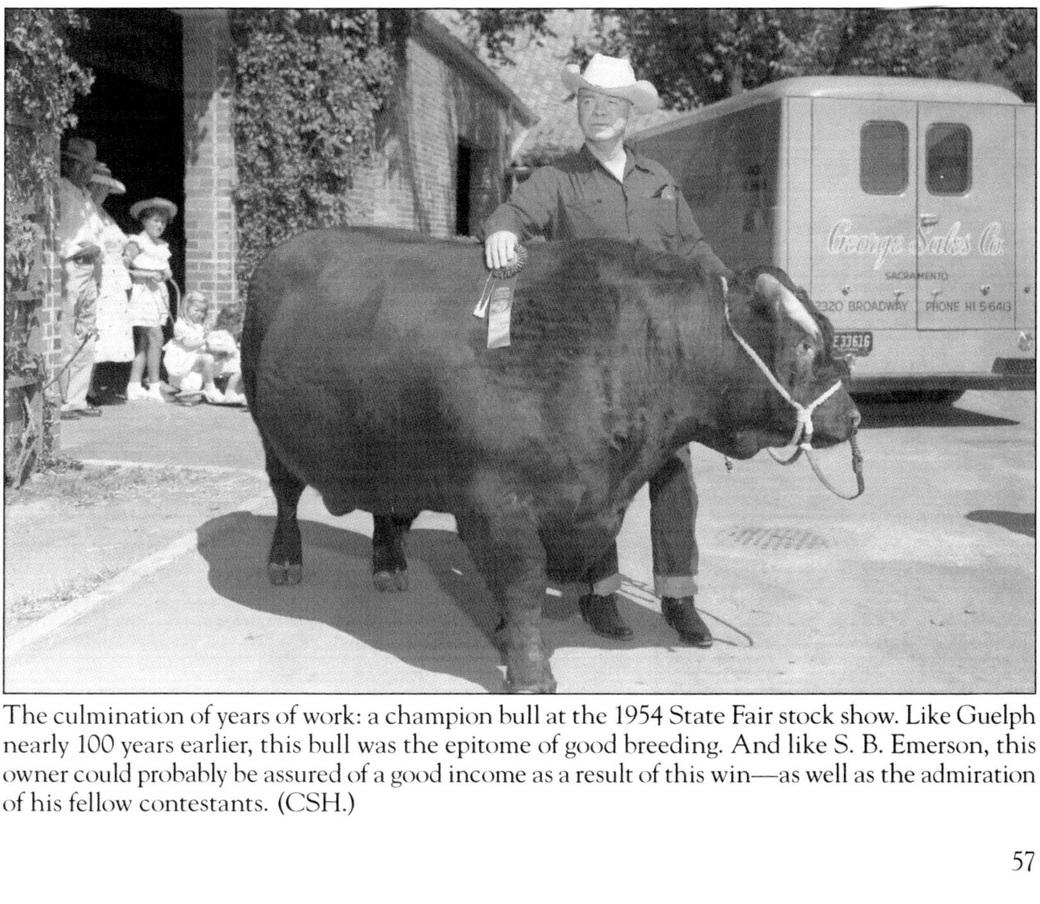

The culmination of years of work: a champion bull at the 1954 State Fair stock show. Like Guelph nearly 100 years earlier, this bull was the epitome of good breeding. And like S. B. Emerson, this owner could probably be assured of a good income as a result of this win—as well as the admiration of his fellow contestants. (CSH.)

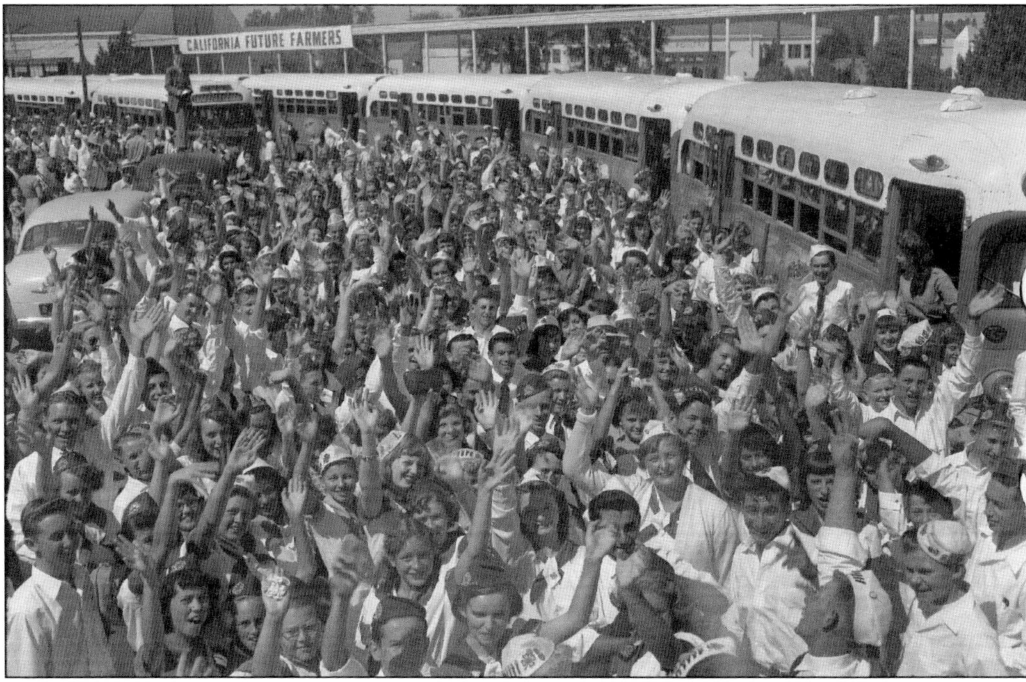

4-H is always a part of the stock show. This *c.* 1953 photograph shows the 4-H contingent disembarking from buses at the main entrance of the fair. And as the sign in the background indicates, the Future Farmers of America also attend the fair. (CSH.)

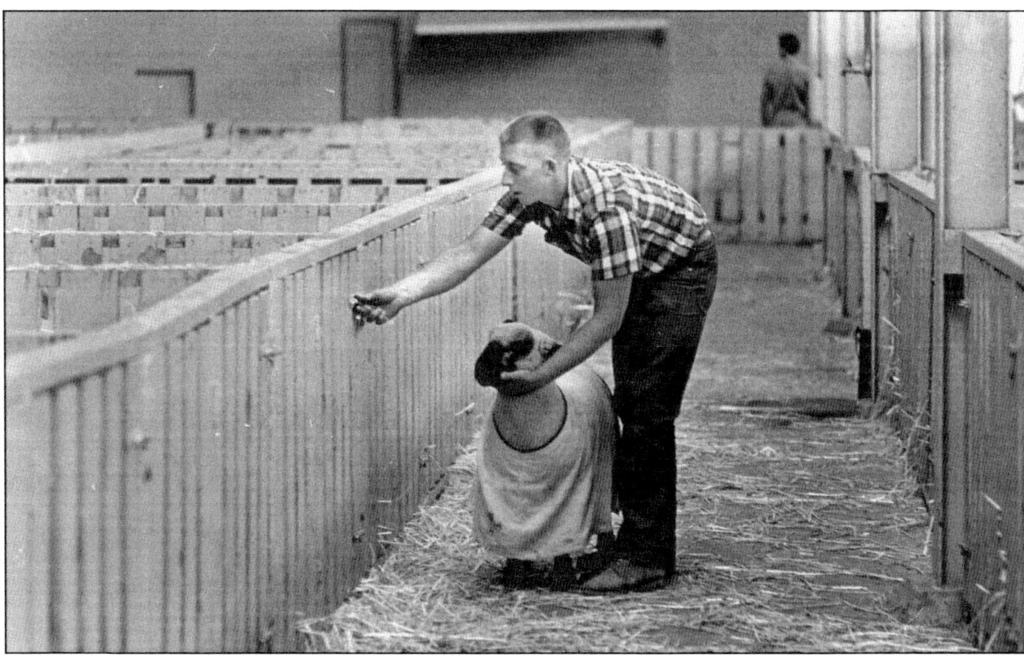

Norman Lincoln, a member of the Future Farmers of America (FFA), was one of the first to arrive for the 1967 State Fair. He is shown here herding his prize Hampshire sheep into the stock pens. Members of the FFA at this time were assisting with the planning for the new site at Cal Expo. (CSH.)

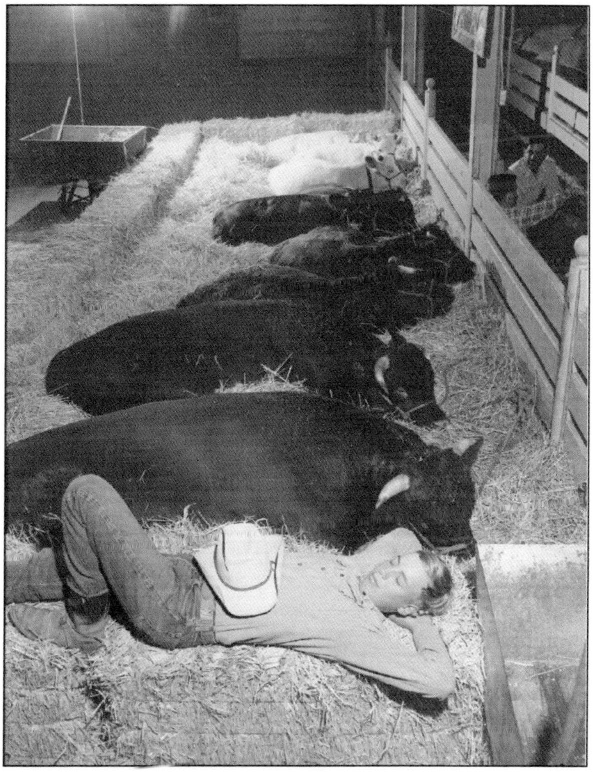

Preparing for the stock show can be very tiring. This photograph from 1954 captures a competitor in the show catching up on his sleep next to his small herd of eight shorthorns. This is a common sight to this day at the State Fair. (CSH.)

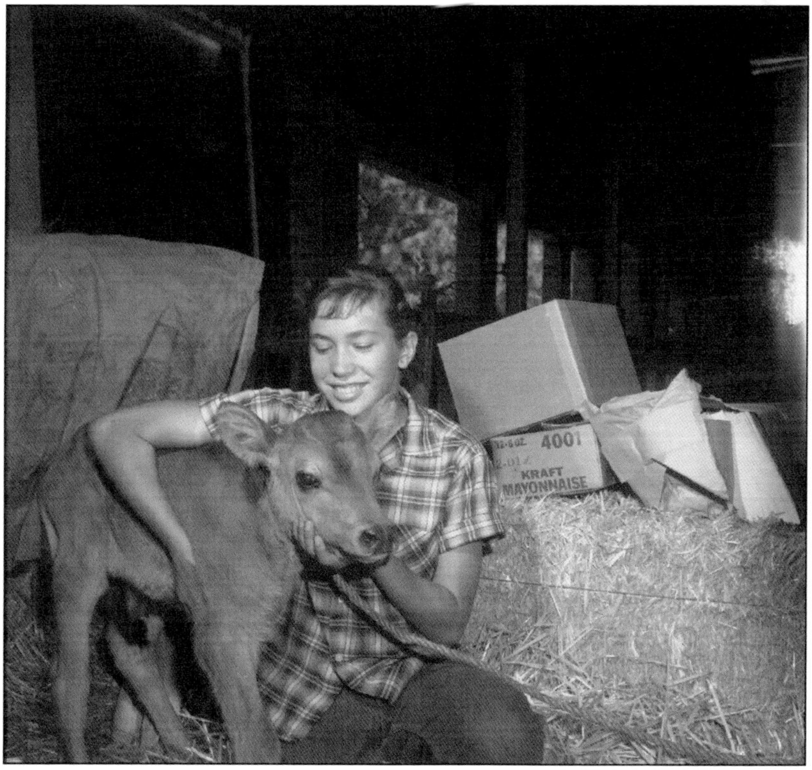

The photograph at left shows the first calf born at the State Fair in 1960. The girl in the photo is unidentified. Both the girl and the calf were potential attendees at future State Fairs. (CSH.)

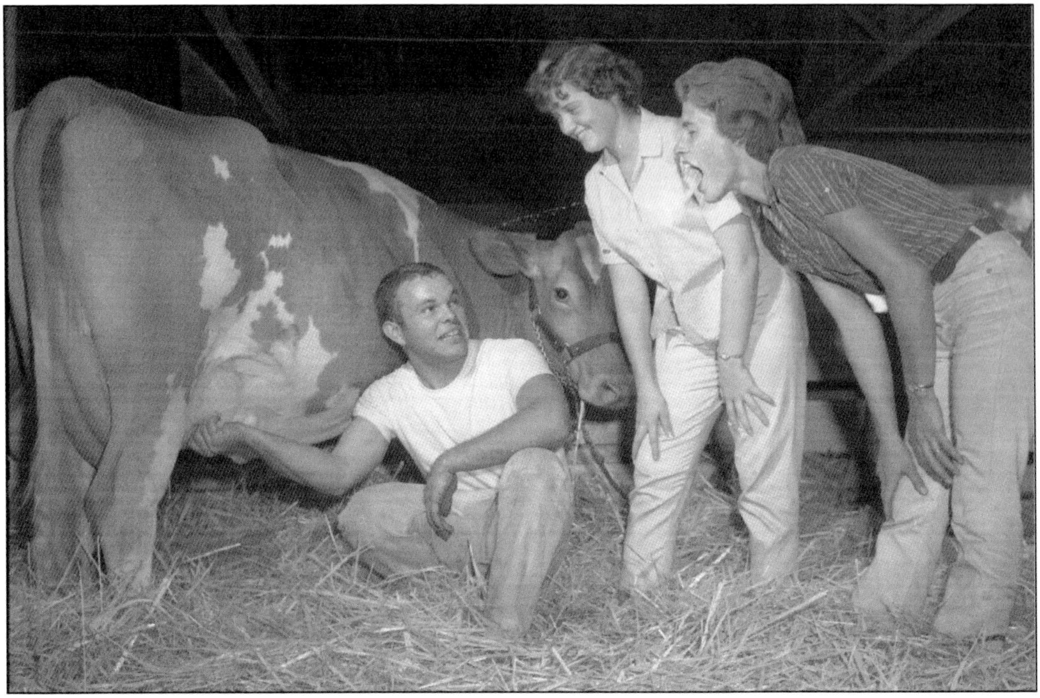

While the stock show is considered very serious to all the entrants, that does not mean they cannot have a bit of fun. In 1960, two visitors to the fair got a taste of the freshest milk possible from one of the entrants in the stock show. (CSH.)

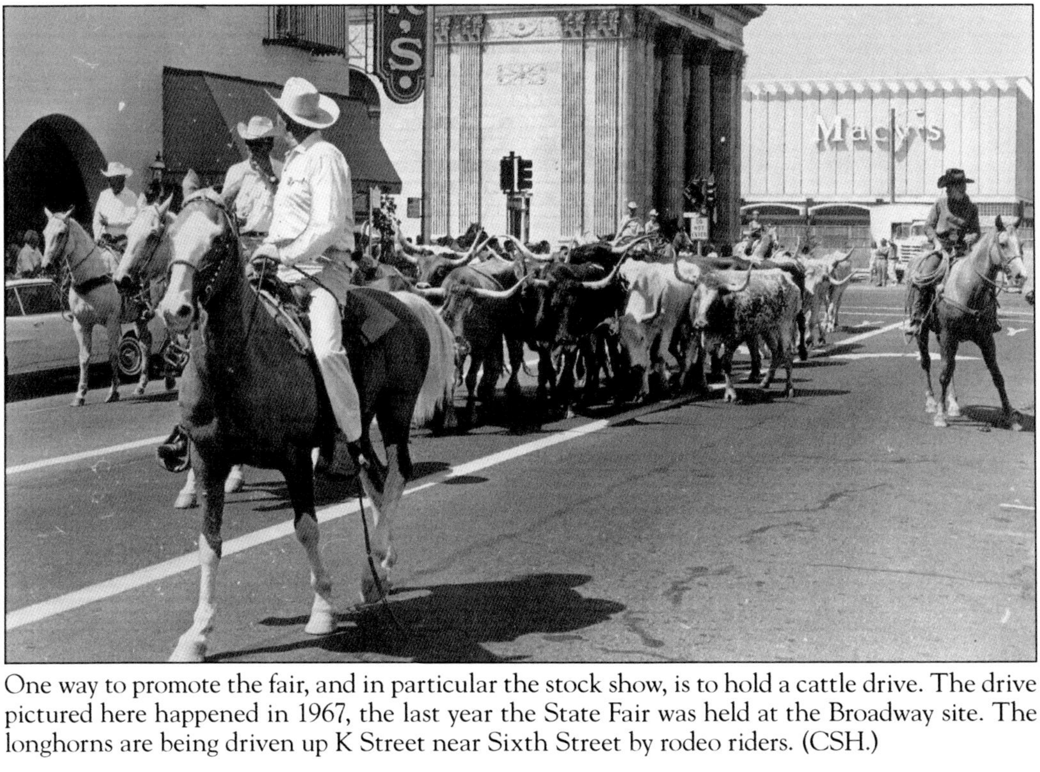

One way to promote the fair, and in particular the stock show, is to hold a cattle drive. The drive pictured here happened in 1967, the last year the State Fair was held at the Broadway site. The longhorns are being driven up K Street near Sixth Street by rodeo riders. (CSH.)

Who said world politics and farm animals do not go together? In 1962, Krushchev the bucking mule, along with his owner Cotton Rosser, was a star of the show. He was given the name after only 4 out of 350 had successfully ridden him. It was claimed he was the only mule in the world capable of throwing rodeo riders. The claim seems correct. (CSH.)

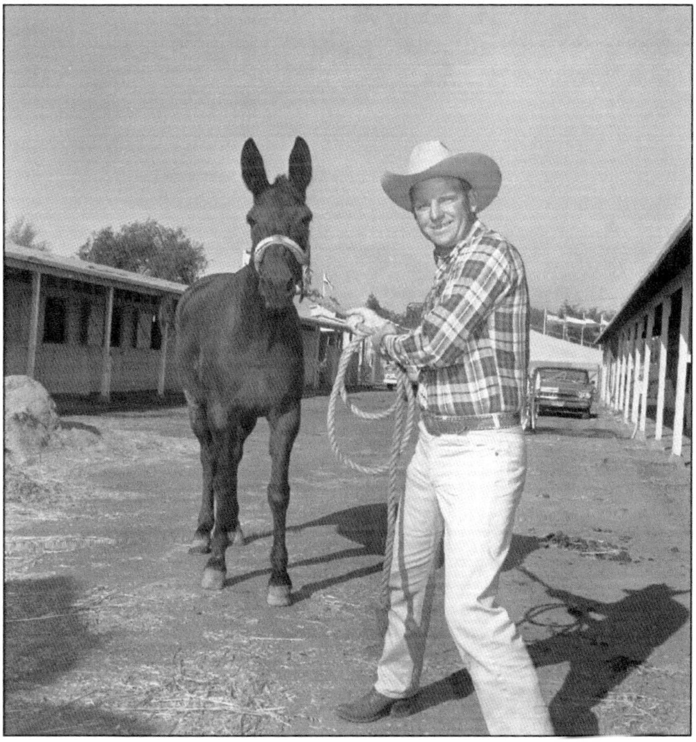

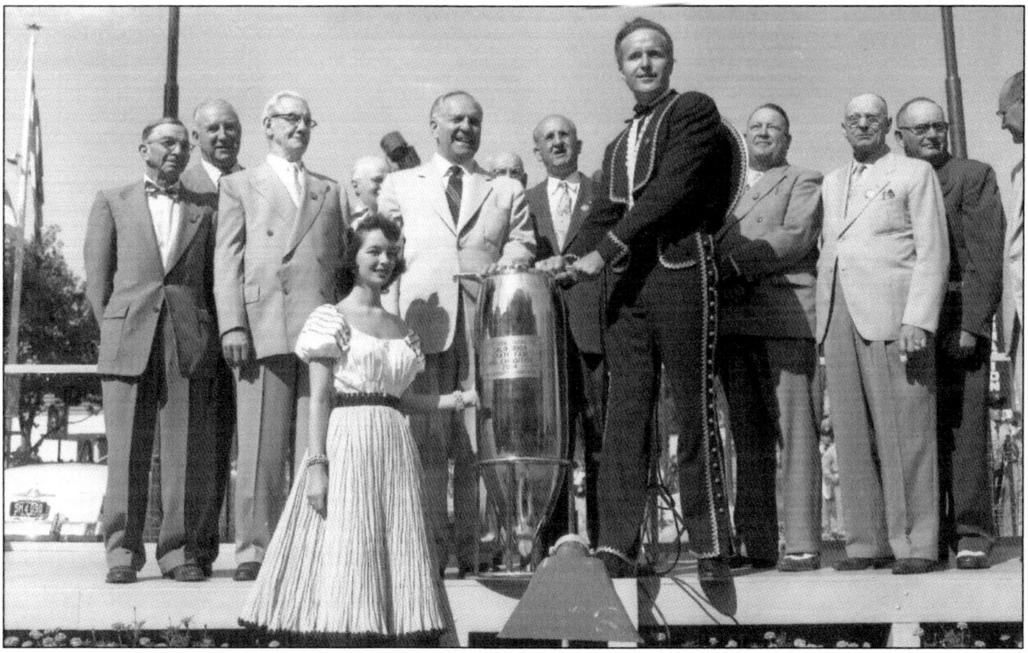

The State Fair celebrated 100 years in 1954 with a time capsule. Governor Knight and the "Californian," portrayed by actor Bill Meigs to represent California history, have their hands on a bomb-shaped container with 100 years of fair history inside. They are surrounded by fair officials, including fair president William P. Wright (center) and the 1954 Maid of California, Phyllis Yarwood (front). (CSH.)

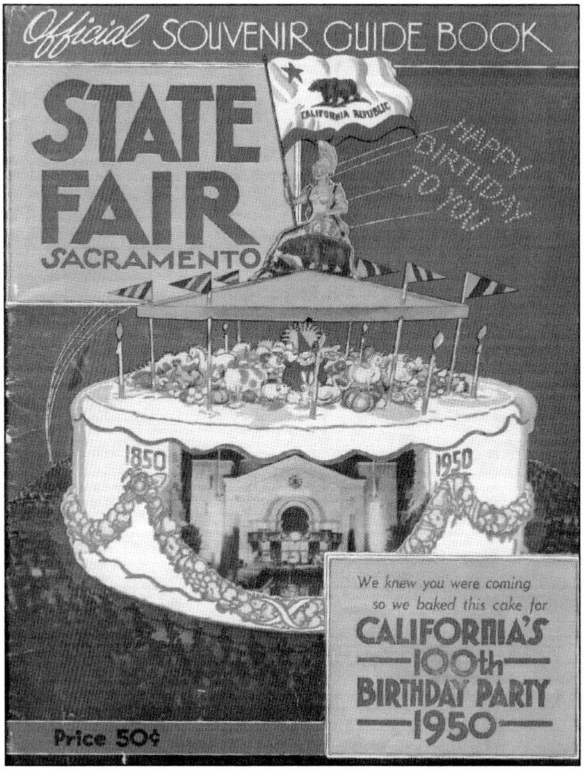

In 1950, California celebrated its centennial and the State Fair was central to the festivities. The 100th Birthday Party was the theme of the fair that year, as seen here on the cover of the "Official Souvenir Guide Book." (Sacramento Room, Sacramento Public Library.)

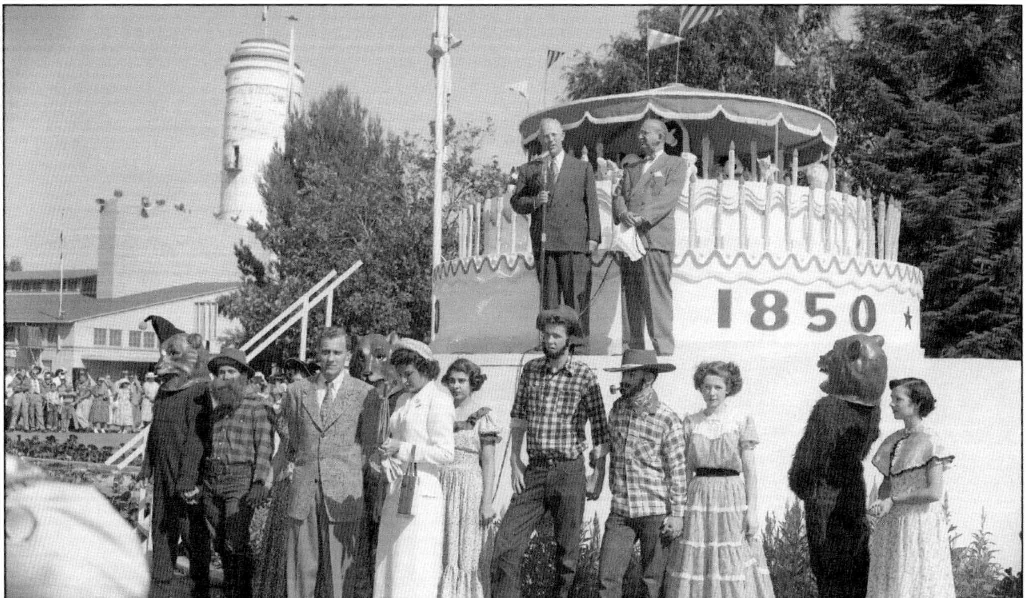

Gov. Earl Warren is seen here addressing the crowd on opening day in 1950, on the cake that graces the cover of the souvenir guide book. In front of the cake are characters representing the miners and pioneers who came for the Gold Rush, along with the state symbol, the bear. This photograph is by Pulitzer Prize–winning photographer Joseph Benetti, when he worked for the *Sacramento Union* newspaper. (CSH.)

In 1954, Phyllis Yarwood of Orange County was chosen as the Maid of California to represent the California State Fair for the year. The runners-up were from Yolo and San Francisco Counties. (CSH.)

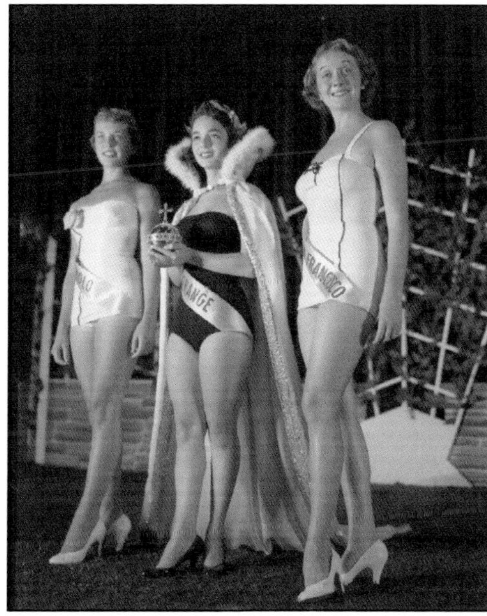

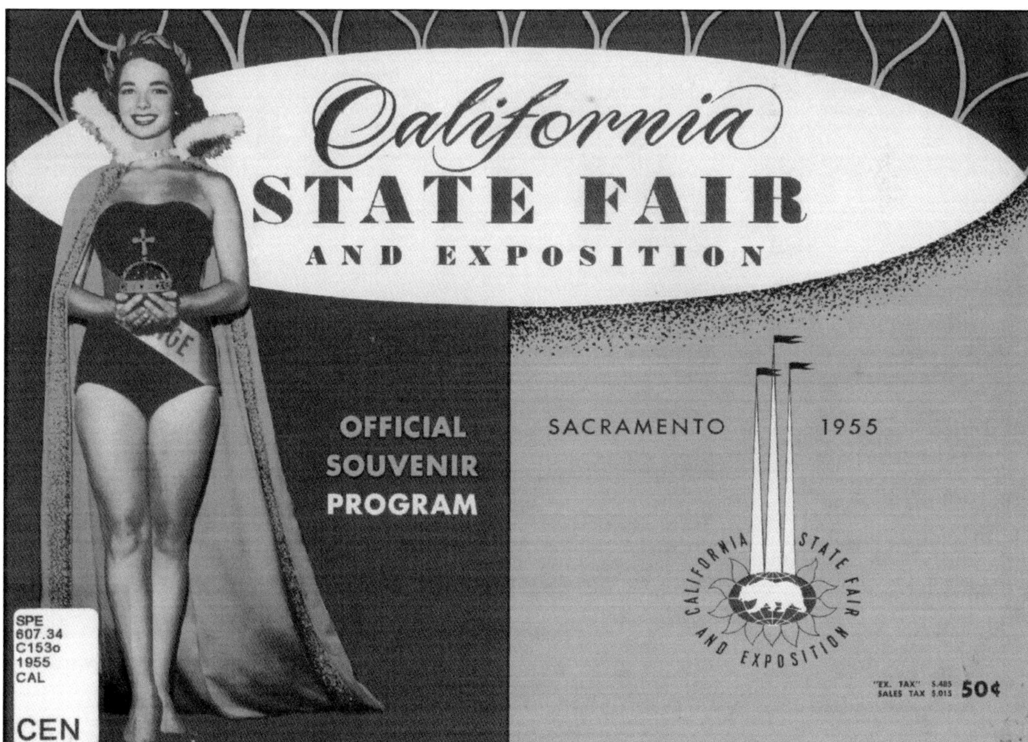

One of the benefits of being selected as the Maid of California is the winner's photograph appearing on all sorts of promotional items. Phyllis Yarwood, the 1954 Maid of California, is shown on the cover of the 1955 "Official Souvenir Program," seen and purchased by thousands of fairgoers. (Sacramento Room, Sacramento Public Library.)

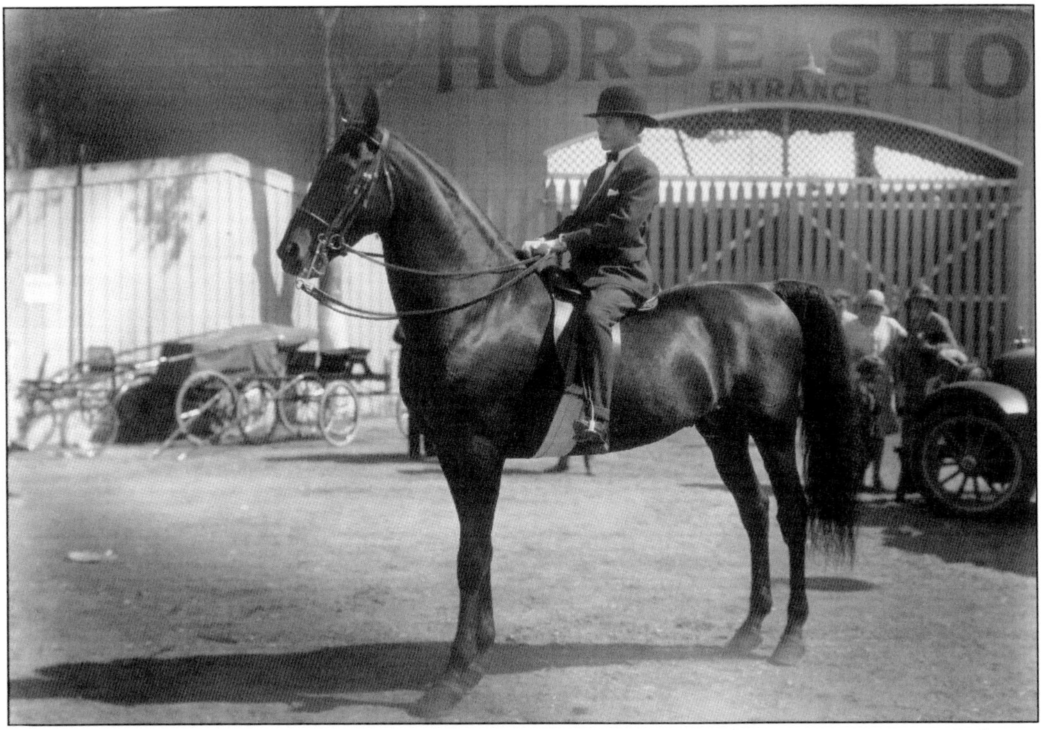

The horse show at the California State Fair is one of the oldest in the western states and always attracts the best riders. In 1926, Barbara Worth, 14, entered the show with her horse, Waveland's Choice. Worth had a long and successful career training horses, and her affiliation with the State Fair, as a competitor and horse owner, lasted for decades. (CSH.)

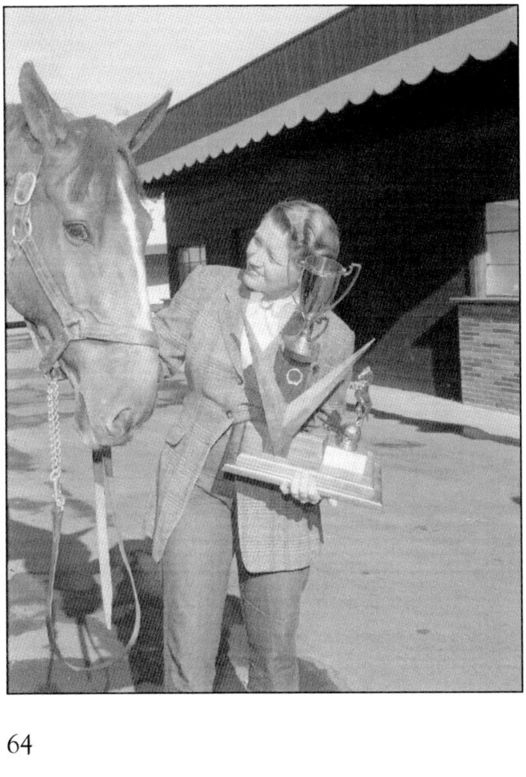

In 1959, Barbara Worth's 18-year-old giant chestnut gelding, Balbriggan, was the champion jumper at the State Fair horse show. Standing 18 hands, or six feet high, Balbriggan was one of the largest horses at the show. In 1994, Worth was inducted into the Show Jumping Hall of Fame. And Balbriggan is still remembered as a great horse. (CSH.)

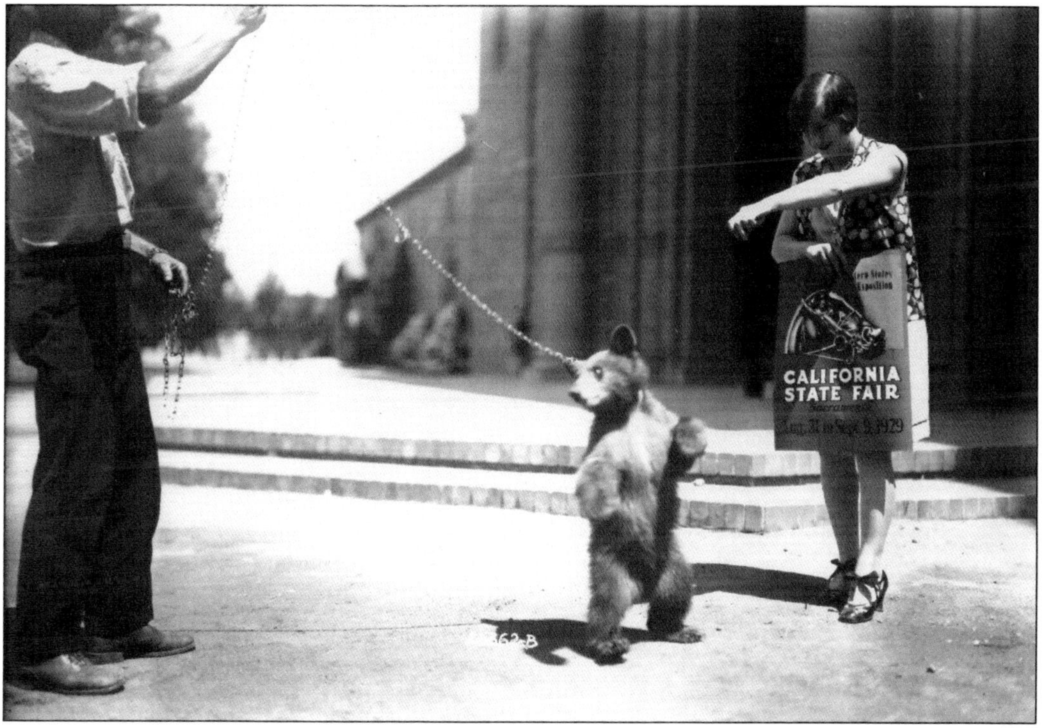

This August 1929 photograph of the mascot of the State Fair was taken to promote the fair that year. (CSH.)

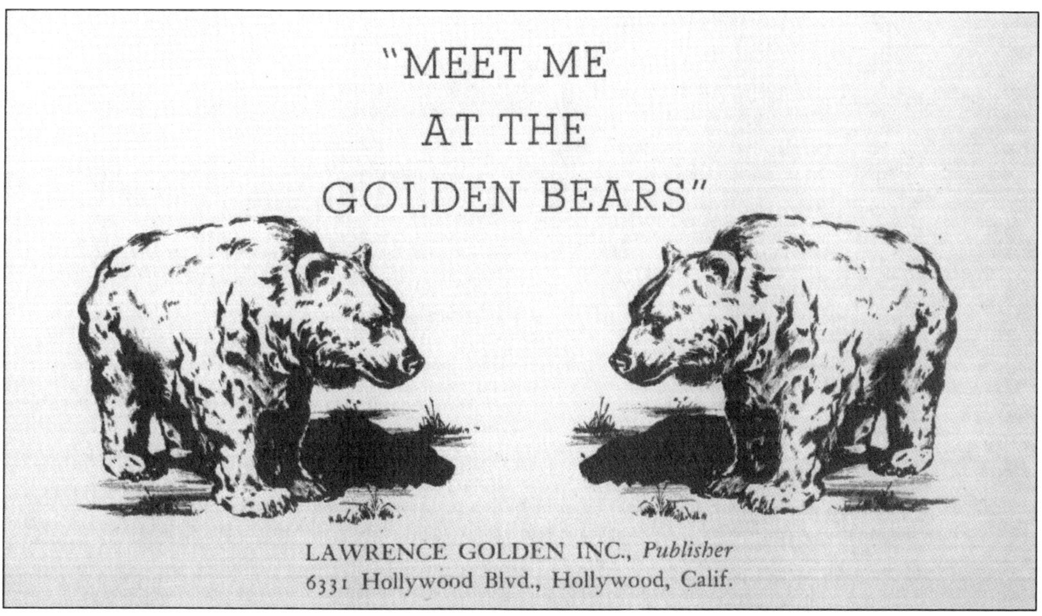

"Meet Me At The Golden Bears" is the phrase to use when meeting up with friends at the State Fair. The bears were installed in 1929 at the front of the main Agricultural Hall. This image was inside the front cover of the 1947 souvenir guide. (CSH.)

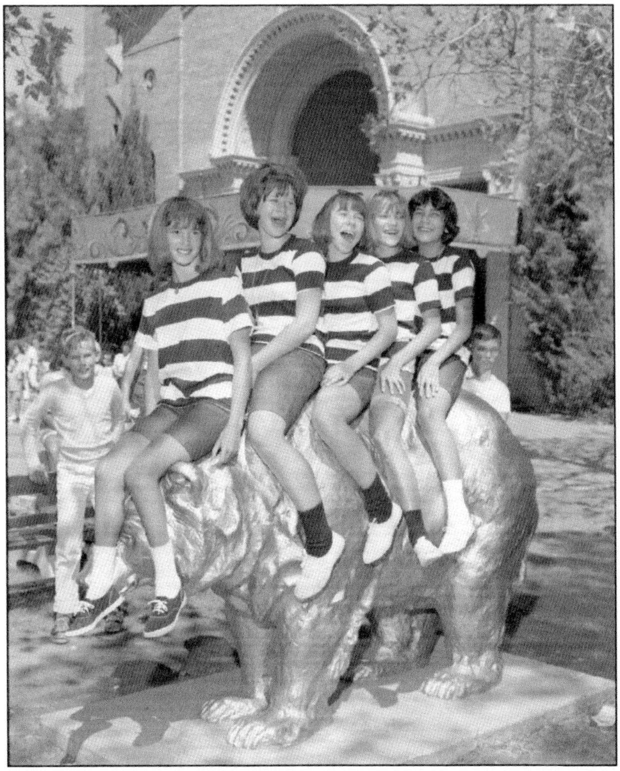

The Golden Bears are more than just a place to meet. They are also very popular for posed photographs. This c. 1964 photograph shows five friends having a lot of fun with the bears. (CSH.)

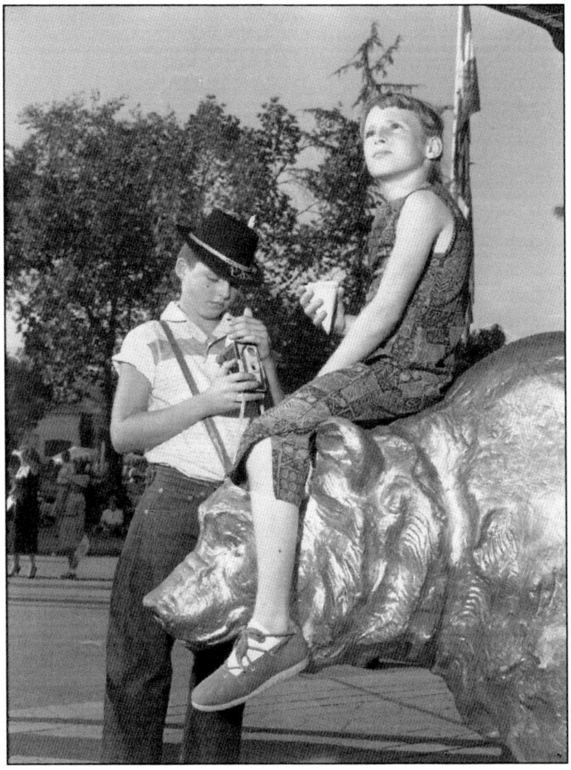

Serious photography featuring the Golden Bears is also encouraged. This late-1950s image shows a young photographer and his model trying to get the perfect shot. (CSH.)

Family photos with the bears are always popular, as seen here in 1957. The cute children are unidentified. (CSH.)

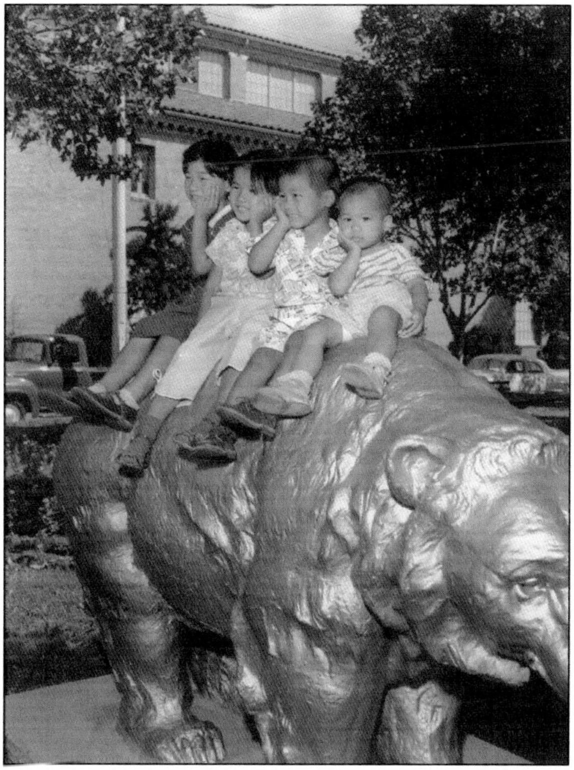

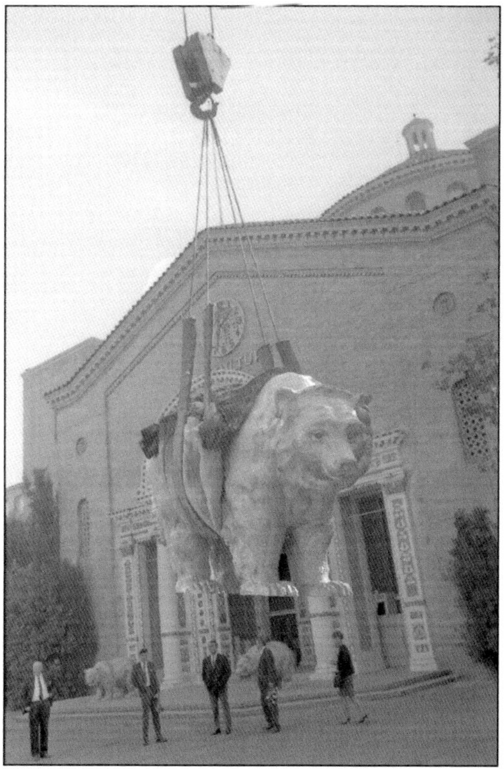

In August 1968, the four Golden Bears were moved from the Broadway site to Cal Expo. Two of the original bears flank the main driveway into Cal Expo on Exposition Boulevard. Two more original bears are located inside the main gate. Cal Expo has since added replica bears near the racetrack and at Gate D. (CSH.)

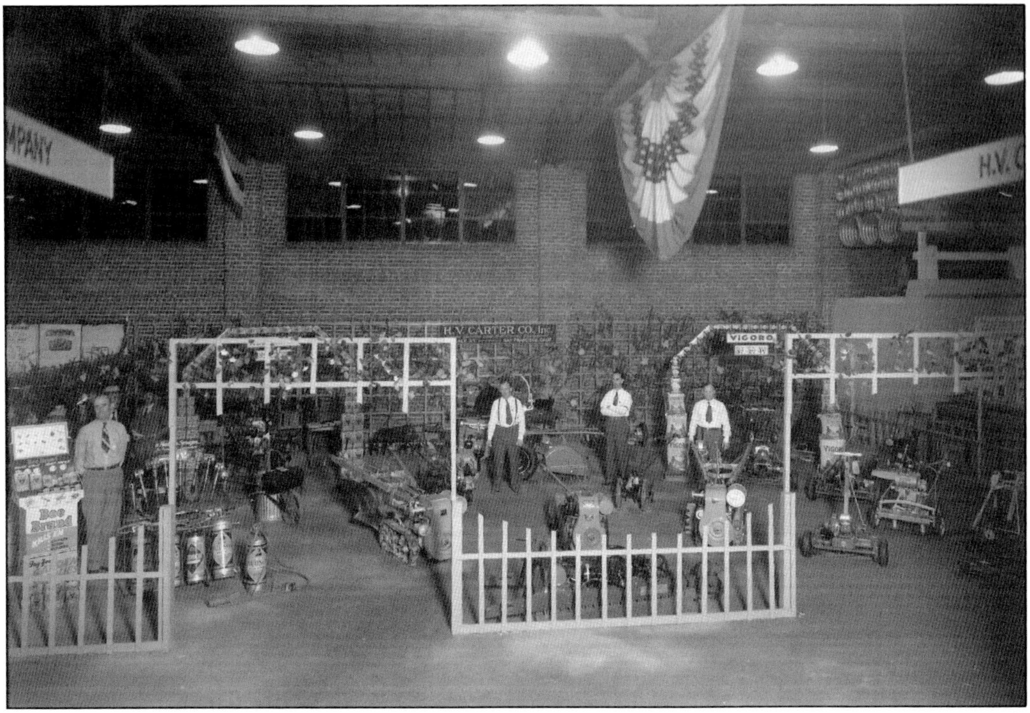

The State Fair encouraged displays of new technology that were useful to farmers and those with smaller tracts of land. The H. V. Carter Company of San Francisco set up this display in 1937 to showcase the wide variety of motorized landscape equipment, insecticides, fertilizers, and grass seed available to maintain golf courses. (CSH.)

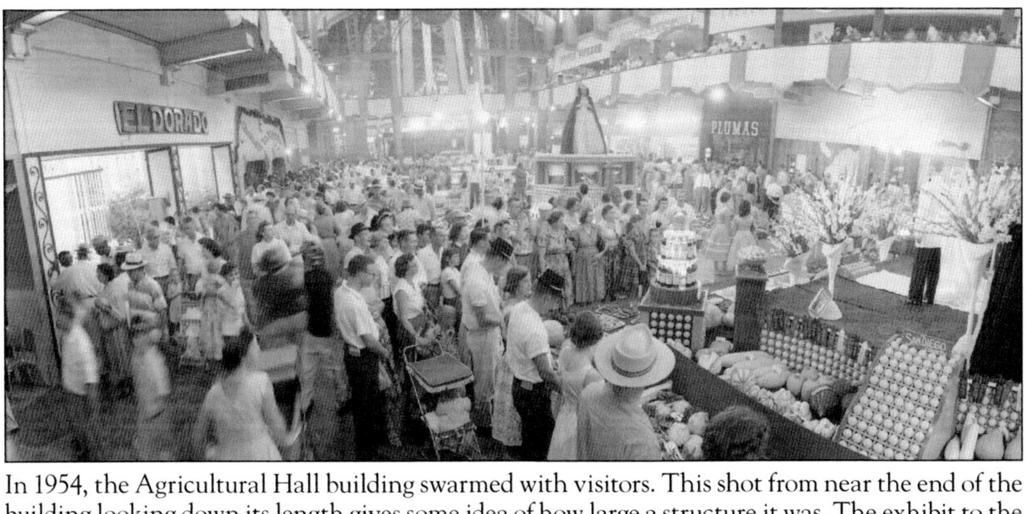

In 1954, the Agricultural Hall building swarmed with visitors. This shot from near the end of the building looking down its length gives some idea of how large a structure it was. The exhibit to the right is for San Diego County, which looks to have had a very successful exhibition. (CSH.)

The 1954 State Fair featured one of the largest county exhibits ever set up. Gov. Goodwin Knight and his wife wave to the crowd from the exhibit for Alameda County. The port at Alameda was one of the largest on the West Coast, where goods from around the world arrived and California's exports to the world were shipped. Note the size of the model ship. (CSH.)

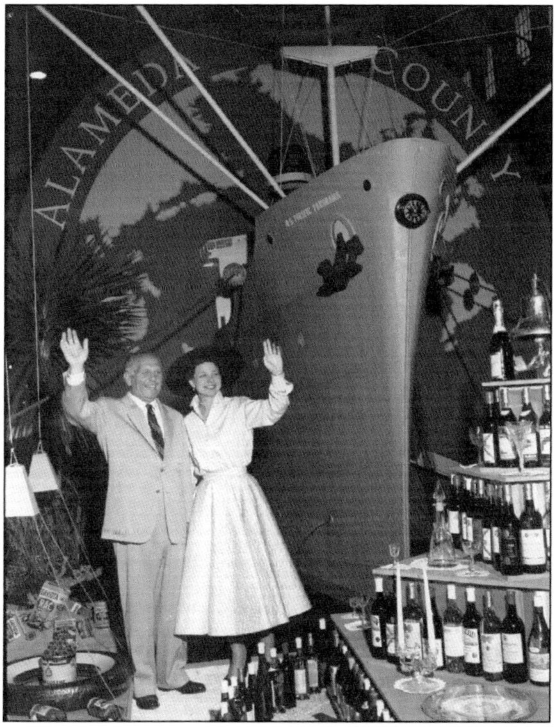

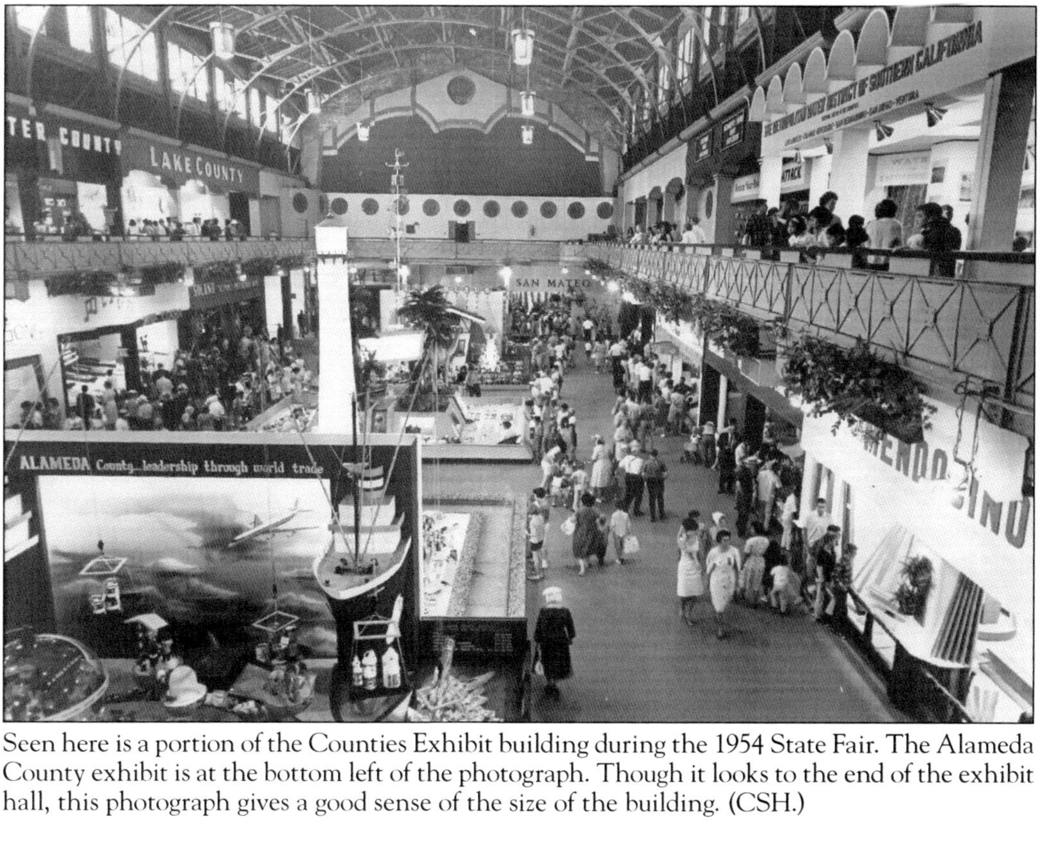

Seen here is a portion of the Counties Exhibit building during the 1954 State Fair. The Alameda County exhibit is at the bottom left of the photograph. Though it looks to the end of the exhibit hall, this photograph gives a good sense of the size of the building. (CSH.)

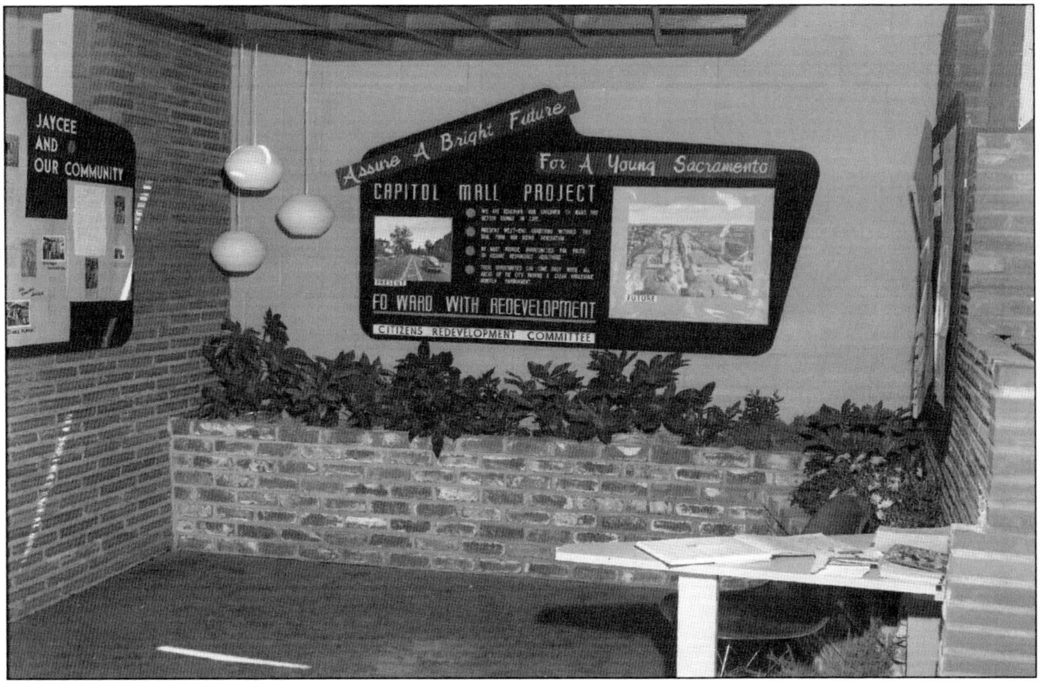

The exhibit hall was also used to promote various projects from around the state. This one, from 1954, was done to promote the proposed Capitol Mall redevelopment project, from Tower Bridge to the state capitol in Sacramento. The project was completed in the early 1960s. (CSH.)

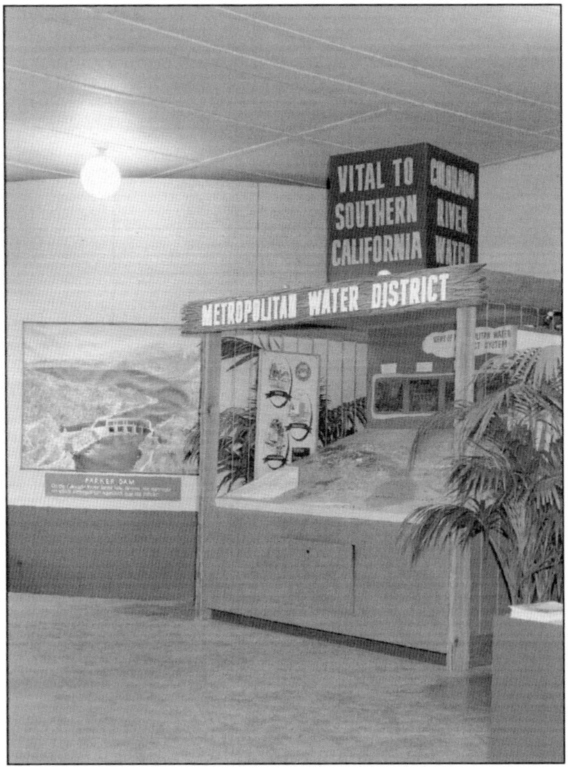

The Metropolitan Water District in Southern California also had an exhibit in 1954. It was used to promote several projects to move large quantities of water from abundant sources in Northern California to the much drier south and its increasing population. Water is still a contentious subject and is often highlighted in county exhibits. (CSH.)

A lot of work goes into setting up exhibits. Shown here are workers and volunteers building the exhibit for Placer County in 1954. The car-icing plant was located in the Roseville railyard, as part of the Pacific Fruit Exchange area. Specially designed rail cars were loaded with fresh fruits and vegetables, then packed with ice for shipping to the rest of the country. (CSH.)

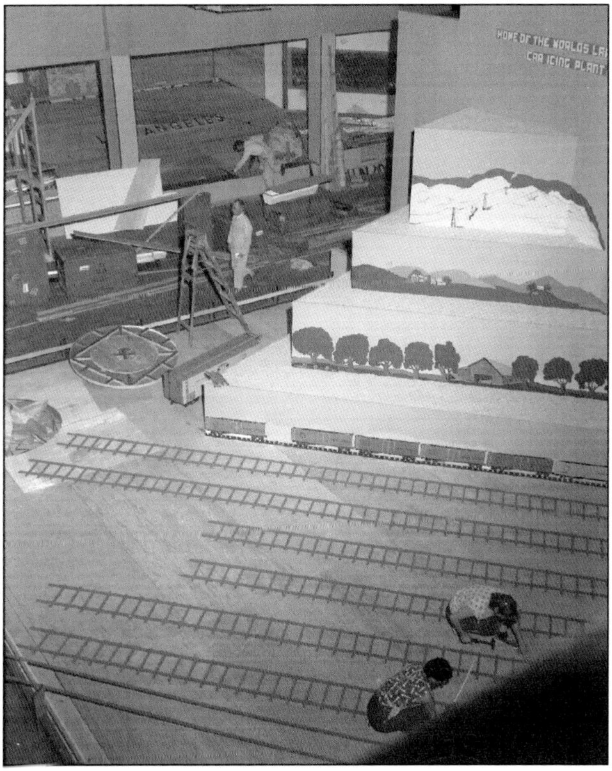

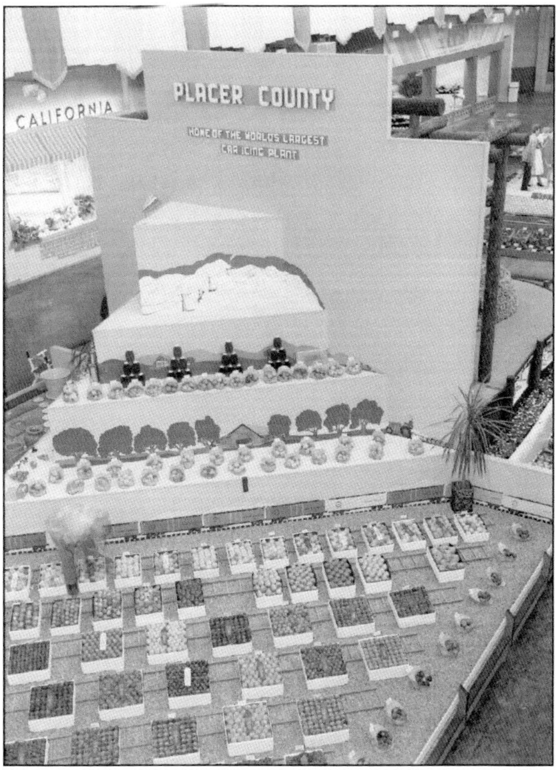

This photograph shows the nearly finished Placer County exhibit. A man is seen putting the finishing touches on a box of fruit. The car-icing plant in Roseville was not in operation for much longer. A few years later, mechanically cooled rail cars were developed, ending the need for ice. The exhibit was an eye-catching way to promote California's agriculture. (CSH.)

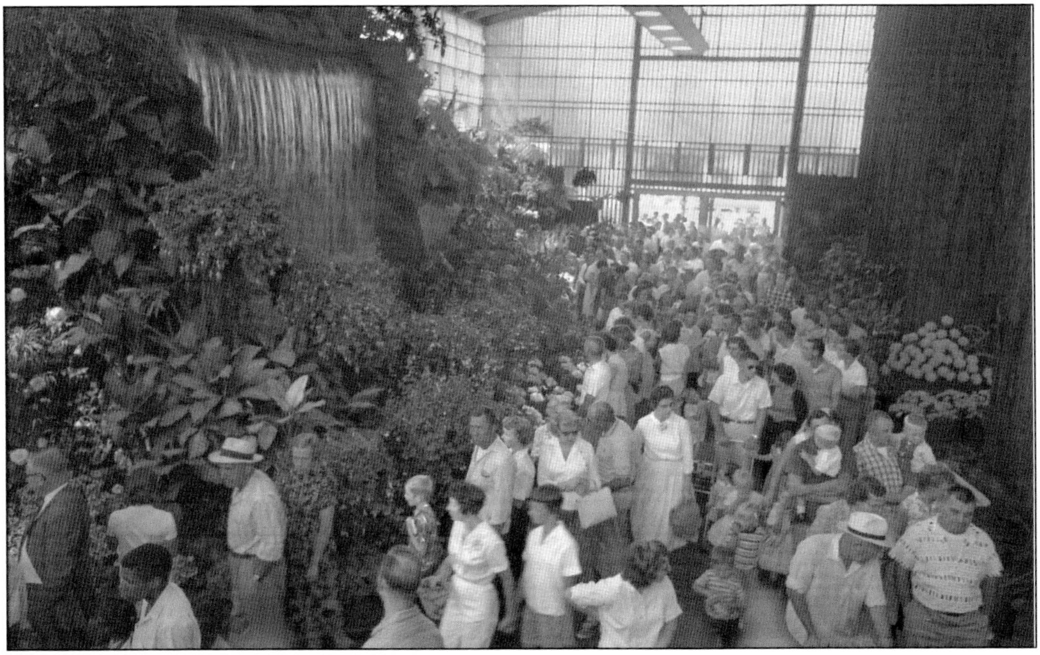

The main entrance to the Hall of Flowers is shown in 1960. This was always one of the most popular exhibits for fairgoers, as the crowd seen here indicates. And it is not hard to understand why. With waterfalls cooling the room and beautiful exhibits of both common and exotic flowers, it was a natural draw. (CSH.)

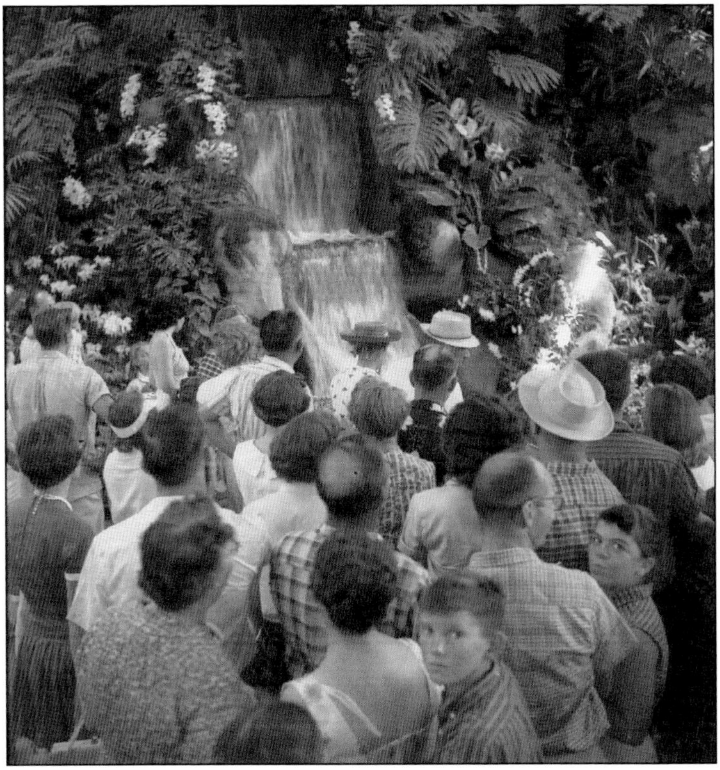

This elaborate exhibit featuring a tiered waterfall in the Hall of Flowers in 1958 draws a large crowd. (CSH.)

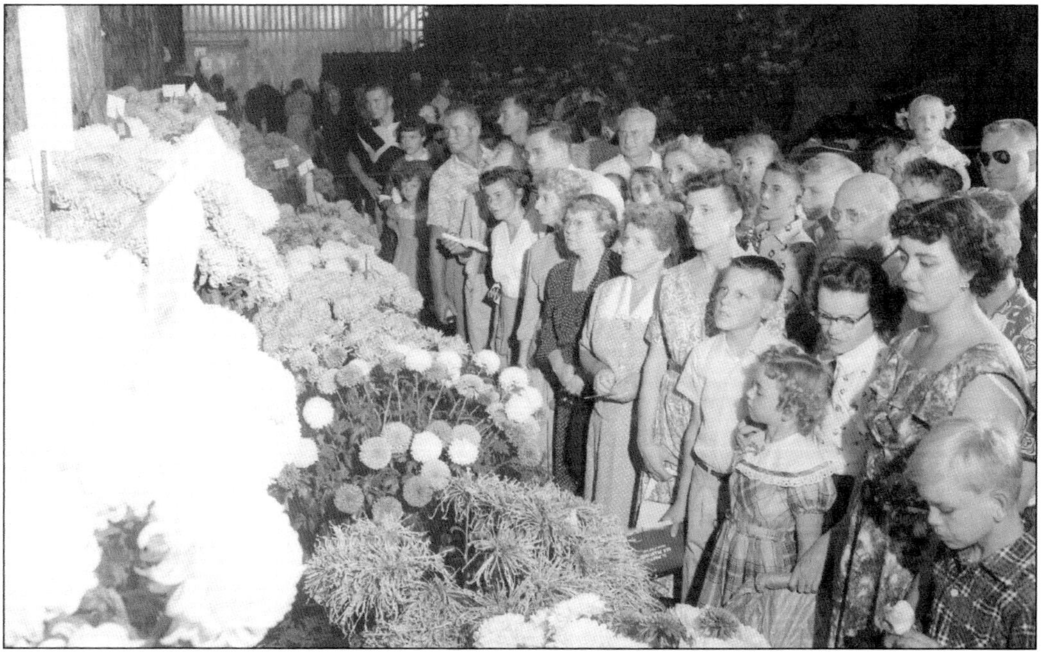

Another exhibit in the Hall of Flowers, this one was photographed in 1954. The crowd viewing the exhibit is of every age, from the very young to the very old. And everyone is entranced. Even though the crowd is large, it appears that it is very quiet. The young man in the middle seems particularly impressed. (CSH.)

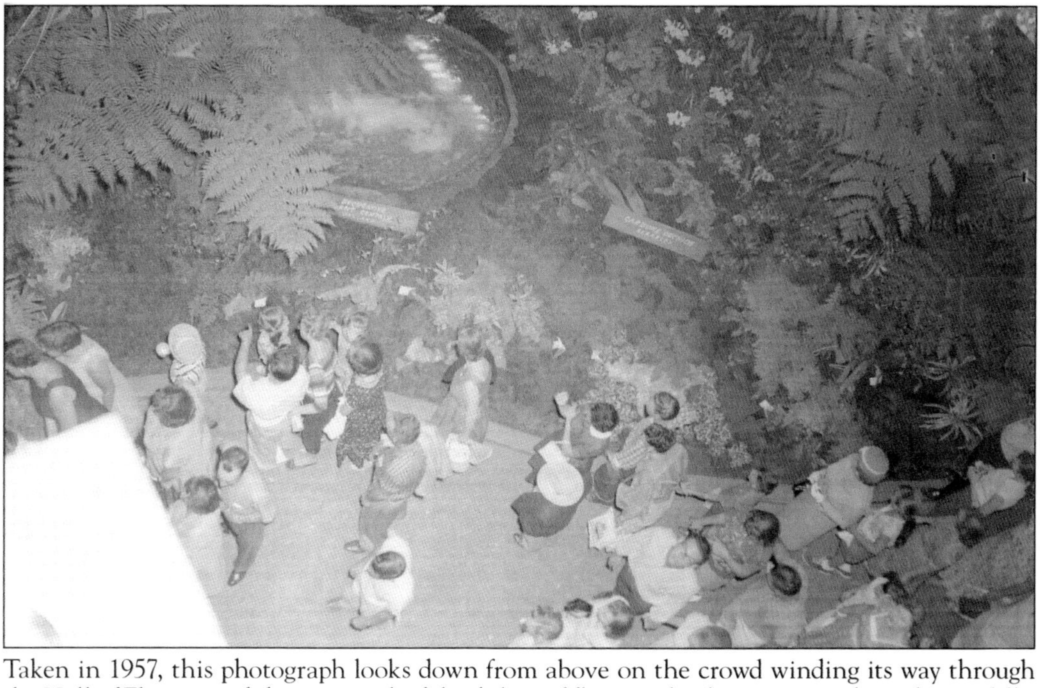

Taken in 1957, this photograph looks down from above on the crowd winding its way through the Hall of Flowers and the many colorful exhibits of flowers, shrubs, trees, ponds, and waterfalls. All of the exhibits had signs indicating the types of flowers and shrubs as well as the suppliers, so that potential customers knew whom to contact. (CSH.)

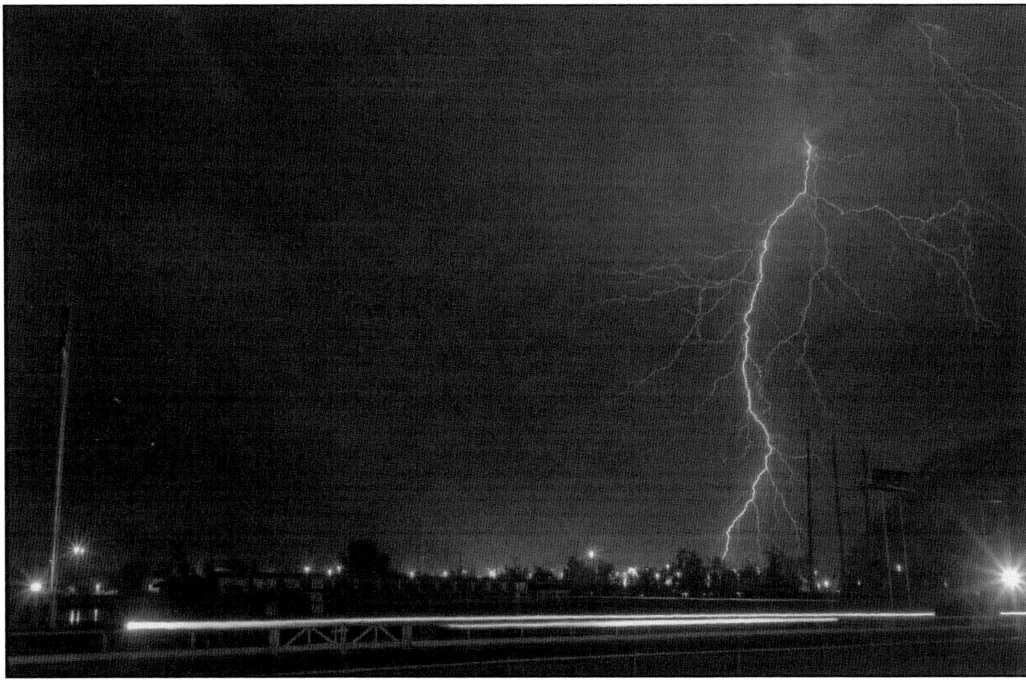

On September 2, 1960, during the State Fair, a series of thunderstorms moved over Northern California. This spectacular photograph captures a large bolt of lightning striking near the south end of the racetrack. Usually, the fireworks seen during a State Fair are man-made. The thunderstorms that night caused over 500 fires throughout Northern California. (CSH.)

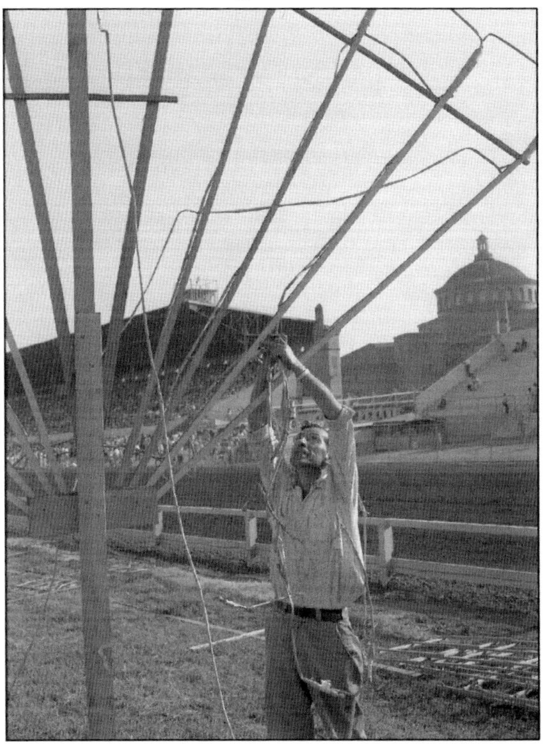

The fair's man-made fireworks require a lot of man-hours to set up displays each night. Seen here on September 6, 1956, State Fair employee George DeAngelous sets up a fan display. It does not look like much here, but when the fuse is lit, the display will become a peacock. (CSH.)

The fireworks fans were popular for many years. A 1954 ground display featuring four of the fans is seen here from the grandstand, which is packed with people. The little girl in the middle of the photograph is very excited. (CSH.)

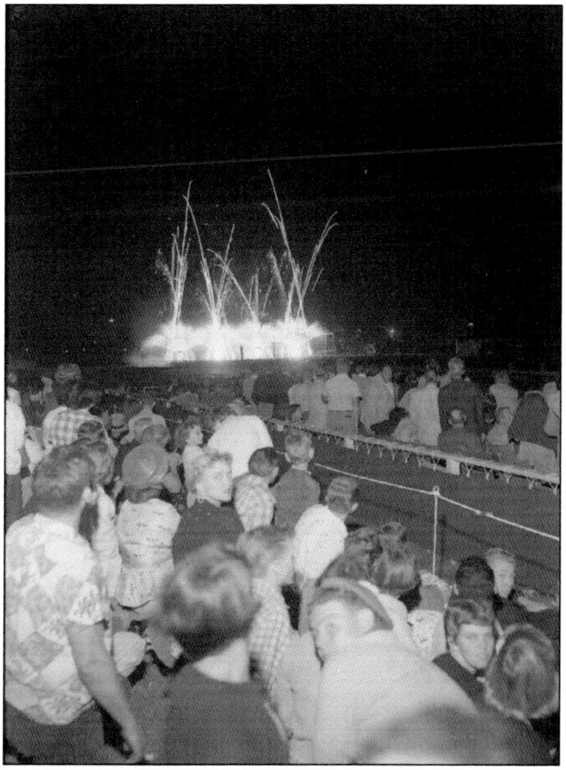

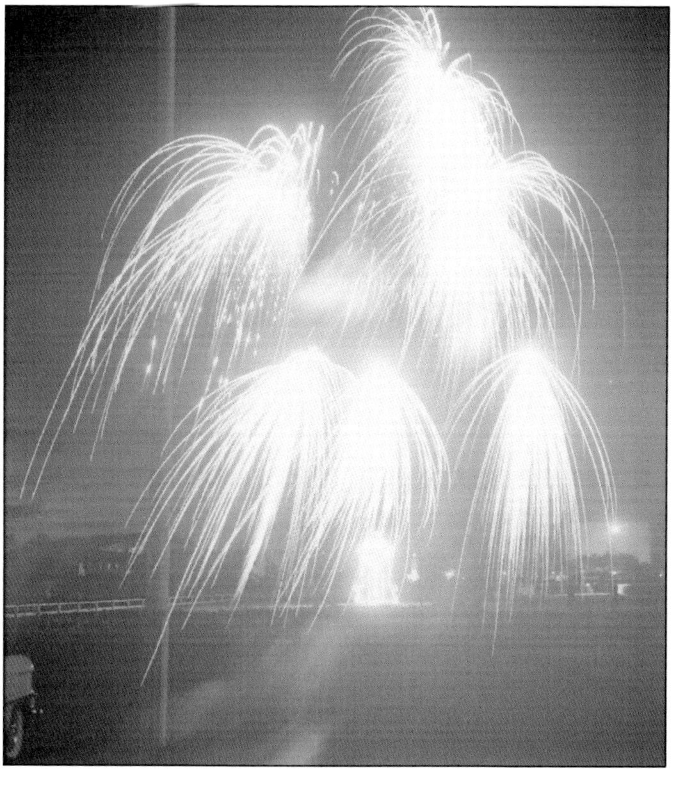

The grand finale to the fireworks display just past sunset on September 2, 1959, is seen from the south end of the racetrack. This timed exposure captured about ten shells going off plus the ground display, featuring a building of some type. Visible in the distance is the water tank. (CSH.)

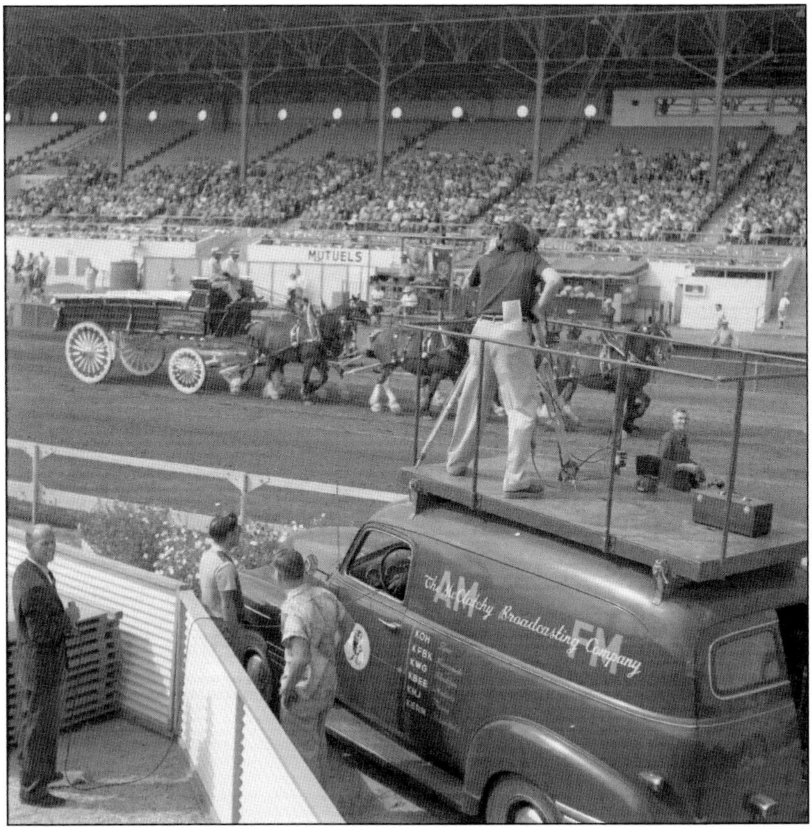

The McClatchy Broadcasting Company was a presence at many State Fairs. Their radio and TV stations covered the Central Valley, so McClatchy was the choice to cover big events at the fair, like the opening stock parade. In this photograph from about 1961, a crew is covering the event. The team of Clydesdales is from H. Castagnasso and Sons in Sonoma, California. (CSH.)

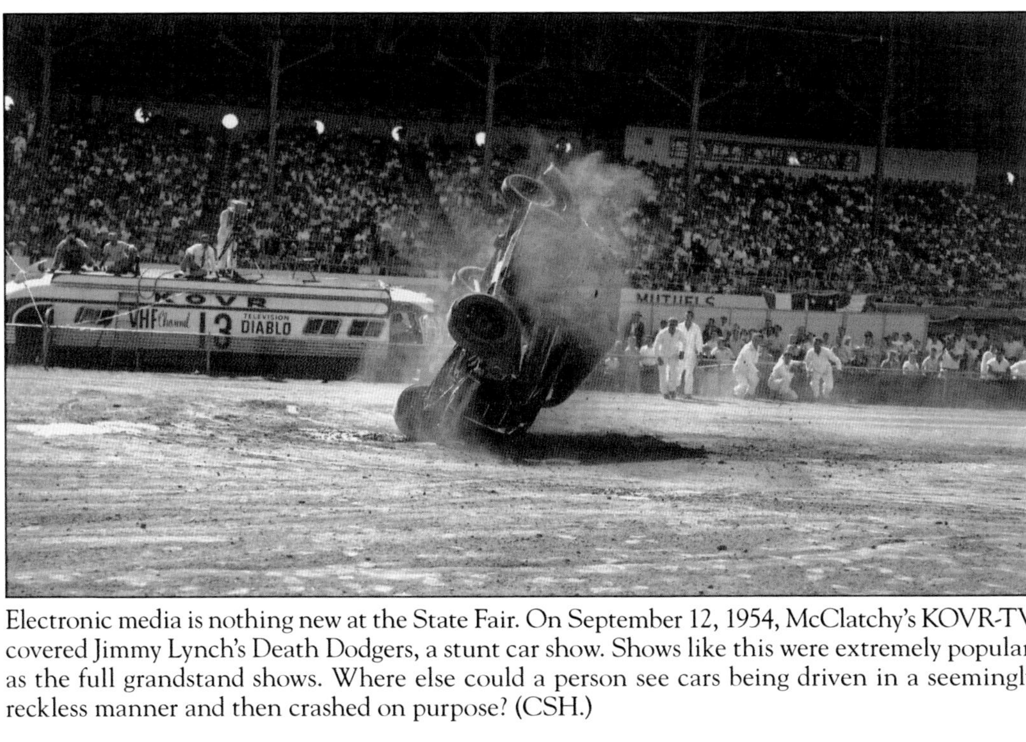

Electronic media is nothing new at the State Fair. On September 12, 1954, McClatchy's KOVR-TV covered Jimmy Lynch's Death Dodgers, a stunt car show. Shows like this were extremely popular, as the full grandstand shows. Where else could a person see cars being driven in a seemingly reckless manner and then crashed on purpose? (CSH.)

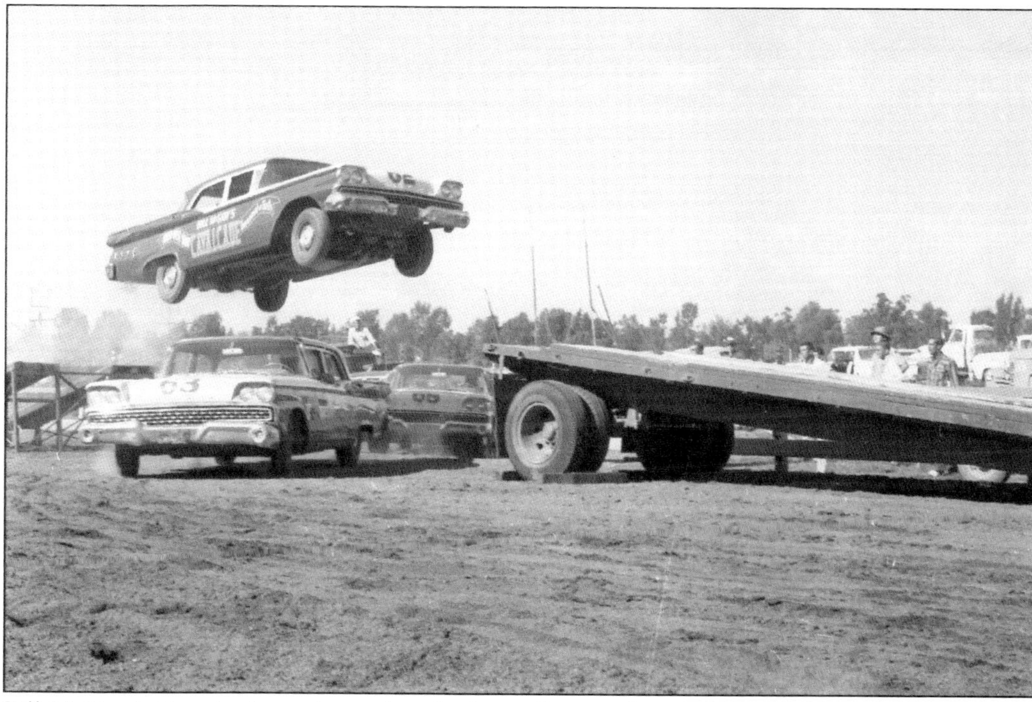

Bill McGaw's Cavalcade performed at the State Fair on September 9, 1959. In this stunt, Ford Fairlanes are driven around and between two ramps while another jumps approximately 50 feet between the ramps. Do not try this at home! (CSH.)

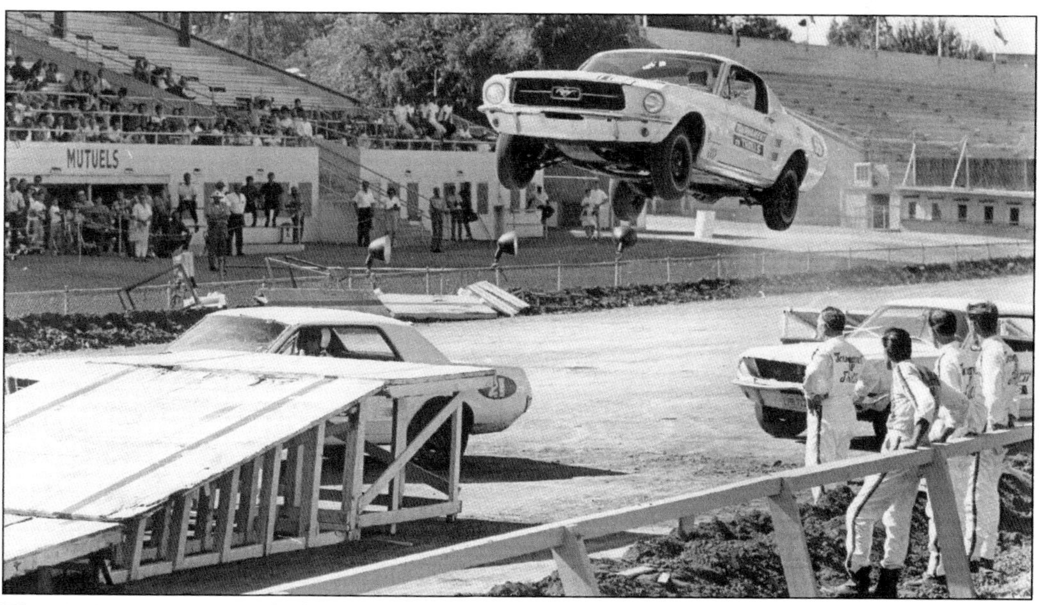

The 1967 Tournament of Thrills featured Ford Mustangs. This is the same type of stunt shown in the previous photo, but in this case, the ramps are built on-site. While still dangerous, it seems safer than using a flatbed truck trailer. (CSH.)

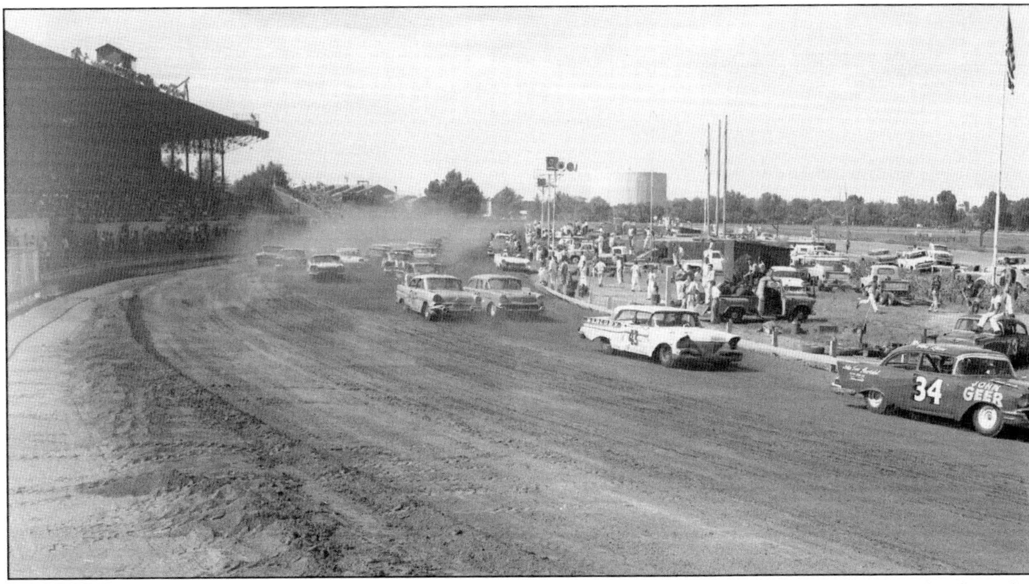

NASCAR sanctioned a Grand National 100-mile race on September 13, 1959. It was the last day of the fair, and the track had to be somewhat modified for the event. The race itself was difficult because of the amount of dust thrown up by the cars. The field is seen here heading into the first turn. (CSH.)

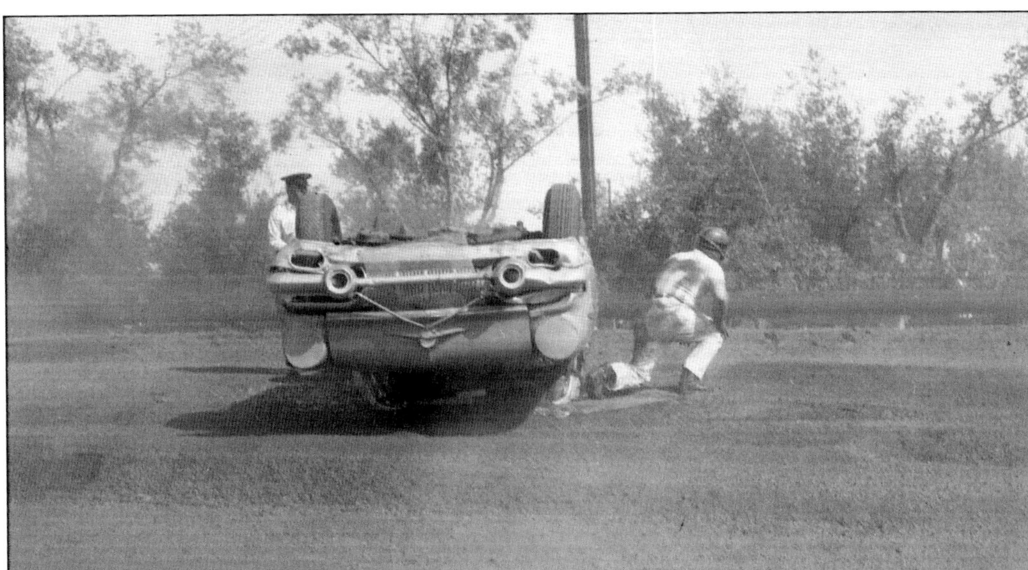

The NASCAR race was not without crashes. Driver Andy Scranton of Compton, California, crawls out of his car after it flipped at the south end of the track. A fireman is seen behind the car. Fortunately, Scranton was able to walk away and avoided serious injury. (CSH.)

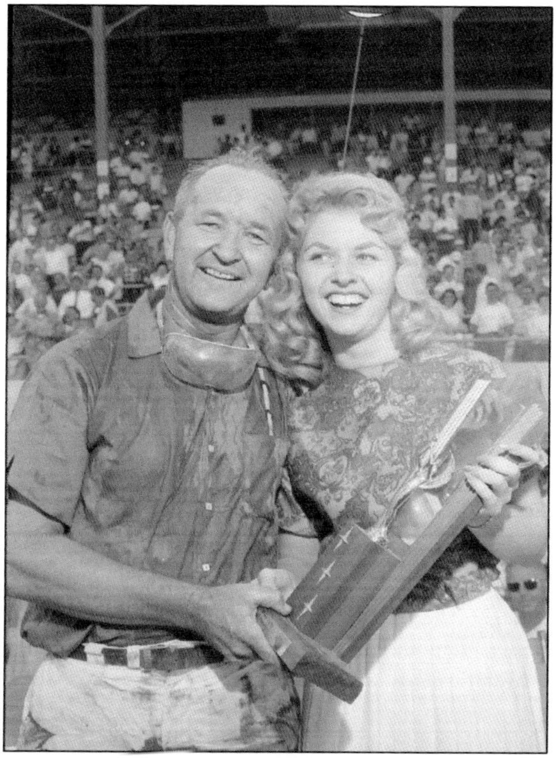

Driver Eddie Gray of Gardena, California, was able to find his way through the dust (note the nearly opaque goggles) and win the race. He is seen here accepting the trophy from Virginia Gere, who was the queen of the day. The photographs of the race were taken by *Sacramento Bee* photographer Irving Camp. (CSH.)

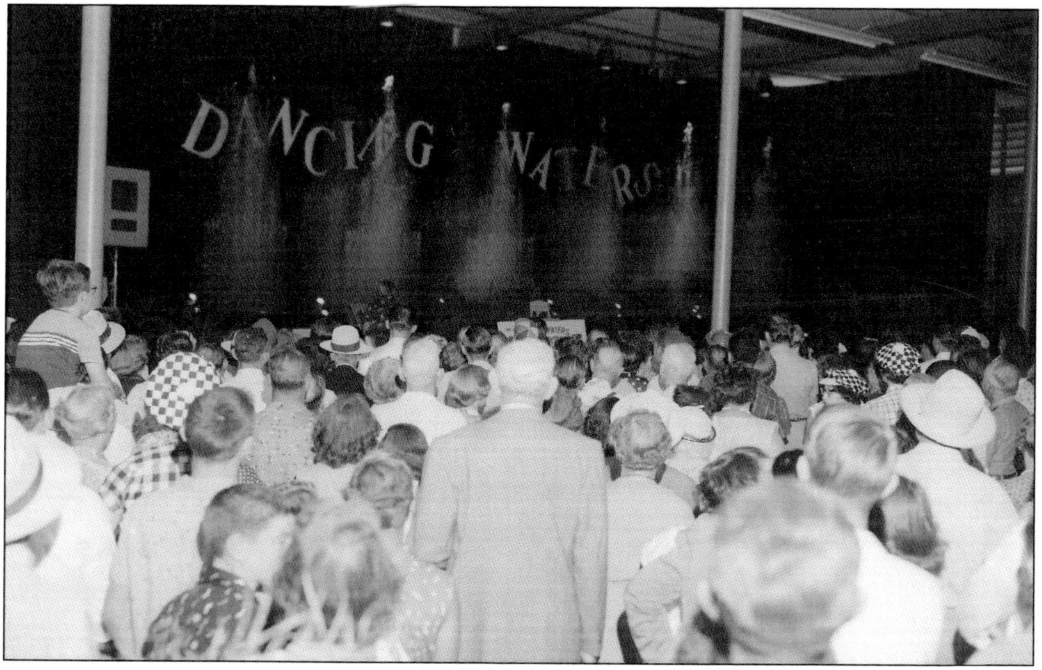

Dancing Waters debuted at the State Fair in 1954 and was an immediate hit. The 38 tons of water could be made to form shapes, appear as Niagara Falls, or mimic fire. This was done using 19 motors, color spotlights, 10,000 feet of wiring, and several thousand feet of steel pipe. Dancing Waters had premiered earlier at Radio City Music Hall in New York City. (CSH.)

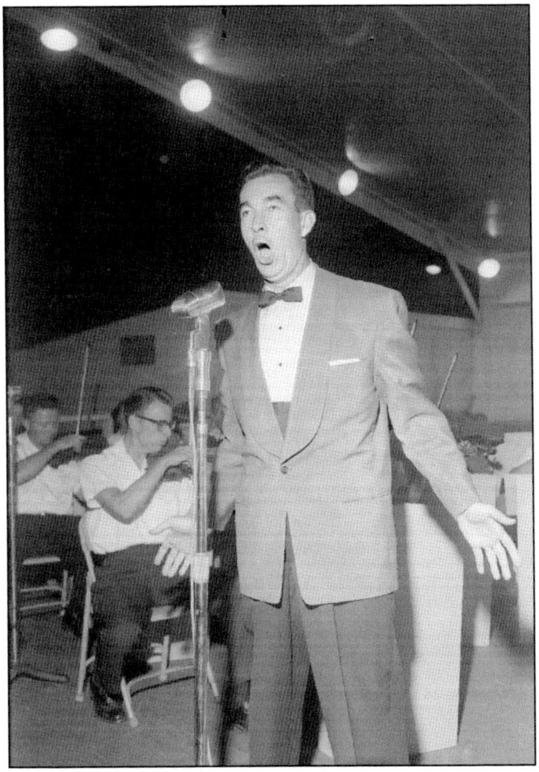

Sacramento native Stan Noonan was named the official vocalist of the 1959 fair. Noonan performed with the Dick Jurgens Orchestra, the San Francisco Opera, on Broadway, and with the San Francisco Symphony. He was also a regular on the Arthur Godfrey Show before his appearance at the State Fair. (CSH.)

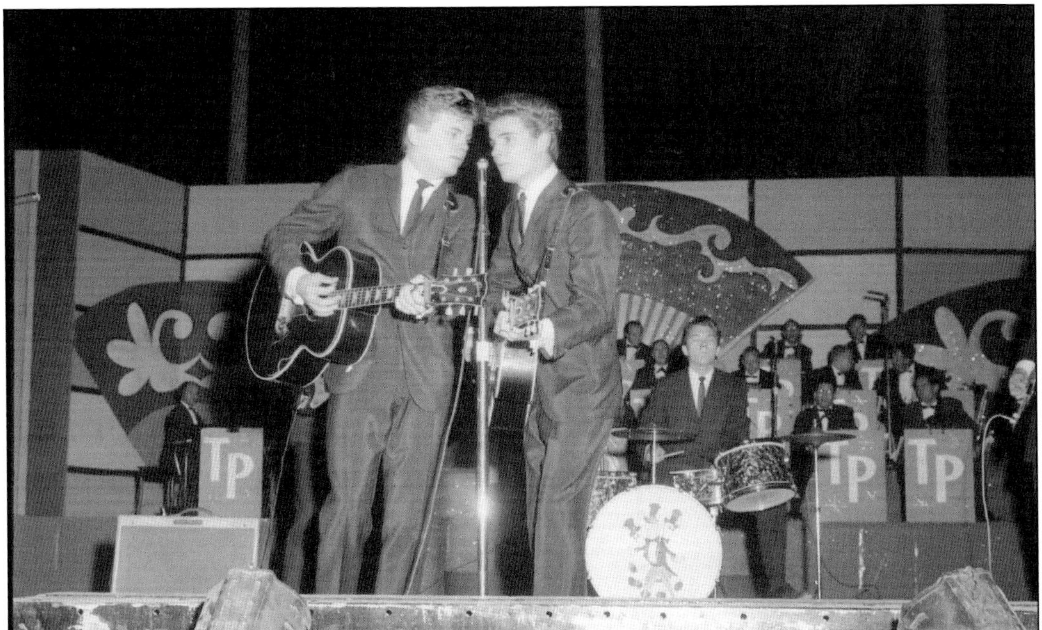

The California State Fair has always had the biggest stars perform. And it was always able to book performers that appealed to all age groups. For the younger crowd in 1959, the fair brought in the Everly Brothers, much to the delight of the many young women who attended the performance. (CSH.)

In 1954, the fair was able to get, among many others, the Marx Brothers to put on a show. Harpo Marx is seen here making life difficult, as usual, for a singer. Harpo was a master harp player, in addition to being one of the funniest people on the planet. (CSH.)

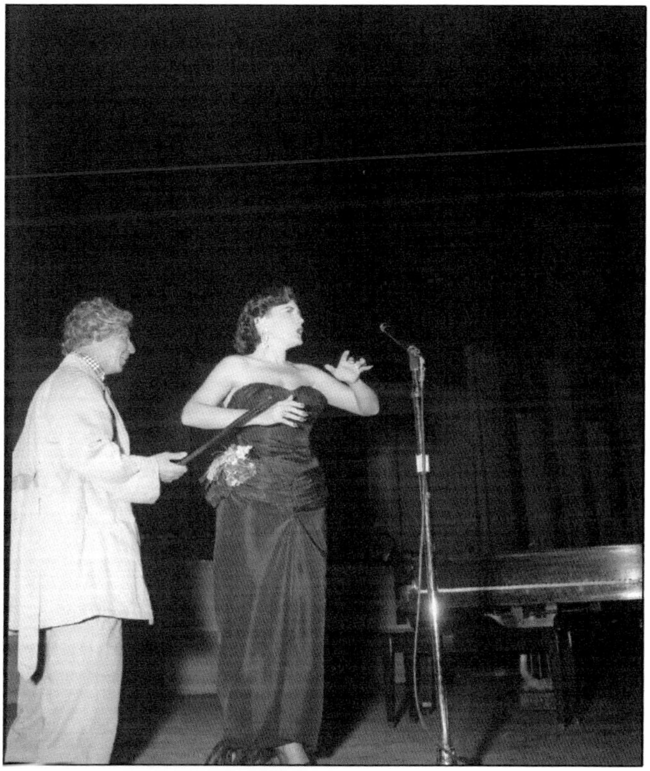

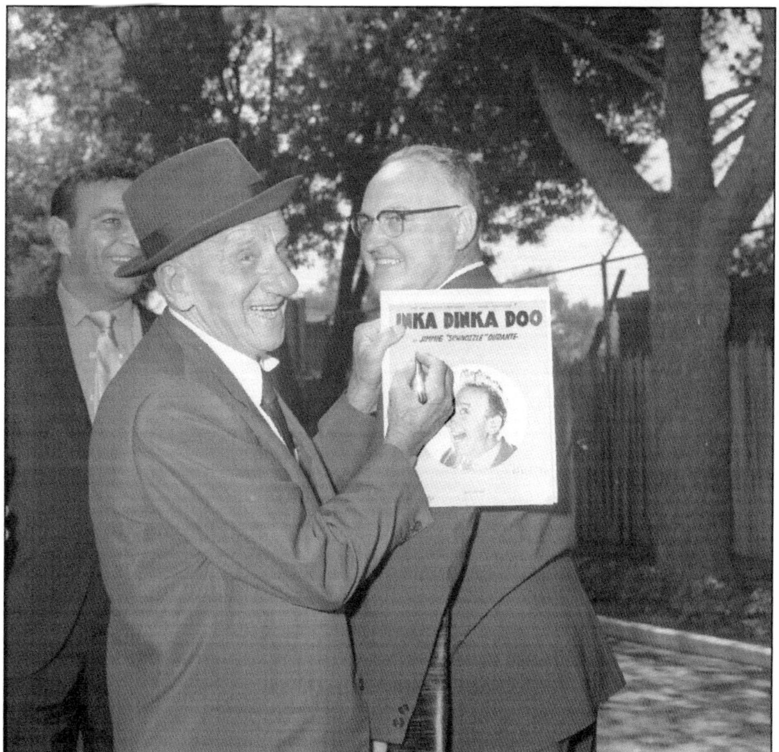

Jimmy "Schnozzola" Durante performed at the State Fair in 1962. He is seen here signing a copy of the sheet music to his most famous song, "Inka Dinka Doo," on the back of Sacramento County Recorder Leonard Hooper. "Good night, Mrs. Calabash, wherever you are." (CSH.)

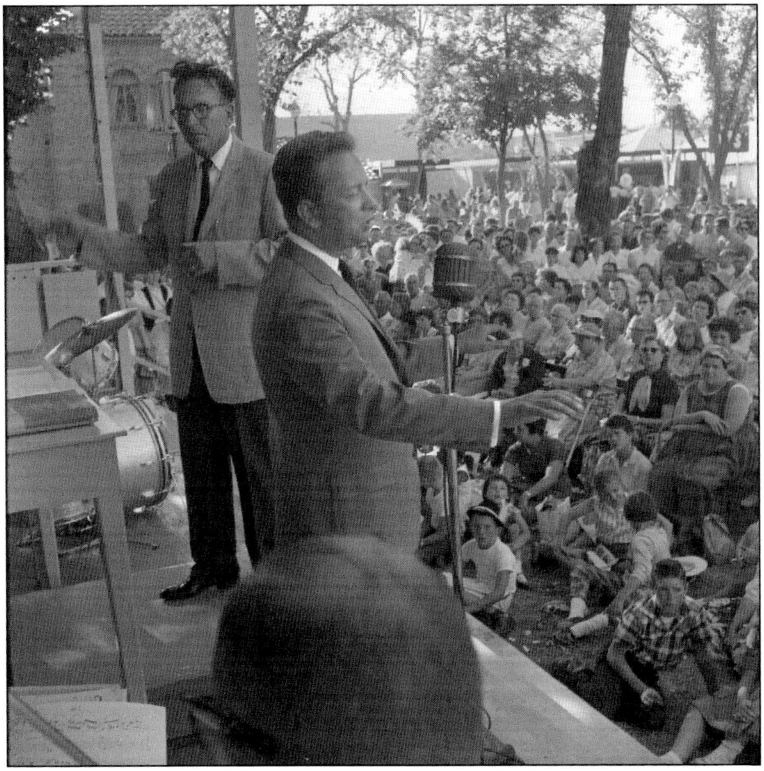

Mel Tormé, known as the "Velvet Fog" for his distinctive voice, performed at the fair in 1960. Tormé, in addition to being an outstanding singer, was also an accomplished drummer. His drum set is seen behind the conductor. Imagine being able to watch a performance by Mel Tormé while sitting under the shade of tall trees! (CSH.)

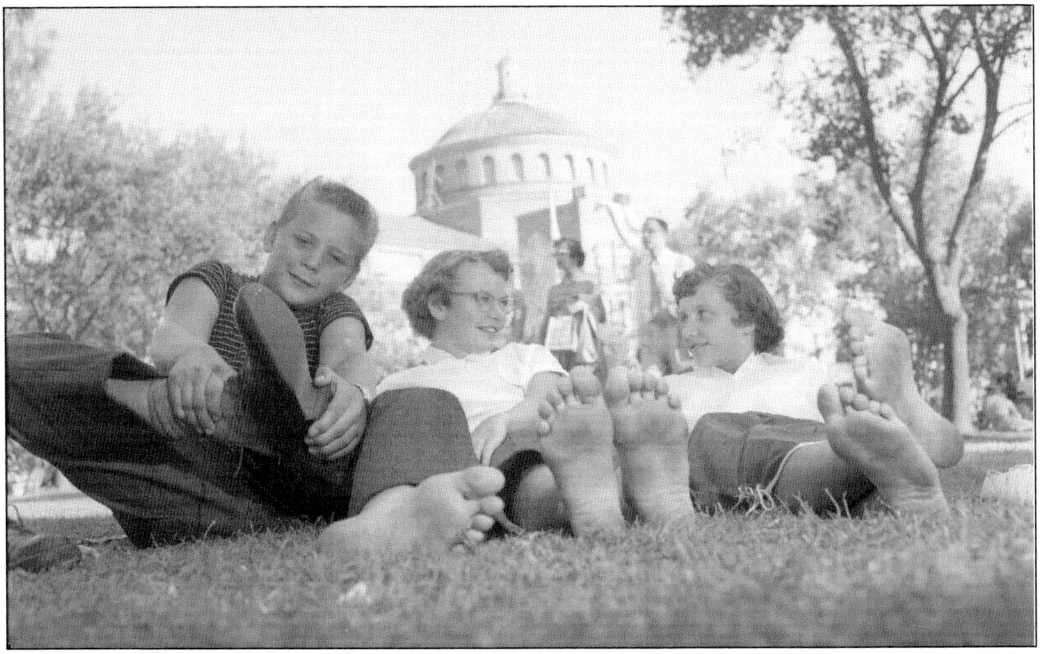

Because there is always so much to see at a State Fair, resting your feet is a big part of the experience. Fortunately, the fair sees to it that there is plenty of space and places to do this. These three unidentified young people do just that on the lawn near the front of the Agriculture Hall in 1954. (CSH.)

The midway as seen from near its entrance in 1952. Note the set of four Ferris wheels in the background. While the number and type has varied over time, Ferris wheels have been a fixture on the midway for many years. (CSH.)

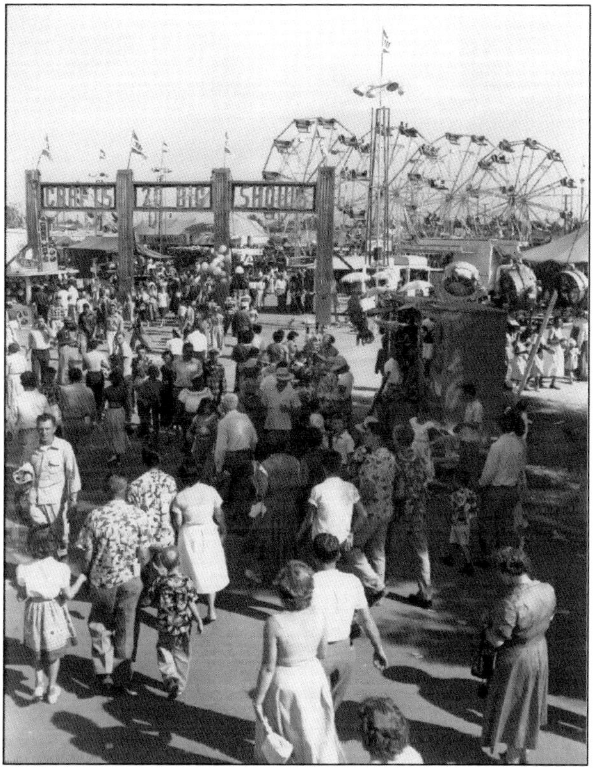

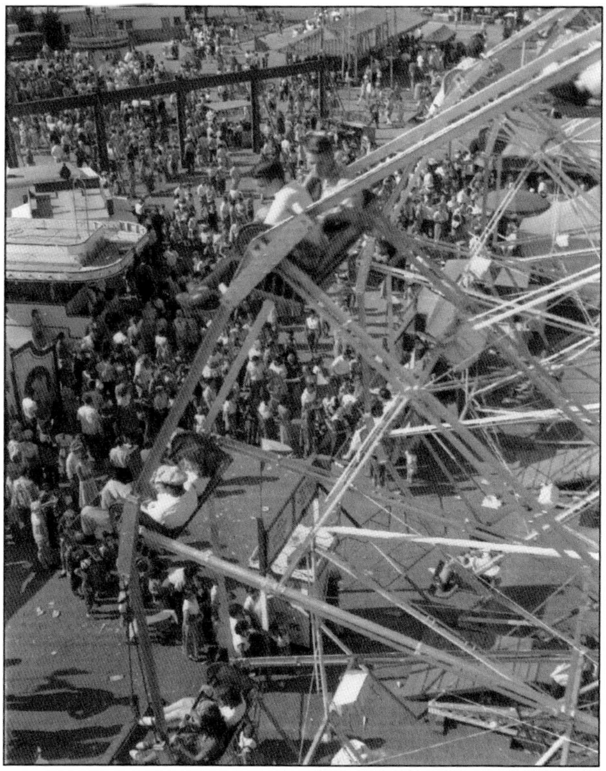

This photograph captures the scene at the midway in 1953. The image must have been taken from one of the four Ferris wheels seen in the previous image. (CSH.)

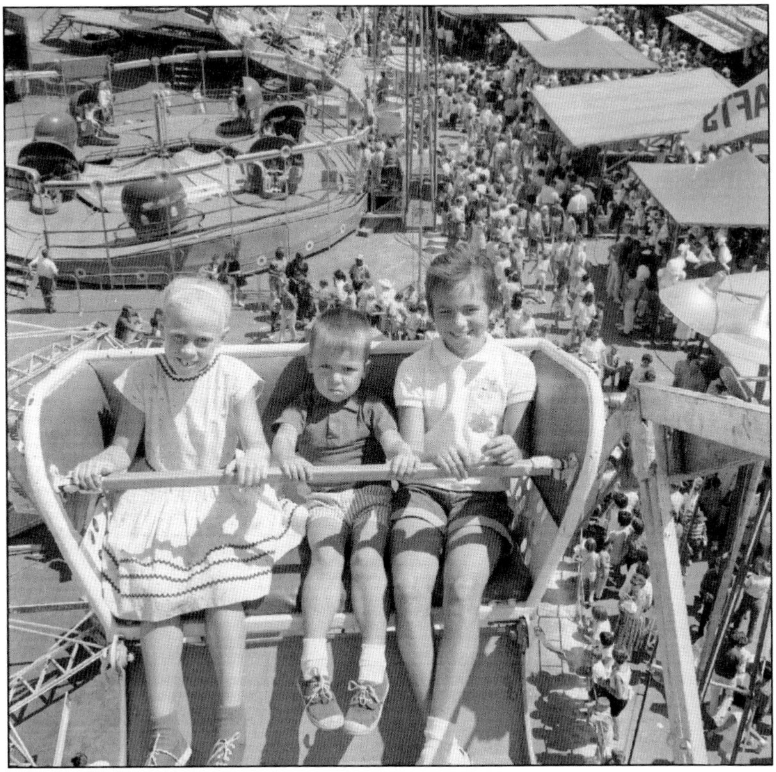

While the various Ferris wheels are fun, they are not fun for everyone. While the two girls are enjoying themselves, the boy in the middle does not look to be having as much fun. One wonders what could be causing his apparent unhappiness in this photograph from 1962. (CSH.)

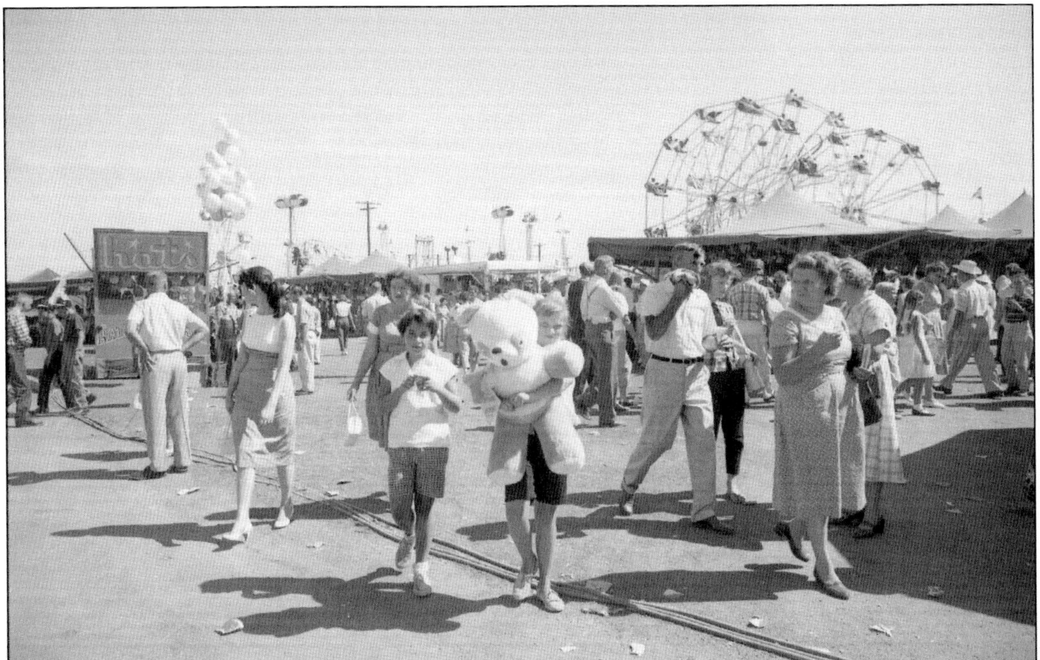

In 1959, the number of Ferris wheels had shrunk to three, possibly to make room for another thrill ride. Christine Vasa (left) and Robbin Rogers look to have had a successful day at one of the many games, if the size of Rogers's bear is any indication. The woman to the right looks jealous. (CSH.)

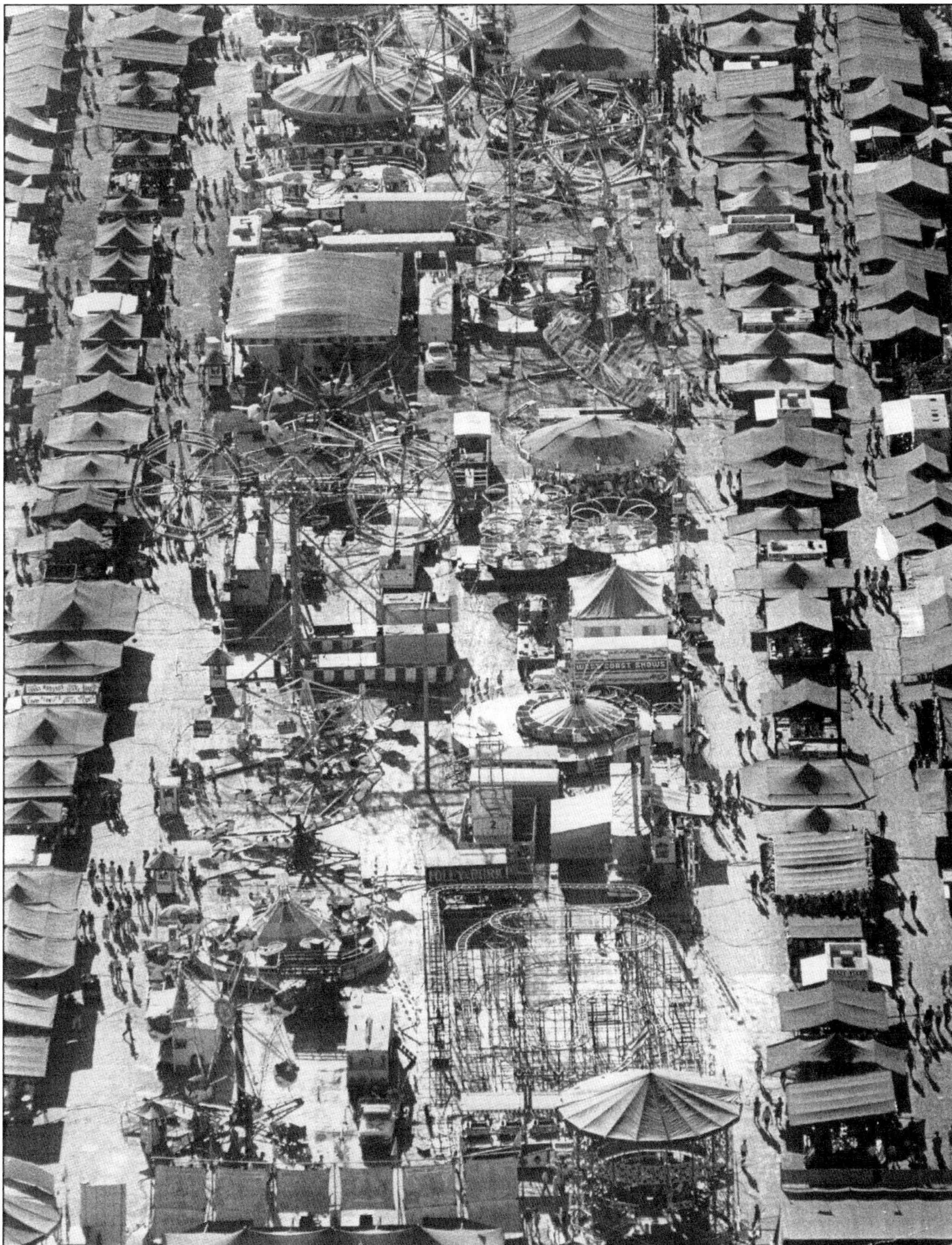

An aerial view of the midway in 1966. This angle gives a good idea as to just how much there was to do in this portion of the fairgrounds. It also shows how crowded the fair had become. There is barely room for all the games, attractions, and rides. This indicates why fair officials had started looking for a larger site nearly 20 years earlier. At the time of this photograph, the start of construction on the new Cal Expo was just months away. Plans had been drawn up and nearly finalized for the new site. (CSH.)

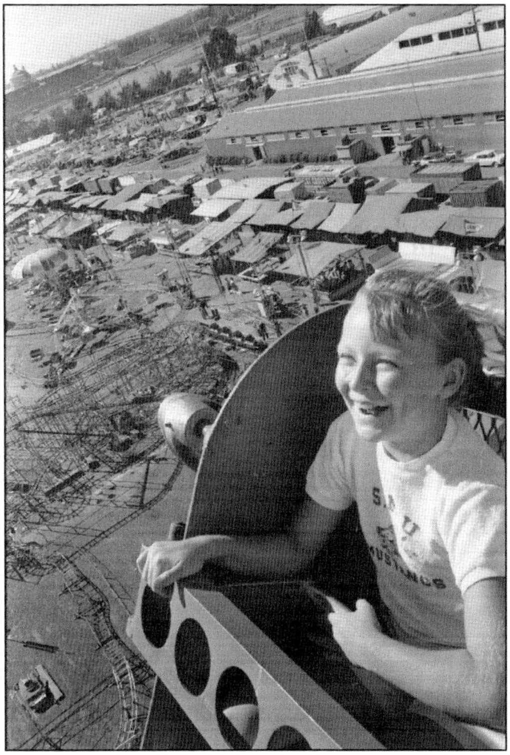

In 1961, Carol Jean Percy, on her first visit to the fair, decided to ride the Sky Wheel with *Sacramento Bee* photographer Robert Hansaker. The Sky Wheel had two Ferris wheels at each end of a boom and could take riders 100 feet high. That is about the point where Percy's photograph was taken. She looks about as happy as a person can be. (CSH.)

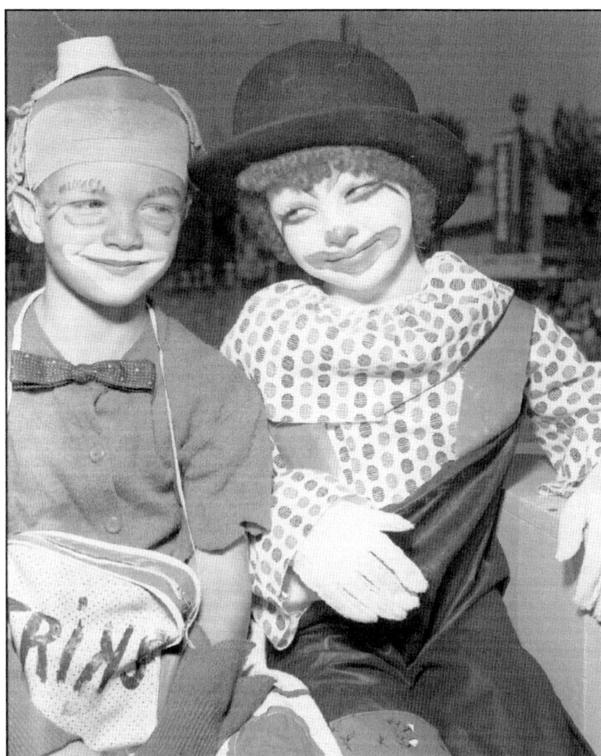

The 1957 Children's Day at the State Fair featured a clown contest as part of the program. The winners in the ages three to six group were Jerry Turley (left) and Laurie Kroll, seen here in their winning costumes and makeup. (CSH.)

Souvenirs for the kids are a must-have item. The two unidentified girls here are happy with the fanciful hats they purchased, possibly at the souvenir stand behind them. The photograph is from 1956 in front of the Counties Exhibit building. (CSH.)

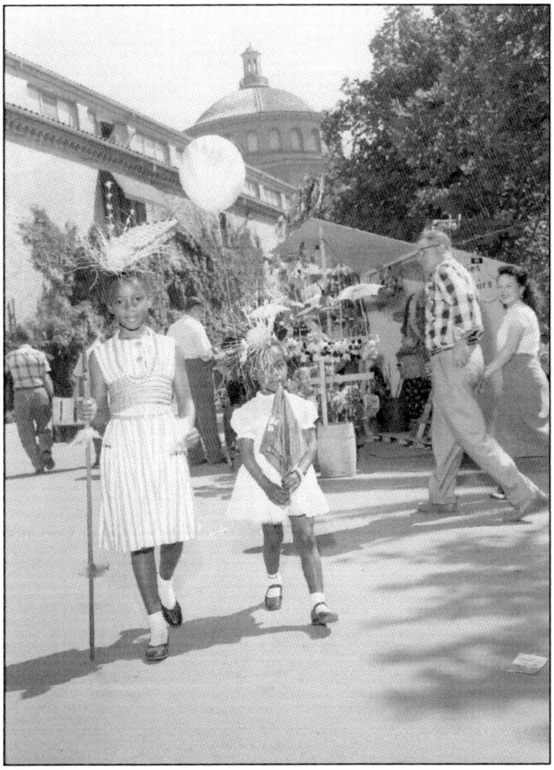

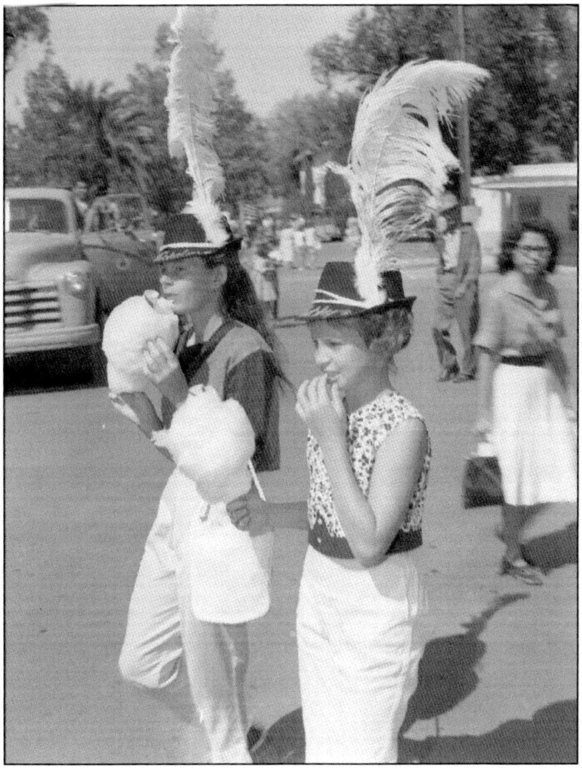

Souvenir hats are always popular. Michalene DeLong (left) and Katherine Crump are seen here in 1960 with their new hats that look to be embroidered with their names. They are also enjoying cotton candy, one of the State Fair food groups. (CSH.)

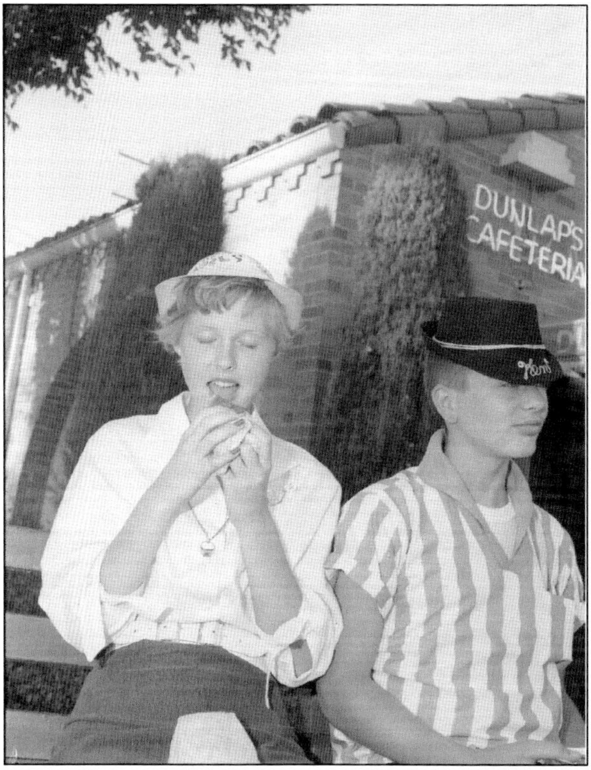

Two young people, with their new, embroidered hats, enjoy a break outside of Dunlap's Cafeteria in 1956. Dunlap's Dining Room, in nearby Oak Park, was a Sacramento institution for decades. Gov. Earl Warren was a patron, as were many, many others. Dunlap's ran this concession during the fair for a number of years. (CSH.)

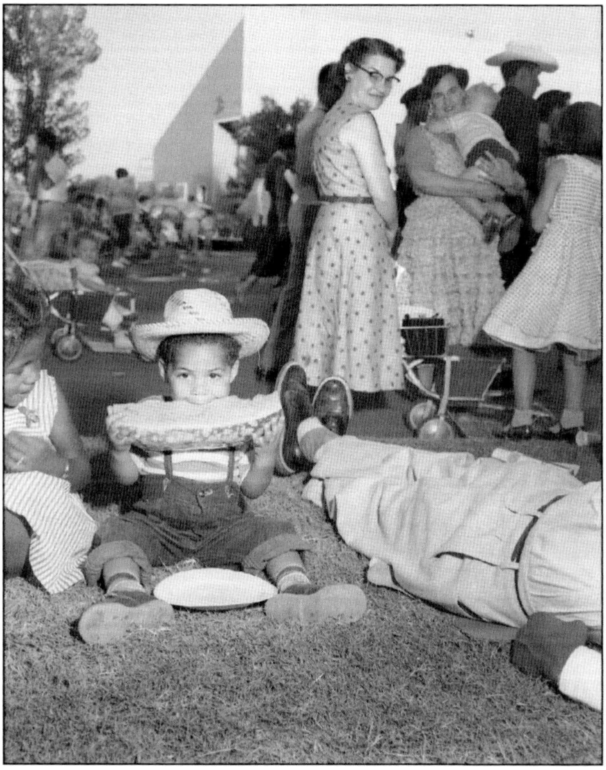

Another big favorite during the fair is watermelon. Marion Hunter, the son of Mr. and Mrs. Douglas Hunter of Richmond, California, enjoys a huge slice of watermelon in 1954, as amused fairgoers look on. (CSH.)

Hot dogs are popular, too—and the bigger, the better. In 1960, Dennis Duarte of Sacramento works his way through a hot dog that appears to be almost as big as he is. (CSH.)

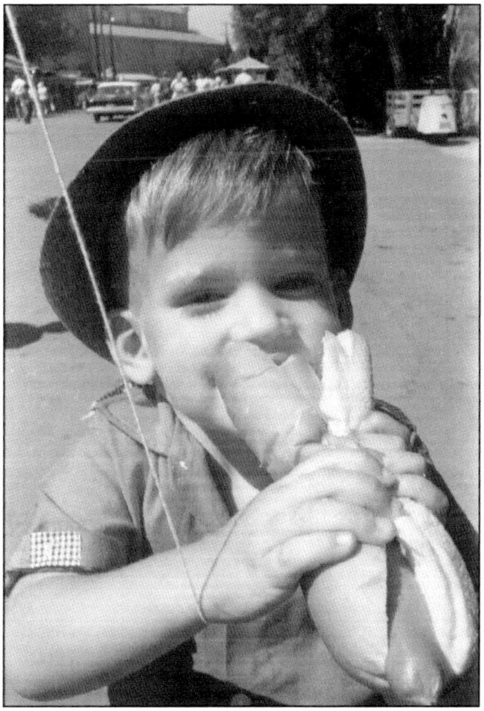

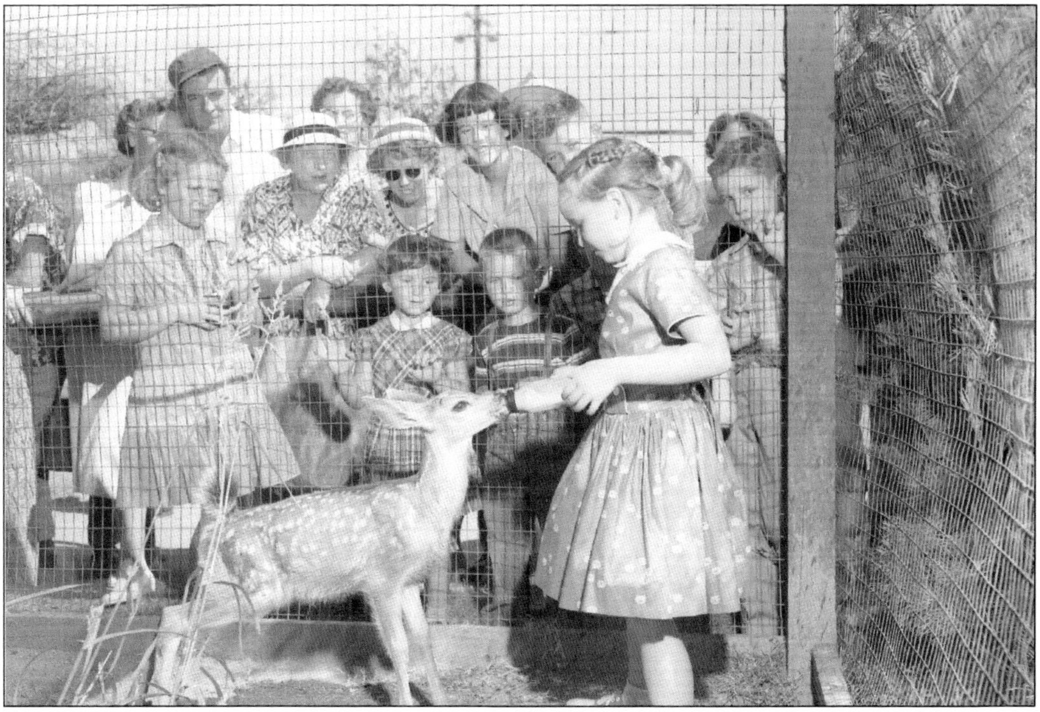

Children of all types love to eat at the State Fair. Alice Moore is shown feeding a fawn by hand in 1955 at the exhibit of the California State Division of Natural Resources. This exhibit is always considered one of the ways the State Fair educates the public about California's natural resources. (CSH.)

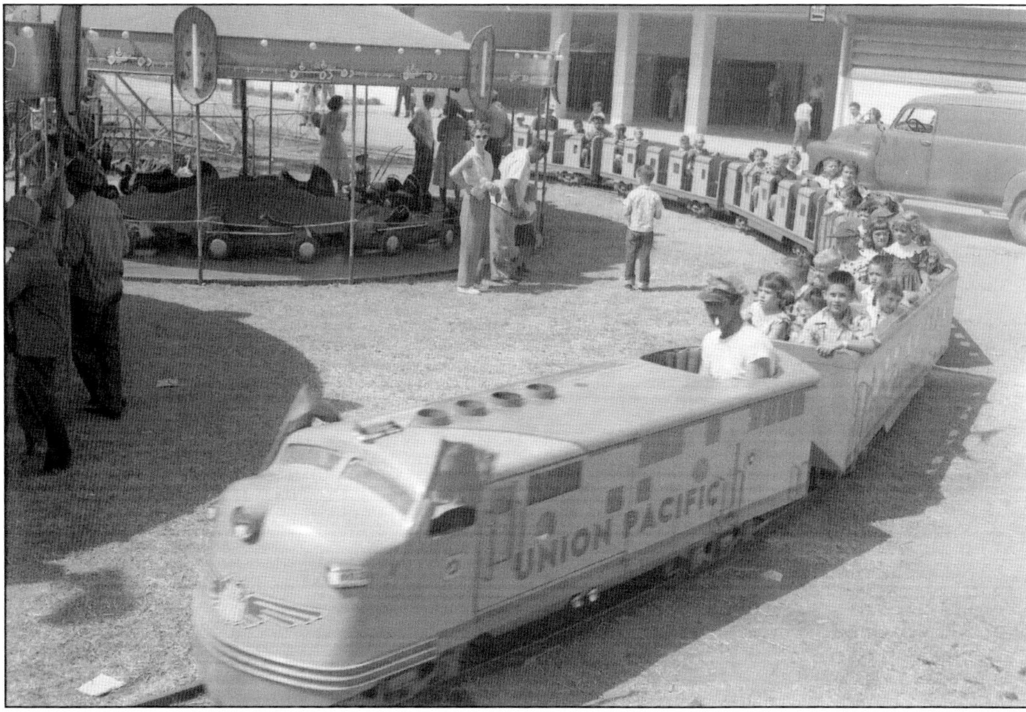

A popular attraction for children during several State Fairs was a model of a Union Pacific train offering rides around the midway. This photograph was taken in 1953. (CSH.)

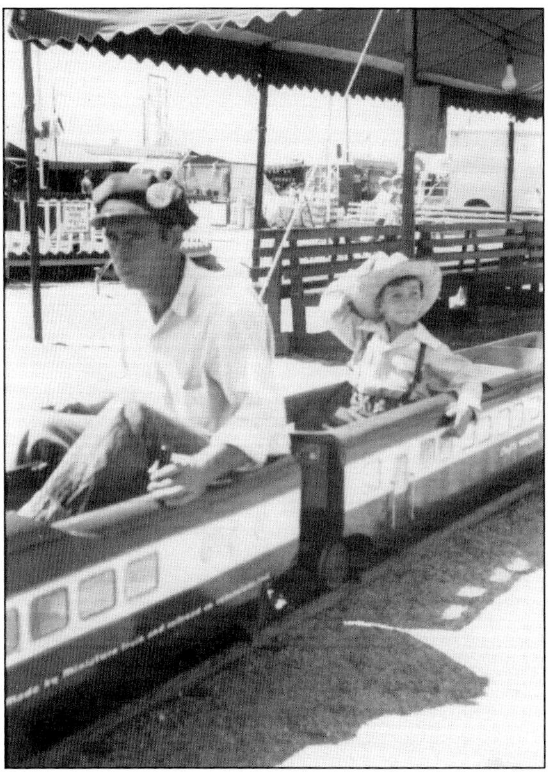

In 1951, a slightly different train was being used. Here, John Morgan of Sacramento takes a tour of the midway. (Sacramento Room, Sacramento Public Library)

Balloons are a big item for children. In front of the Counties Exhibit Hall in 1962, Mike Crippe prevents Dean Vayder from being carried away by his helium balloons. (CSH.)

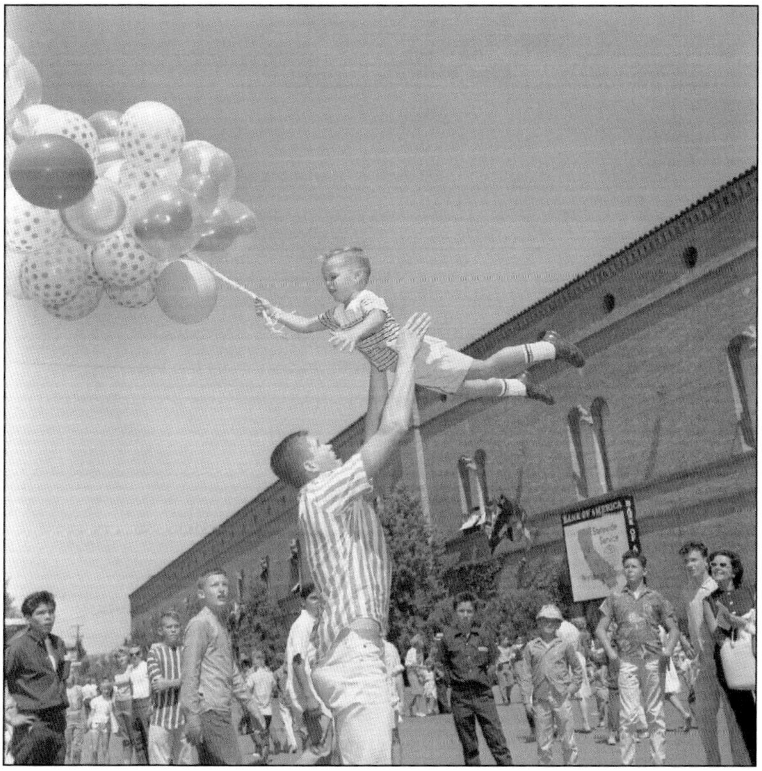

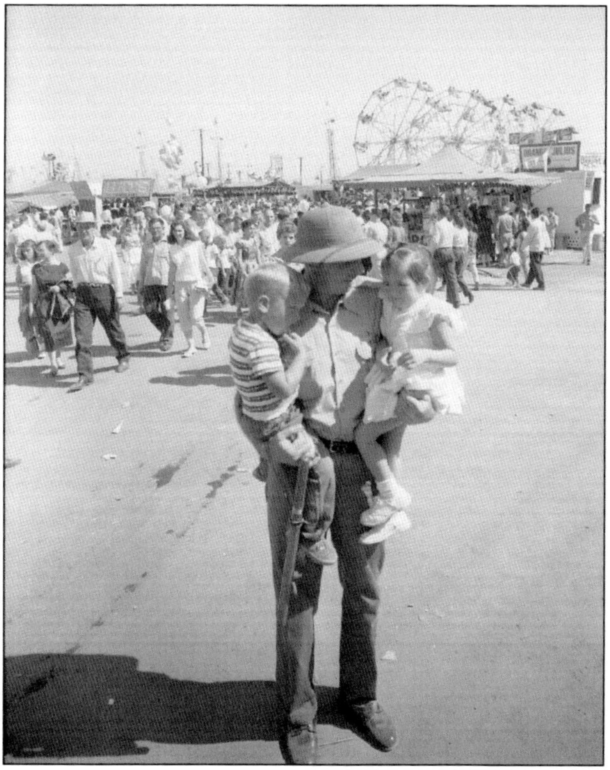

Lost parents are occasionally an issue at the fair. But thanks to the State Fair police, it is not an issue for long. In 1957, California State Fair Police Officer Harry Curry (center) helps two children look for their missing parents. The unidentified children were reunited with their parents shortly after the photograph was taken. (CSH.)

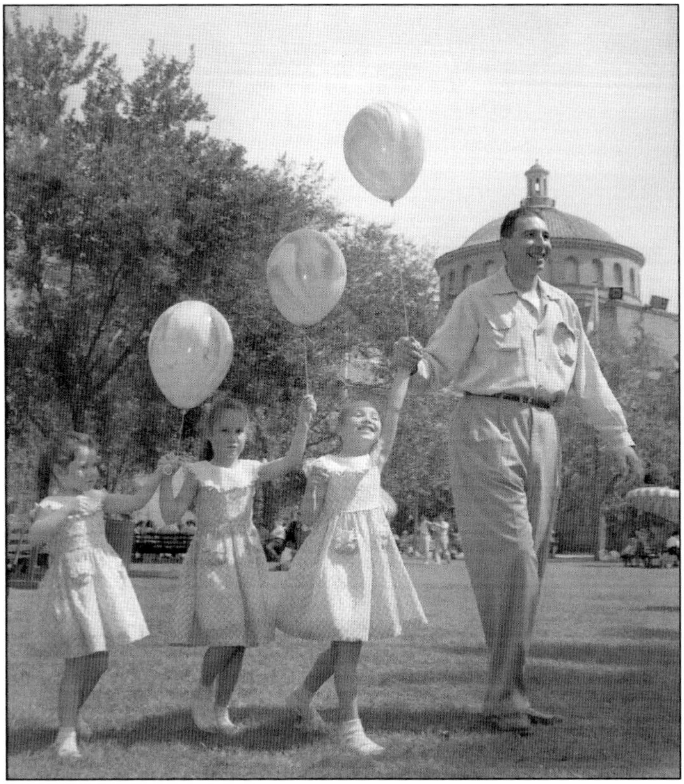

The State Fair is designed for family fun. This photograph from August 30, 1956, captures that feeling beautifully. Seen here on the lawn in front of the Counties Exhibit building are Alfred Rosenzwieg and his three daughters, from left to right, Julie (3), Jill (4), and Marcie (5). They lived in South Sacramento. (CSH.)

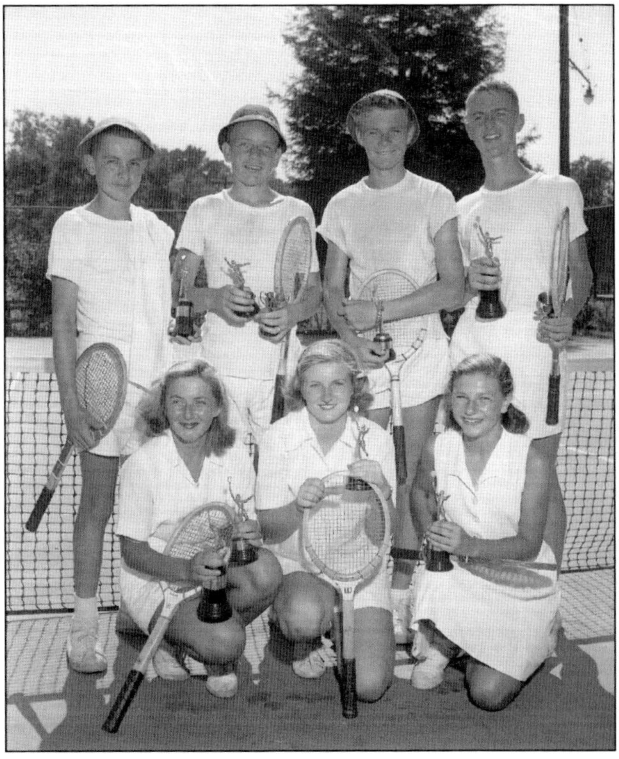

Sports contests have been a part of the fair for a number of years. These unidentified tennis players were all champions of the 1948 Tennis Tournament. There is also an annual golf tournament. (CSH.)

In the 21st century, satellite communication is so common that we barely give it a thought. In 1962, however, Telstar was a revelation. Gov. Edmund Brown, on the phone, places a call to the St. Eriks fair in Sweden using the orbiting Telstar satellite. To the governor's right is Alf Ros, Sweden's consul general in San Francisco. (CSH.)

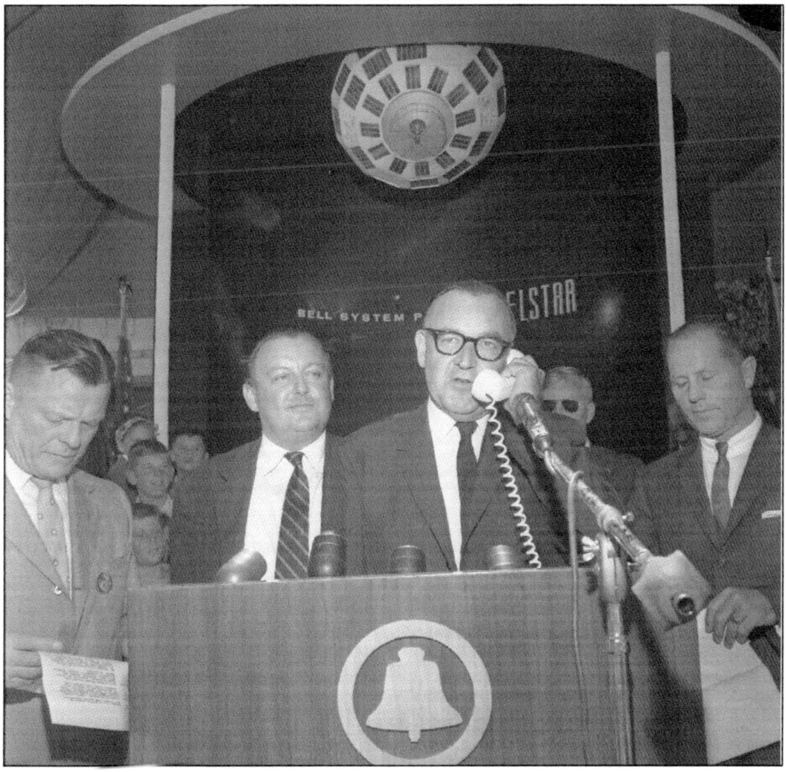

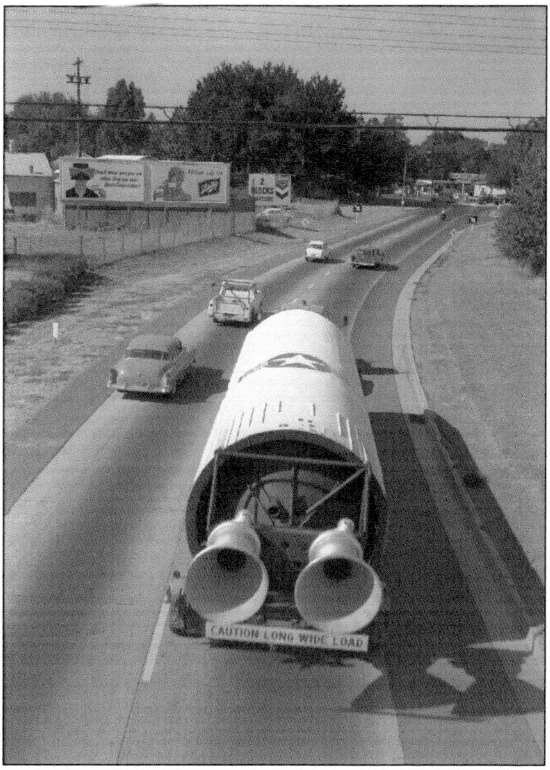

Military technology is always a big hit at the State Fair. On August 29, 1960, part of a Titan rocket is seen on a flatbed truck being transported for display at the fair. One can only imagine what the drivers of the passing cars were thinking. (CSH.)

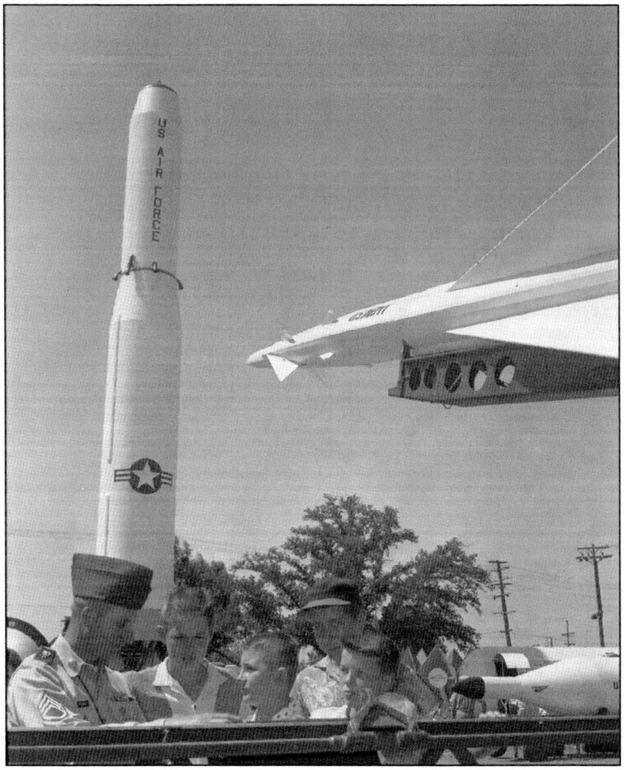

The Titan missile, without its payload, is seen on display on August 30, 1960. A Nike Ajax, the first successful anti-aircraft missile, is at the upper right. Staff Sergeant George Bryant (far left) from Travis Air Force Base, discusses the display with, from left to right, Lynn Wright and David Gatt, both of Quincy, and Tom Wentzell and John Ashley of Sacramento. (CSH.)

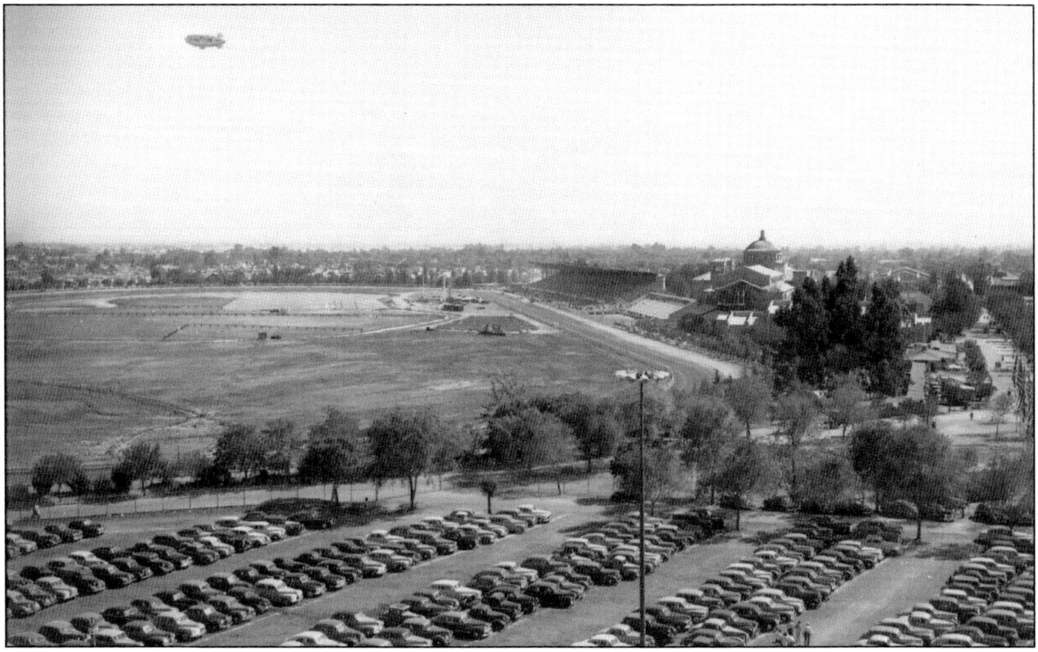

This image, from about 1948, was probably taken from atop the water tank on the north end of the fairgrounds. The lake in the infield is quite small, compared to its size in 1950, and the parking lot is full. Note the Goodyear blimp in the upper left of the photograph. It is towing a banner which is, unfortunately, not legible. (CSH.)

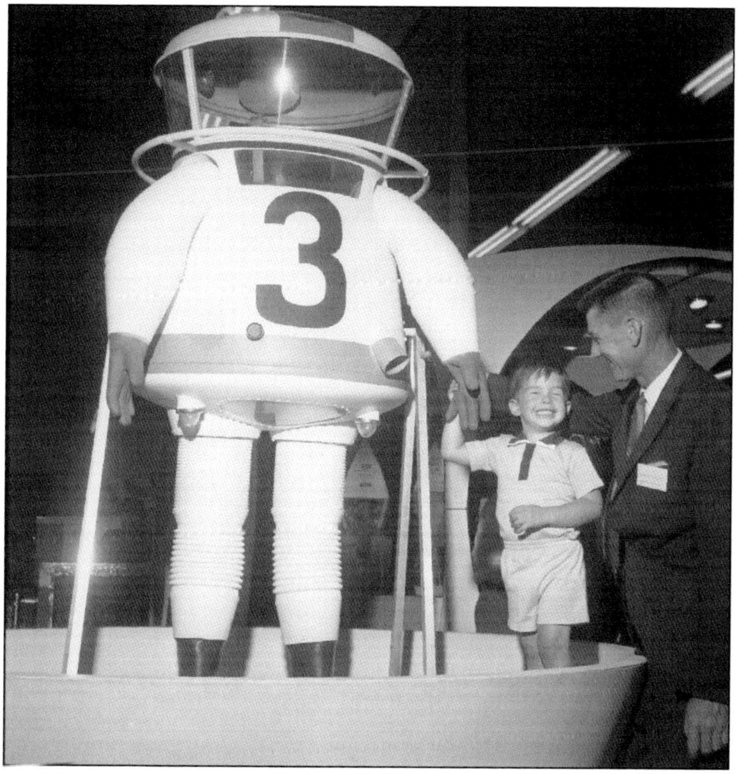

The 1962 fair featured Aerojet's version of a space suit. This space suit never made it to production for use by NASA. Perhaps this concept was not for actual travel in a spacecraft, but rather for exploration on the Moon or Mars. The boy next to the suit seems very impressed. (CSH.)

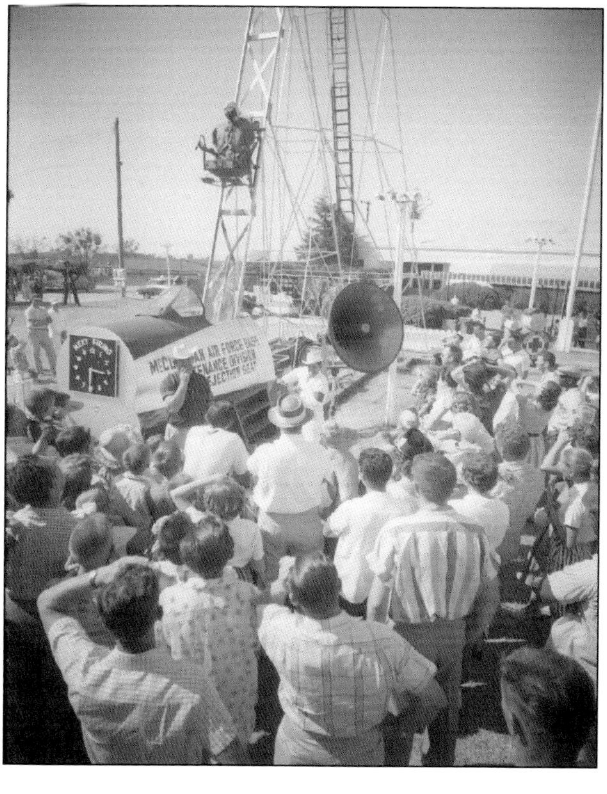

The 1957 fair had this exhibit of an ejection seat from a fighter plane. The exhibit is from McClellan Air Force Base and actually fired the seat, with a dummy pilot, from the model cockpit. Frank Hilliard, in the white hat and dark shirt, was at the microphone explaining exactly how this technology worked. (CSH.)

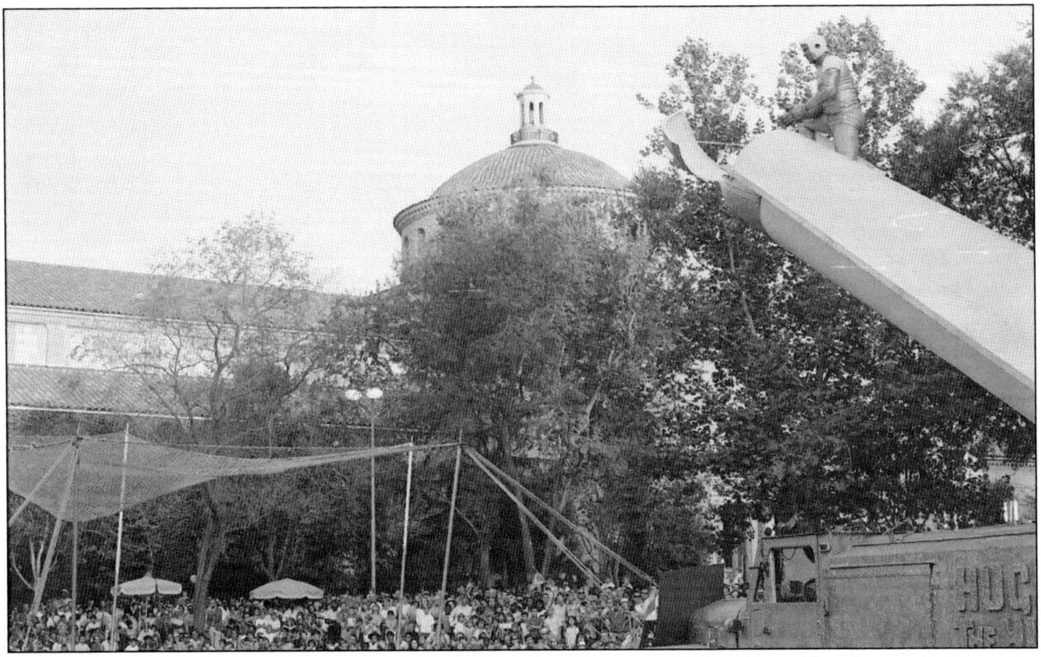

All of the stops were pulled out in 1967 during the last year of the State Fair being held at the Broadway site. Hugo A. Zacchini, 22, the human cannonball, prepares to load himself into the cannon that will shoot him into the net to the left. In the background, the top of the Agriculture Hall is visible. (CSH.)

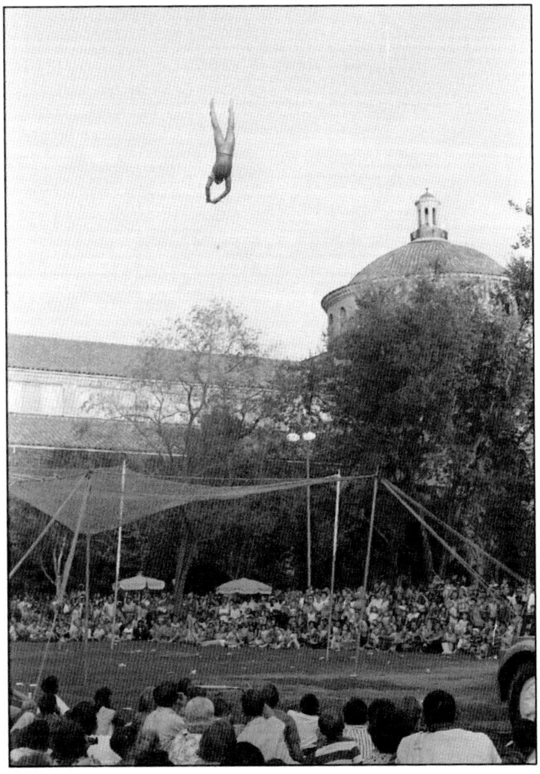

This great photograph captures the human cannonball a split second before he lands in the net. Hugo's father, Hugo T. Zacchini, operated the cannon. This spectacle took place every night at 7:00 p.m. The crowd that gathered to watch this event was huge. (CSH.)

Not all the aircraft at the fair operated as planned. In 1967, this single-engine 1940 Stearman biplane was taking off from the track infield when the engine failed. The pilot, Rober Barr of Sacramento, was able to land the plane in the north parking lot, taking out eight cars. Barr and his passenger, Joel Leach, were both uninjured. The plane and cars, however, fared less well. (CSH.)

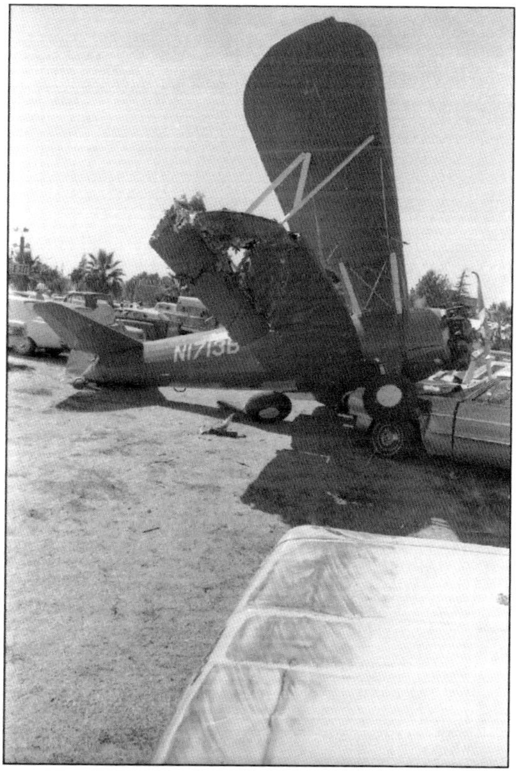

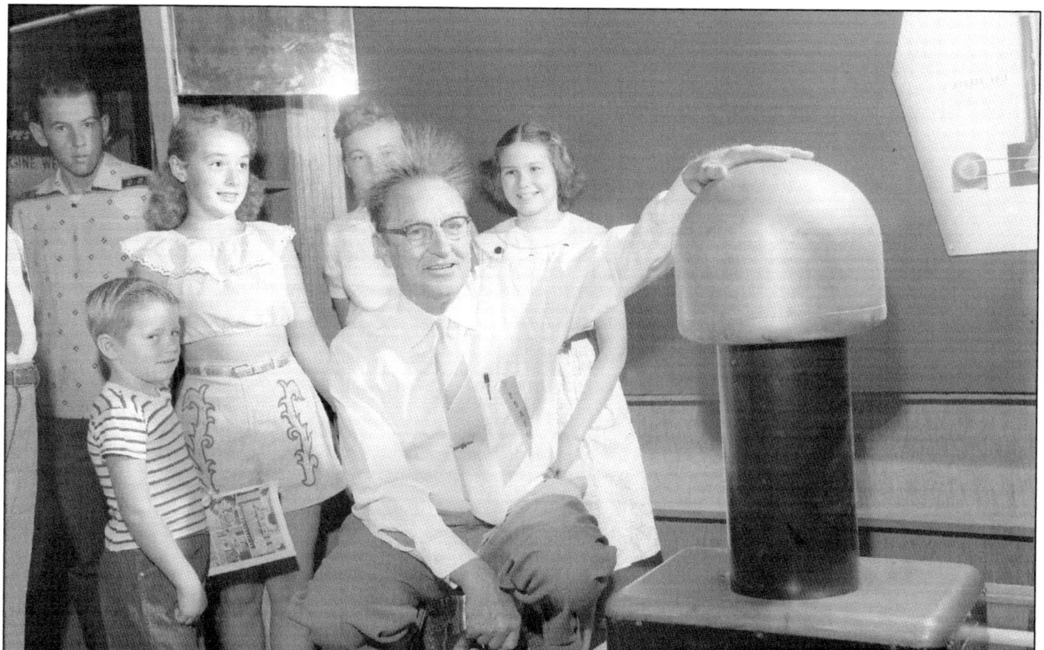

Science exhibits are like magnets for children. Here an exhibitor demonstrates a simple device that explains the concept of static electricity. This was quite amusing to the children gathered around him in 1955. (CSH.)

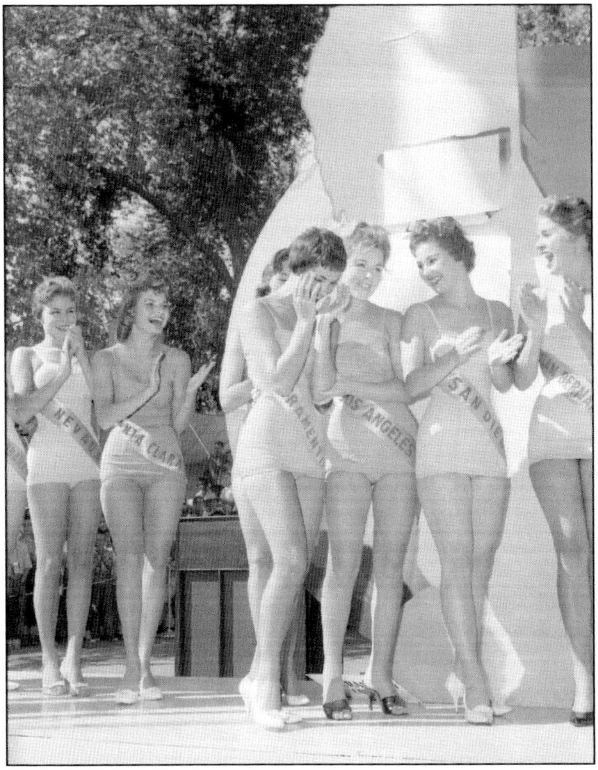

In 1959, Linda Hines of North Sacramento won the Maid of California contest. She is captured here completely surprised and elated a few seconds after her name was announced. Hines was 17 years old and the reigning Miss Sacramento County. (CSH.)

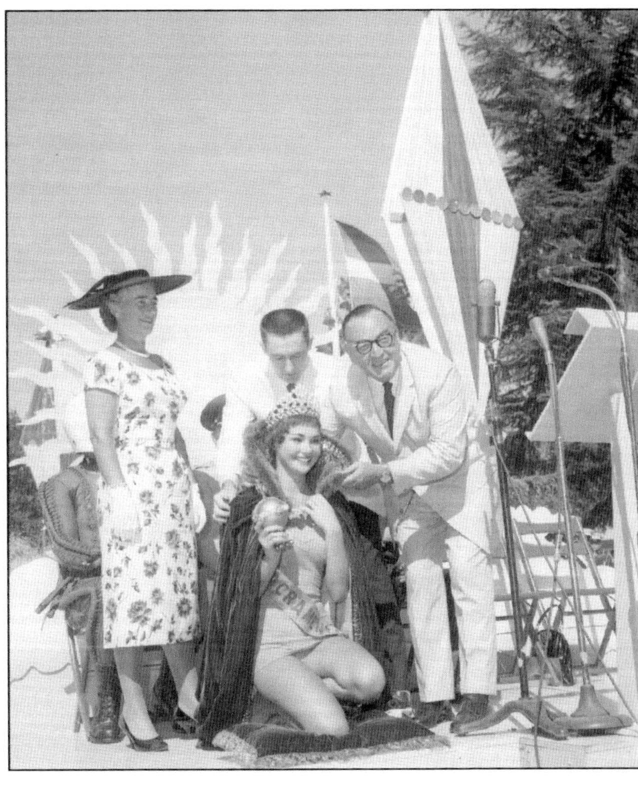

Linda Hines is shown here receiving her crown, cape, and scepter from Gov. Edmund G. Brown on September 2, 1959. The governor's wife is to the left, while an unidentified man adjusts the cape. Other dignitaries, including what looks like a pilot, are behind them. (CSH.)

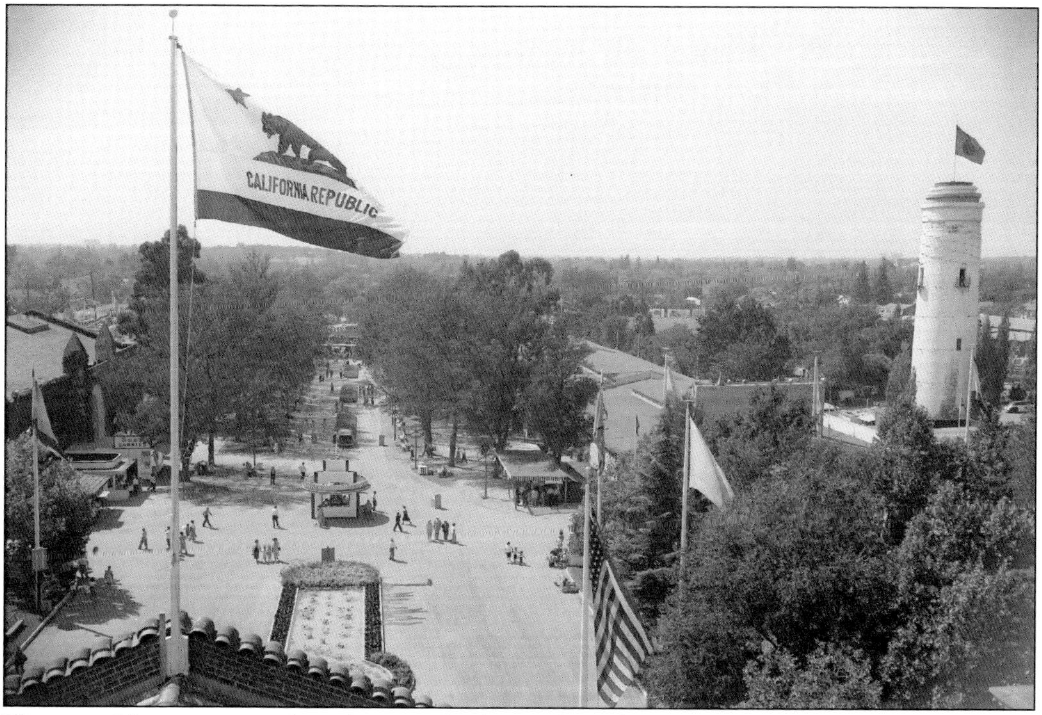

This is a seldom-seen view, from August of 1950. It is from the top of the Agriculture Hall and looks north. The old water tower is seen to the right. The photograph is by Joseph Benetti. (CSH.)

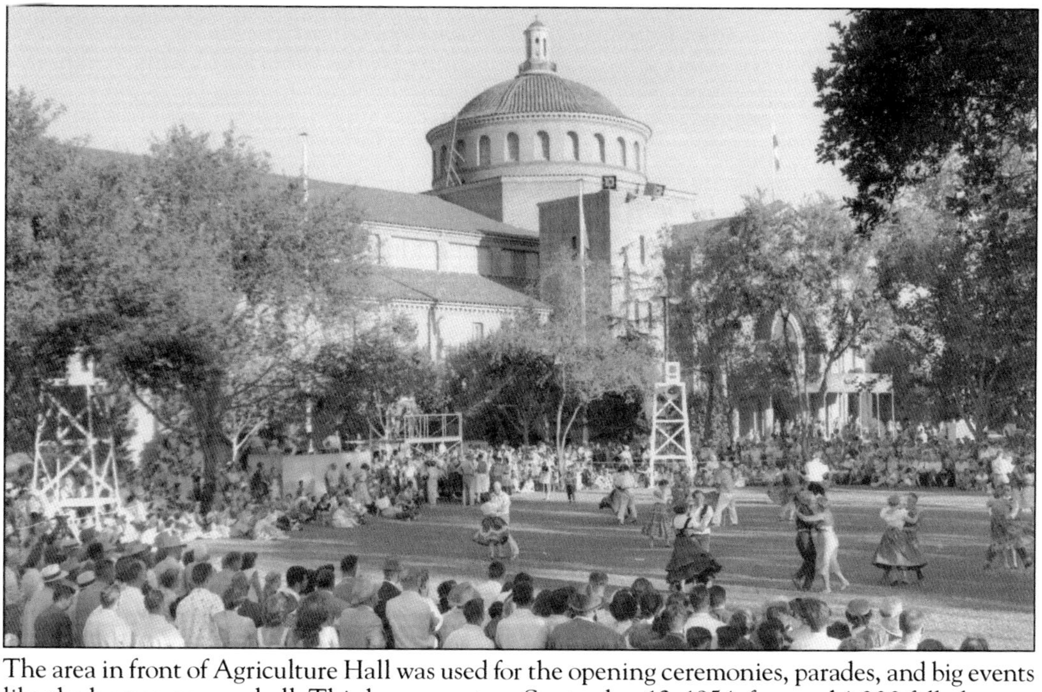

The area in front of Agriculture Hall was used for the opening ceremonies, parades, and big events like the human cannonball. This large event on September 13, 1954, featured 1,000 folk dancers celebrating the last day of the State Fair's 100th birthday. It was yet another record-breaking attendance year. (CSH.)

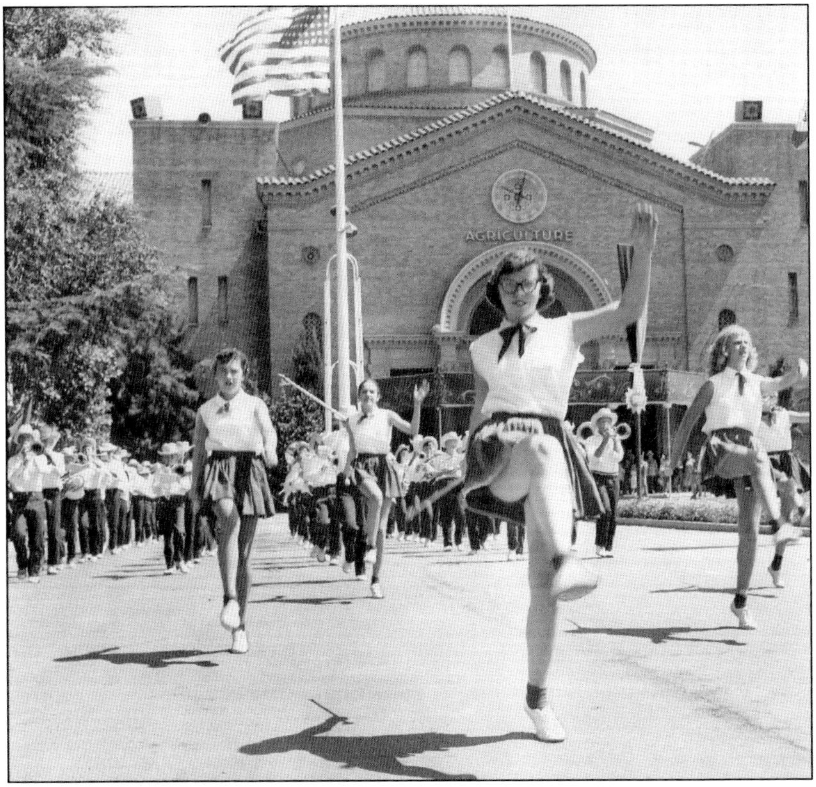

This *c.* 1955 photograph captures an enthusiastic drum majorette leading a marching band. According to the clock, it is 10:00 a.m., so it must be opening day for the fair. (CSH.)

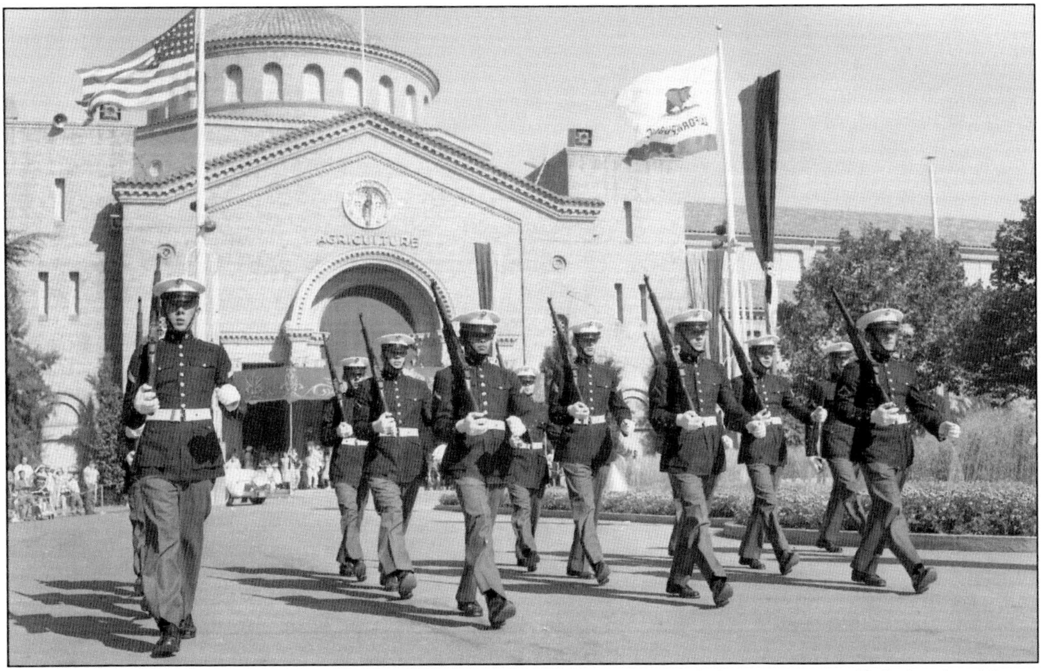

In 1957, a Marine Guard drill team puts on a display in front of the Counties Exhibit building. The State Fair held small parades every day, sometimes several times a day, featuring marching bands, drill teams, and other entertainment.

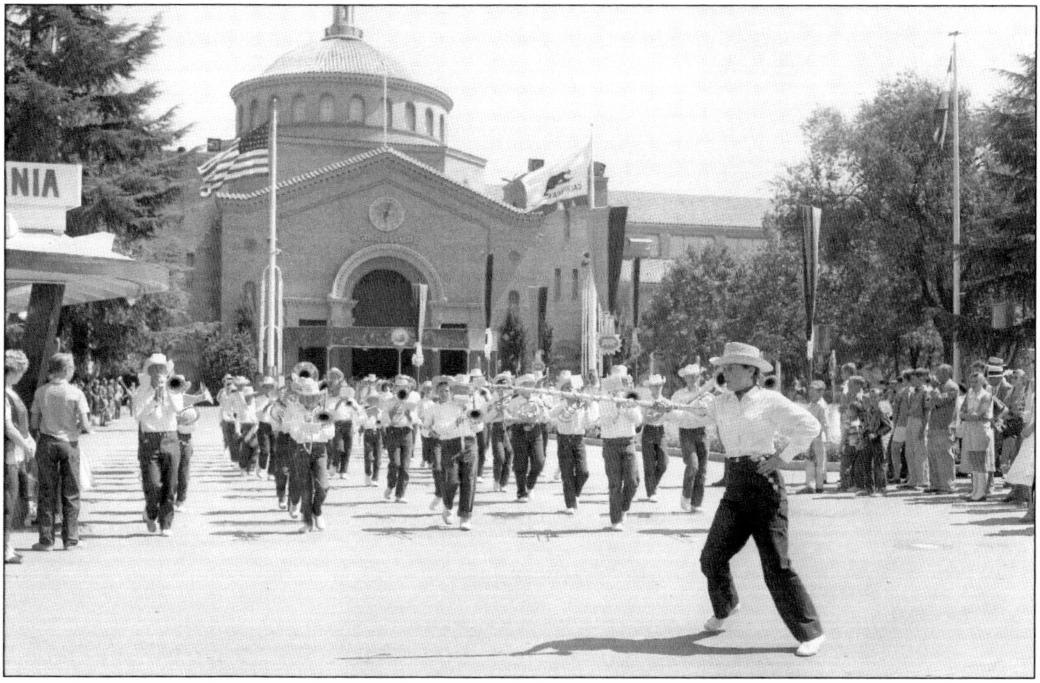

Another photograph from 1957 captures an unidentified band. It may be the same band shown on the previous page, but with a different drum major. This one, though, is equally enthusiastic. (CSH.)

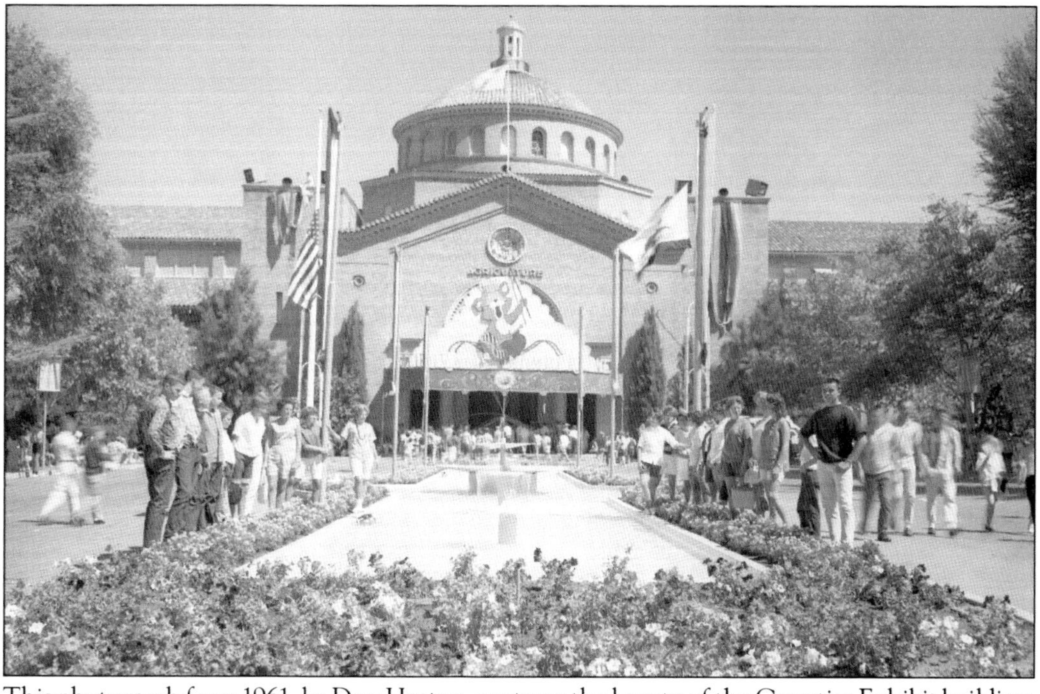

This photograph from 1961, by Don Horton, captures the beauty of the Counties Exhibit building. The fountains in front were a relatively recent addition, having been built about ten years earlier. (CSH.)

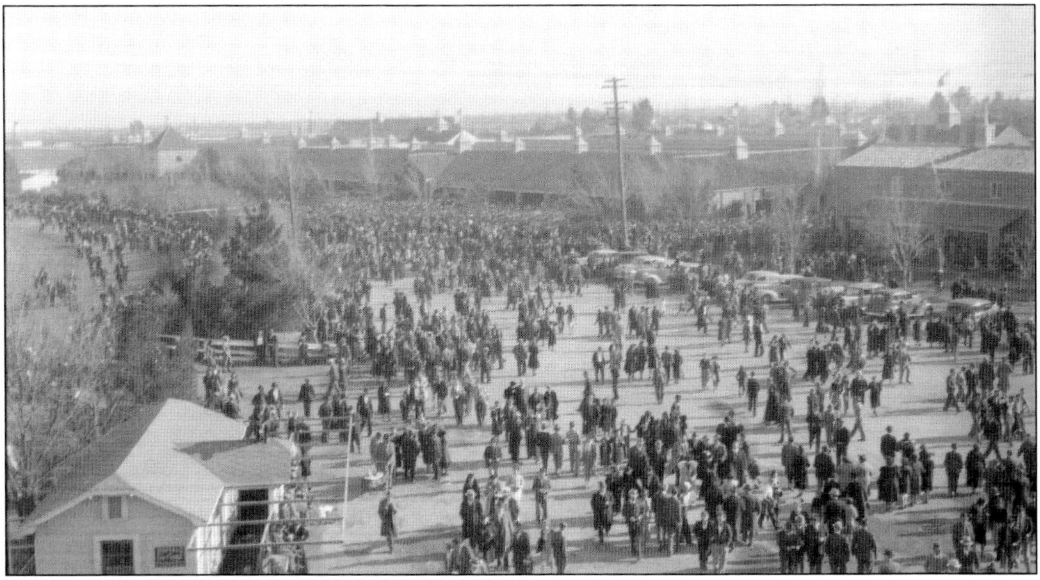

From the early 1930s, possibly taken from the top of the grandstand, this photograph captures a crowd late in the year (there are no leaves on the trees). This image also shows that in the distance to the south, there are few, if any, rooftops visible. This is why the fair was moved to this location: room to grow. (CSH.)

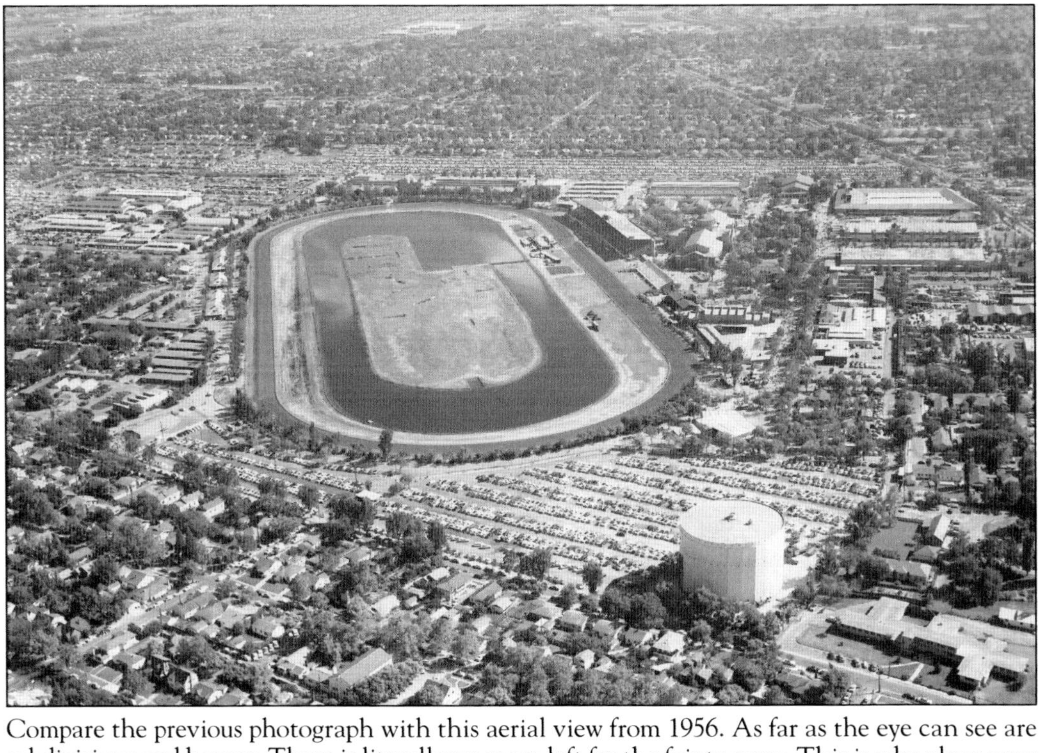

Compare the previous photograph with this aerial view from 1956. As far as the eye can see are subdivisions and houses. There is literally no room left for the fair to grow. This is why plans were already being made to move the fair to a new site. (CSH.)

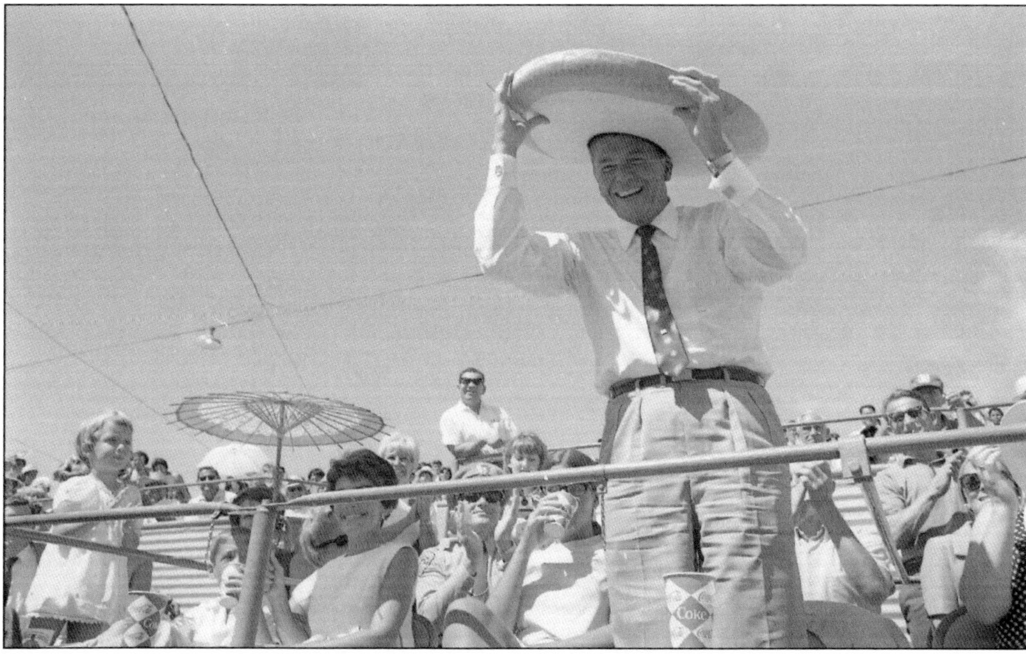

Gov. Ronald Reagan and his wife, Nancy, attended the horse show on the last day of the fair in 1967. The governor received a sombrero as a gift from one of the riders in the show and graciously tried it on. This was the last visit by a governor to the fairgrounds at Stockton Boulevard and Broadway.

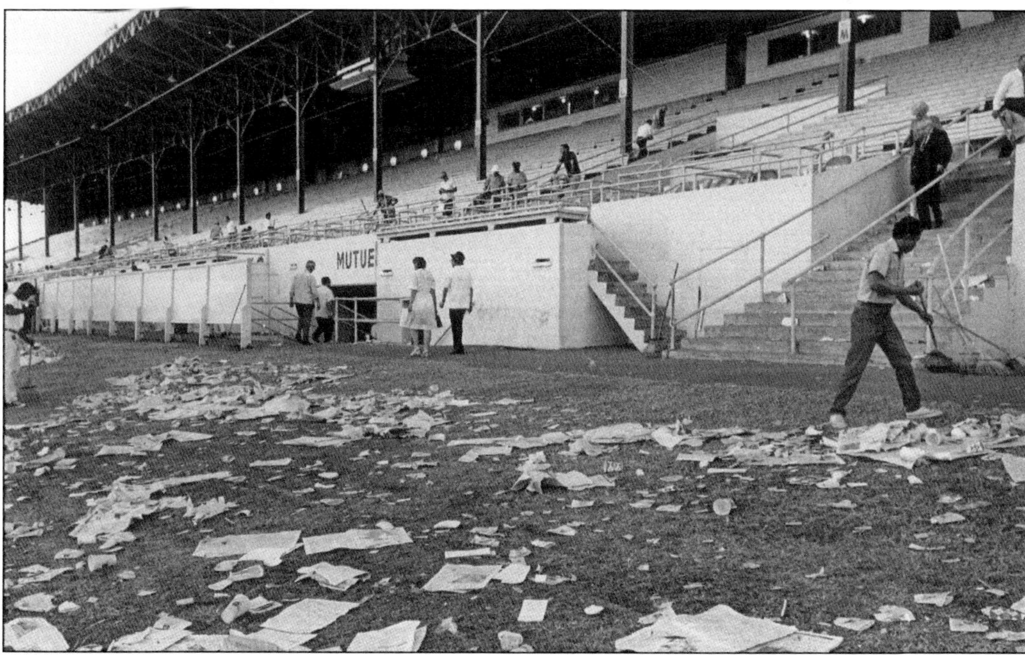

This photograph shows the cleanup after the last race in 1967. After 59 years in the same location, the State Fair was moving. Many consider the run at this site to be the golden age of the California State Fair. If attendance is the only criterion, they may be right. During the last 20 years at Stockton Boulevard and Broadway, the fair set attendance records nearly every year. (CSH.)

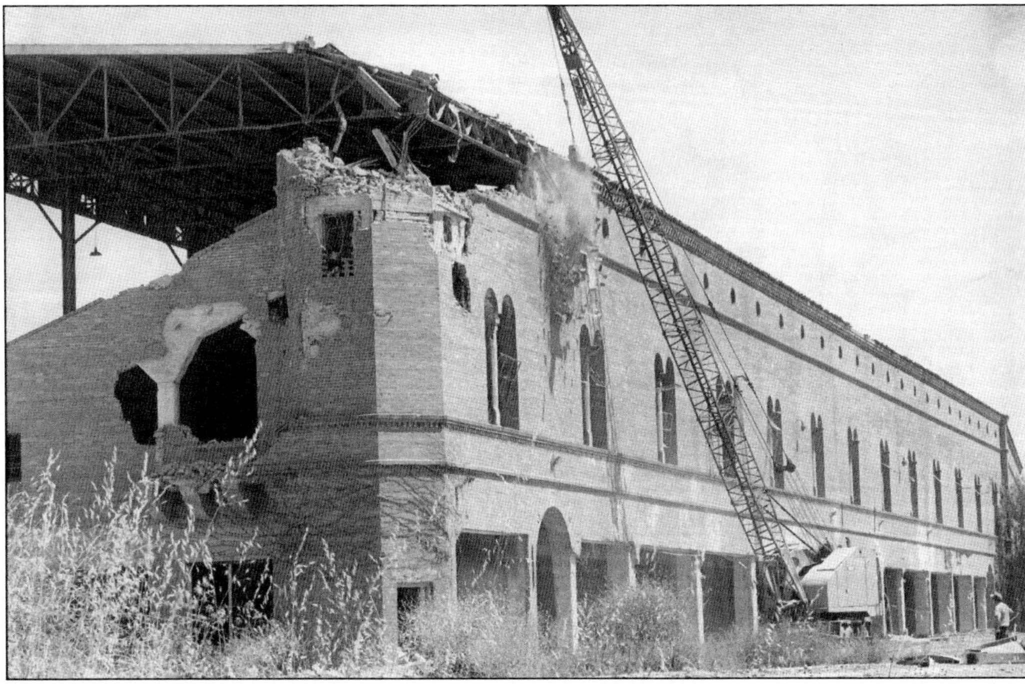

The grandstand is shown being demolished by a wrecking ball around 1974. The back of the photograph states that even better shots would be possible the next day, when the steel canopy was to be knocked down. (CSH.)

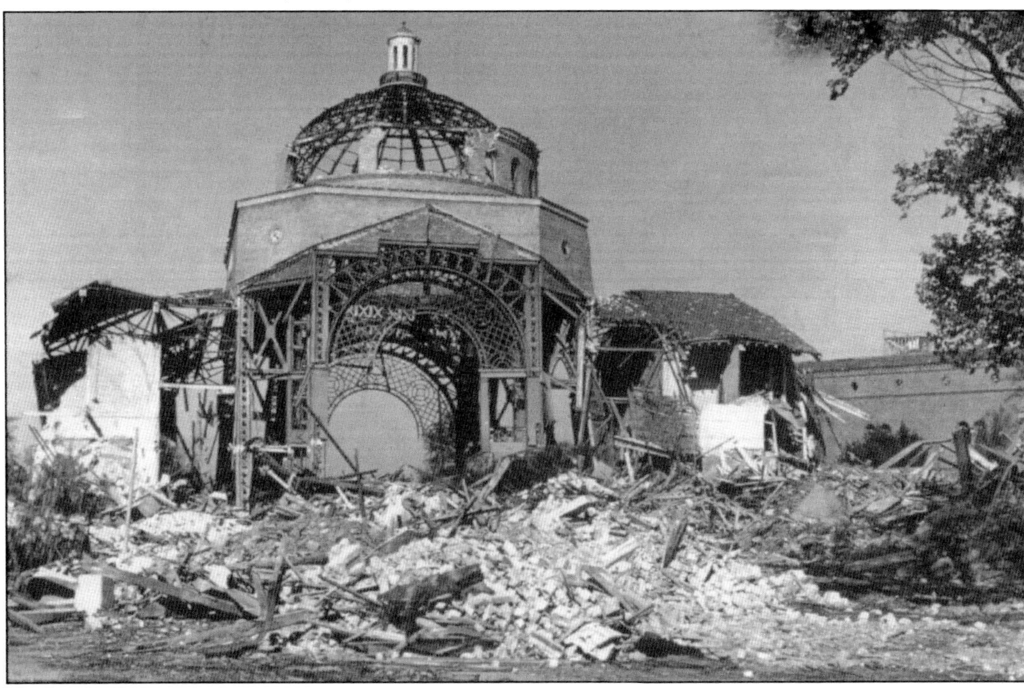

This *c.* 1974 photograph shows the Counties Exhibit building (also known as Agriculture Hall and Governor's Hall) nearing the end of its existence. Tiles from the roof are known to have ended up as roofs for a number of new homes in Sacramento. (CSH.)

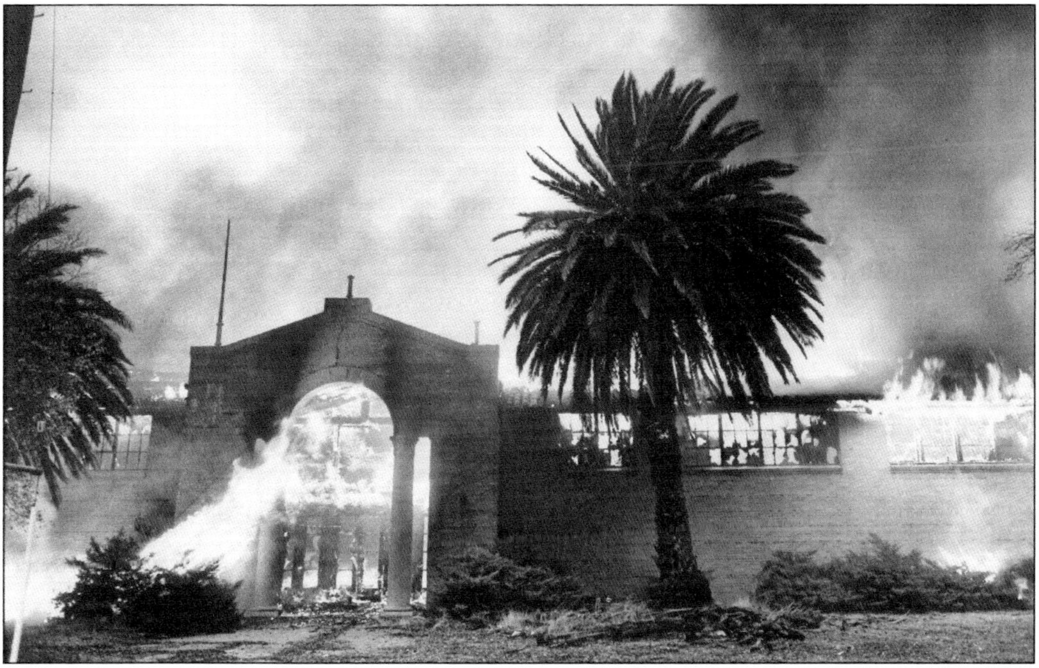

On November 11, 1978, the Women's Building at the old state fairgrounds was destroyed by fire. The building was vacant at the time. The owner of the property was, according to news reports, very upset about the fire. He had been trying to get the area rezoned from residential to commercial for about two years when the fire occurred. (CSH.)

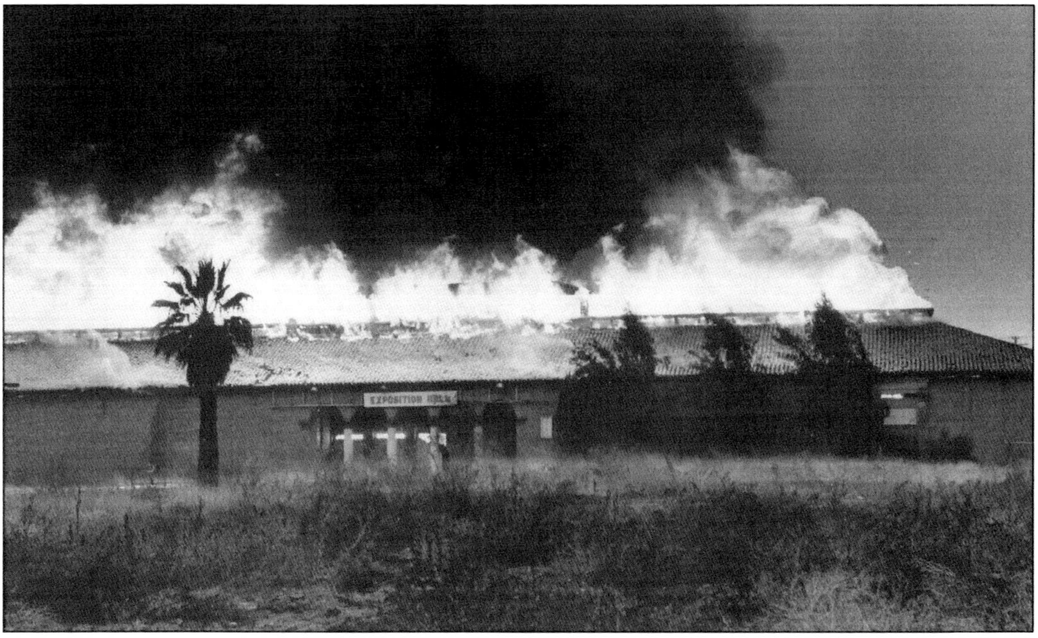

Another view of the fire in 1978. There were plans to convert the building into office space. Constructed in the 1920s, it was formerly the main entrance to the fair and had 96,000 square feet of floor space. At the time of the fire, it was being investigated for consideration as a historical landmark. (CSH.)

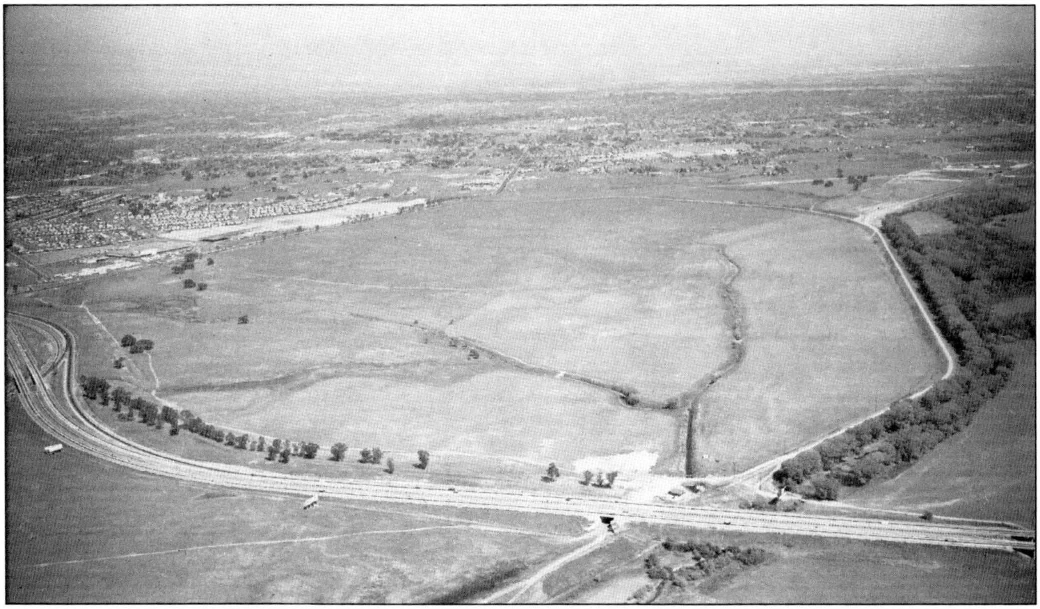

This 1,000-acre piece of land north of the American River was purchased in 1949 as the new site of the California State Fair and Exposition. The American River is to the right, Arden Fair and the new neighborhoods behind it are to the left, and the Elvas Freeway, now Capital City Freeway, cuts through the bottom of the photograph. The photograph was taken by Don Horton in 1959. (CSH.)

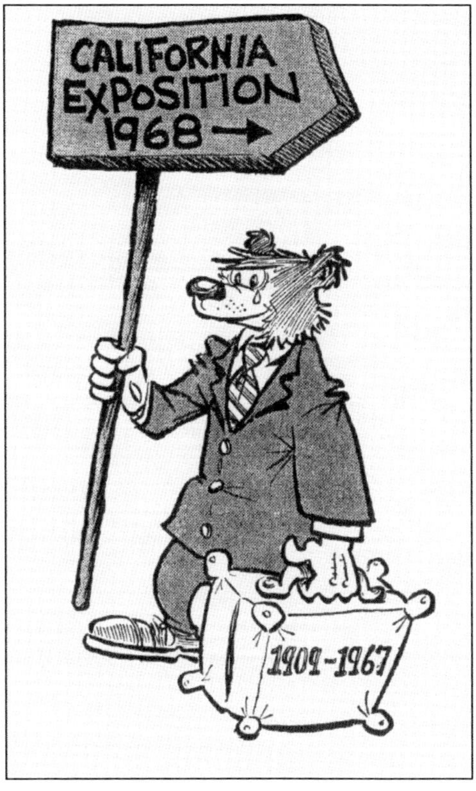

Cartoonist Newton Pratt drew this cartoon in 1967, bidding a fond and tearful farewell to the soon-to-be-referred-to "Old Fairgrounds." (CSH.)

Four

Cal Expo

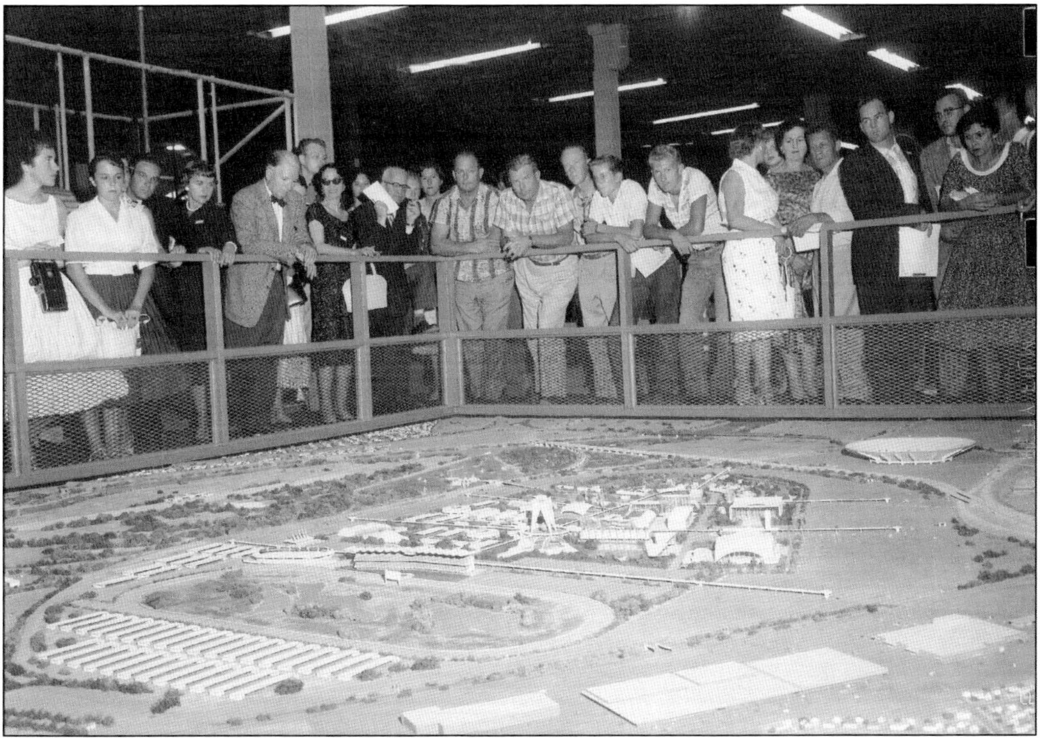

This model of the proposed new fairgrounds for 1961 was on display at the State Fair in 1958. Comments from the crowds were favorable, particularly when it came to transportation. The freeway access and overhead transportation from the parking lots were seen as major improvements. Note the tower in the center and the stadium to the far right. (CSH.)

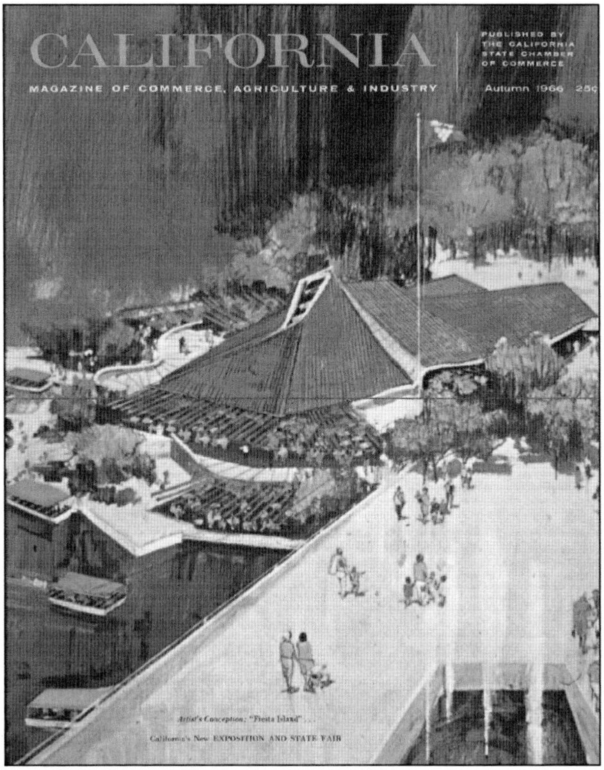

The cover of *California* magazine from Autumn 1966 shows the unrealized "Fiesta Island" at Cal Expo. This sketch, by artist Norman Nicholson, depicts one of the concepts put forth for Cal Expo. Unfortunately, Fiesta Island and another idea, Teen Island, were never built. (CSH.)

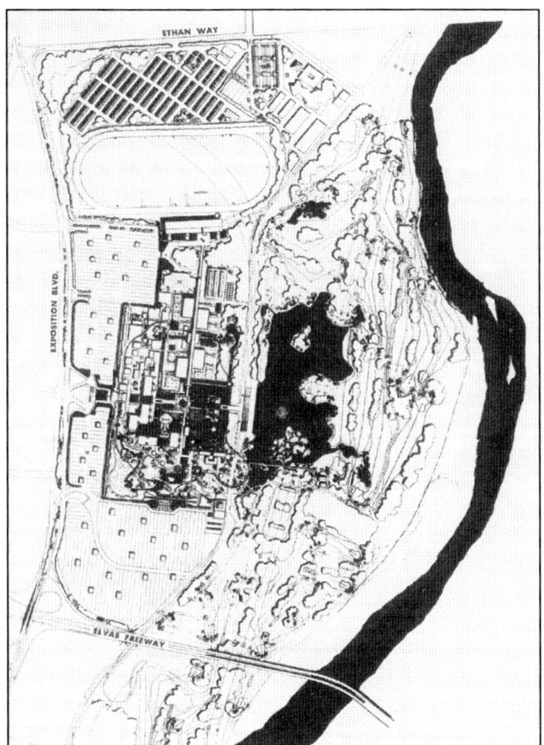

Seen here is the proposed plan for Cal Expo from the May 1966 report by Economics Research Associates. The report covered the design, construction, operating program, and potential economic impact for the exposition. The plan originally called for two golf courses, designed by Robert Trent Jones, alongside the American River, but they were never built. (Sacramento Room, Sacramento Public Library.)

The very informal groundbreaking for the new California Exposition and Fair took place on October 25, 1966. In attendance were, from left to right, Eugene Lemmon, general manager of the exposition; Louis Roth, director of design and construction; Betty Cobb, secretary; and Harry Gravelle, the bulldozer operator. (CSH.)

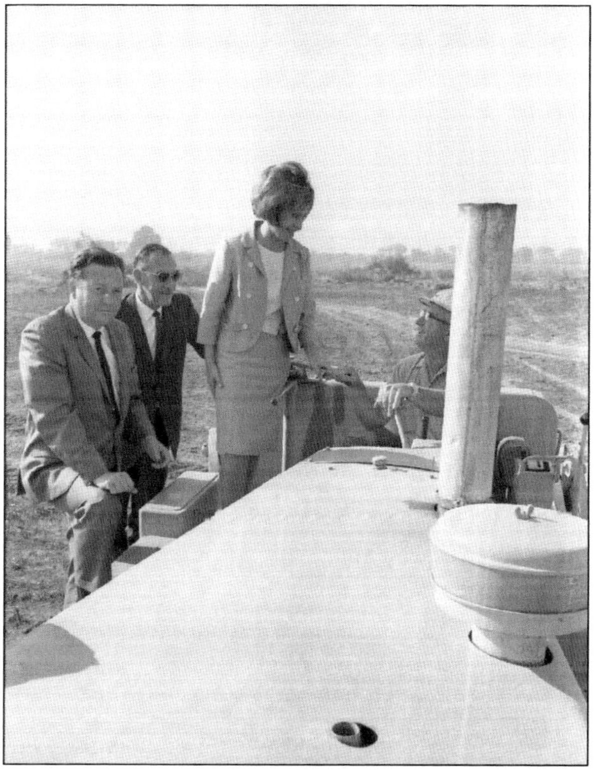

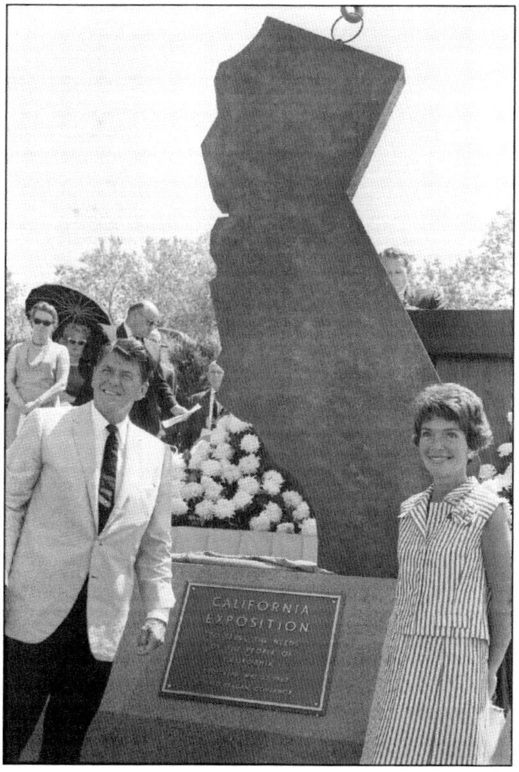

The new California Exposition was dedicated by Gov. Ronald Reagan and First Lady Nancy Reagan on May 22, 1967. The ceremony involved the usual array of dignitaries, speakers, and bands. The highlight was attaching the concrete silhouette of the state by crane to the pedestal with the brass plaque, shown here. (CSH.)

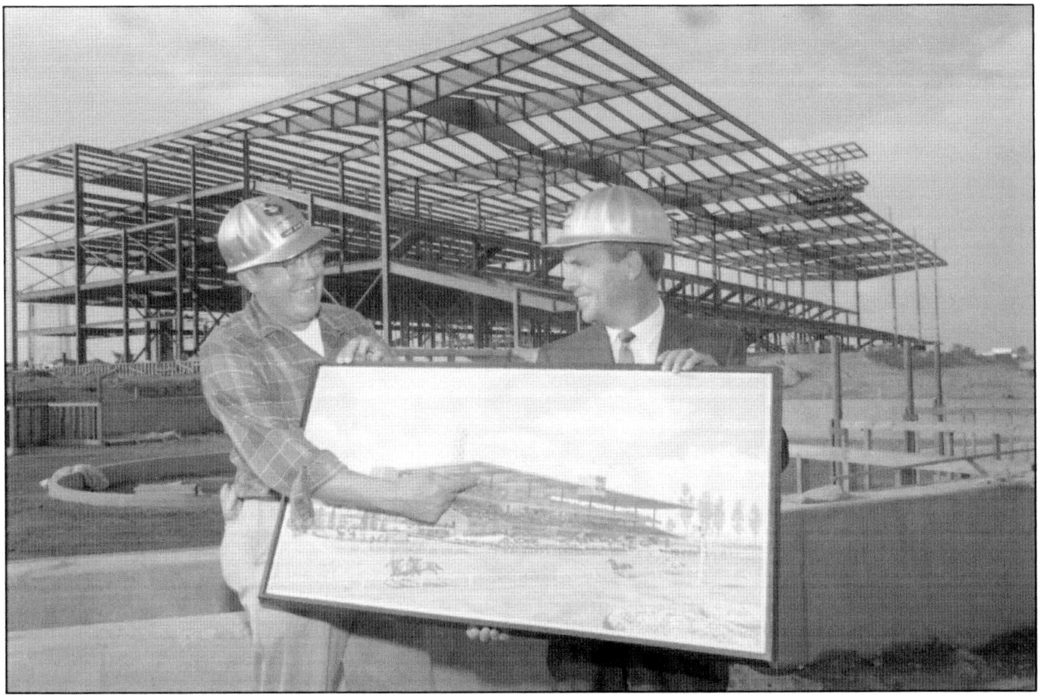

This image shows the grandstand for the racetrack under construction on November 16, 1967. The contractor and a fair official, both unidentified, compare the progress of the construction with the presentation drawing. (CSH.)

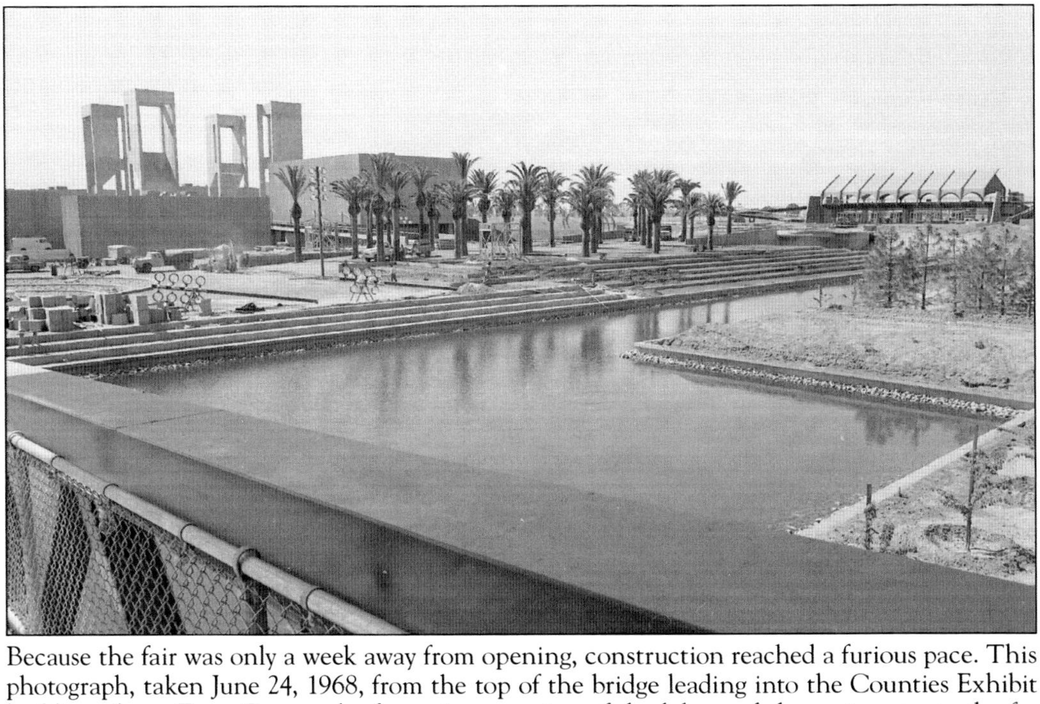

Because the fair was only a week away from opening, construction reached a furious pace. This photograph, taken June 24, 1968, from the top of the bridge leading into the Counties Exhibit building, shows Expo Center, the fountain, a portion of the lake, and the main gate, to the far right. (CSH.)

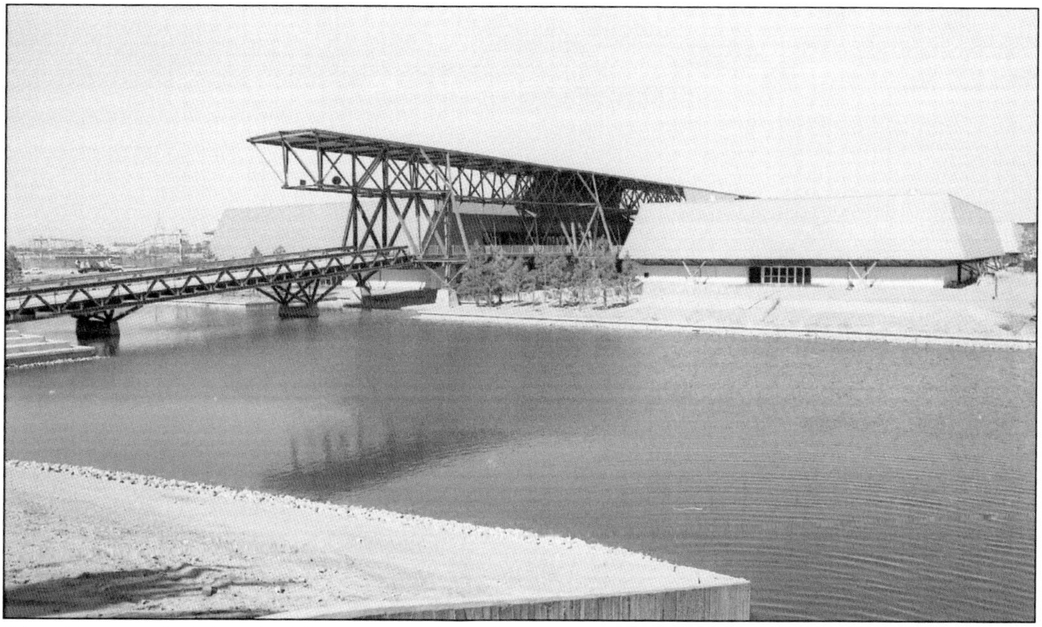

The Counties Exhibits building is seen here from across the man-made lake that separates this structure from Expo Center and the fountain, on June 24, 1968. What looks like two buildings is actually one. The covered walkway sits above the ground floor of the building, where the main exhibit space is located. (CSH.)

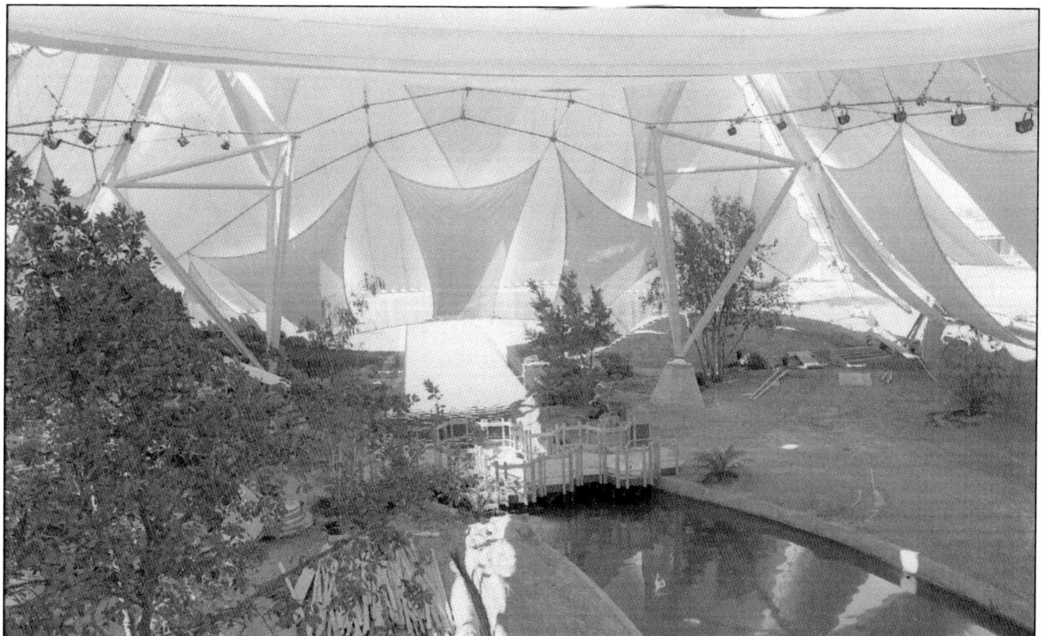

This photograph shows the new Floriculture Pavilion as construction nears completion and the finishing touches are being installed. Unlike the previous Hall of Flowers, this pavilion is open and covered with a large tent-like structure. The image was taken from the elevated walkway into the Counties Exhibit building. The monorail is to the right, out of the frame. (CSH.)

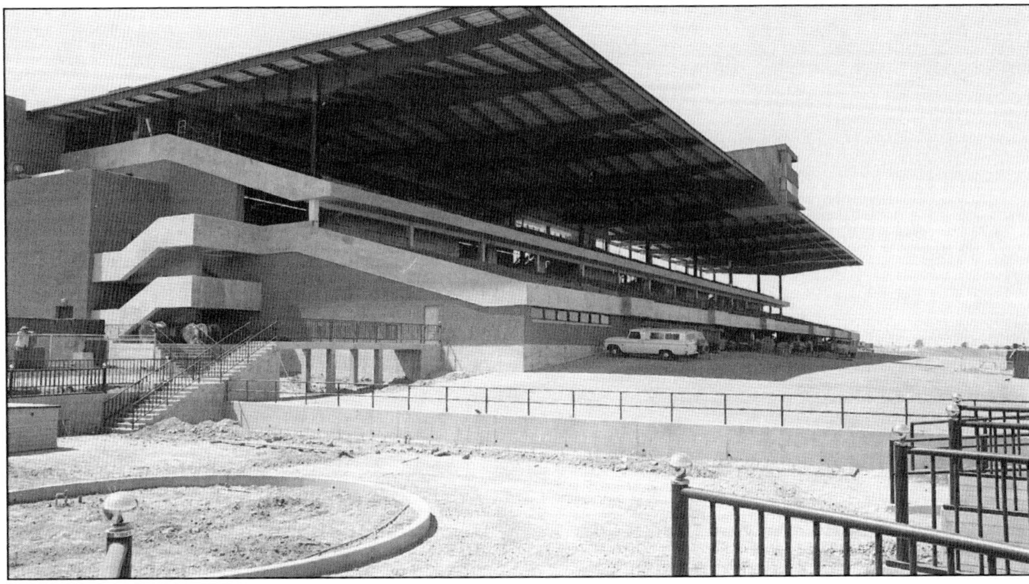

The new Cal Expo grandstand is seen here a week before the opening. The construction is complete and the last details are being attended to. It was quite a tight schedule, but the new California Exposition did open as promised on July 1, 1968. (CSH.)

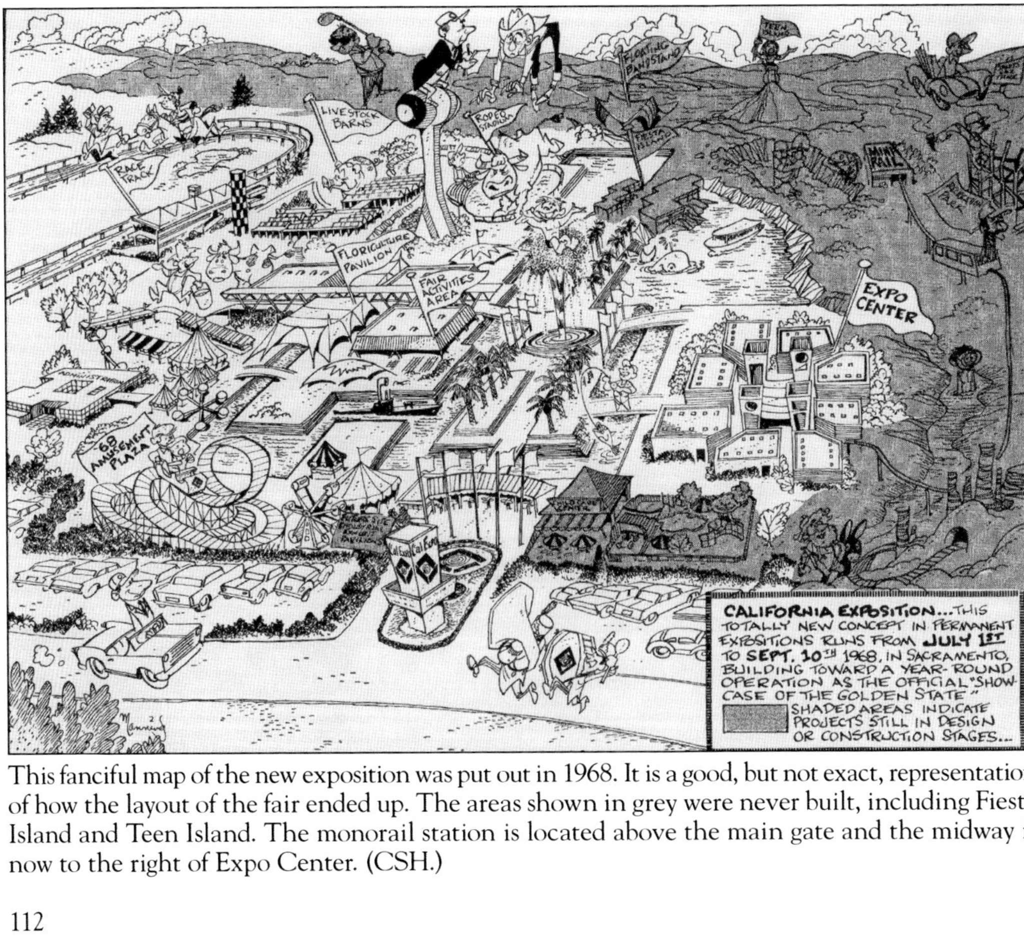

This fanciful map of the new exposition was put out in 1968. It is a good, but not exact, representation of how the layout of the fair ended up. The areas shown in grey were never built, including Fiesta Island and Teen Island. The monorail station is located above the main gate and the midway is now to the right of Expo Center. (CSH.)

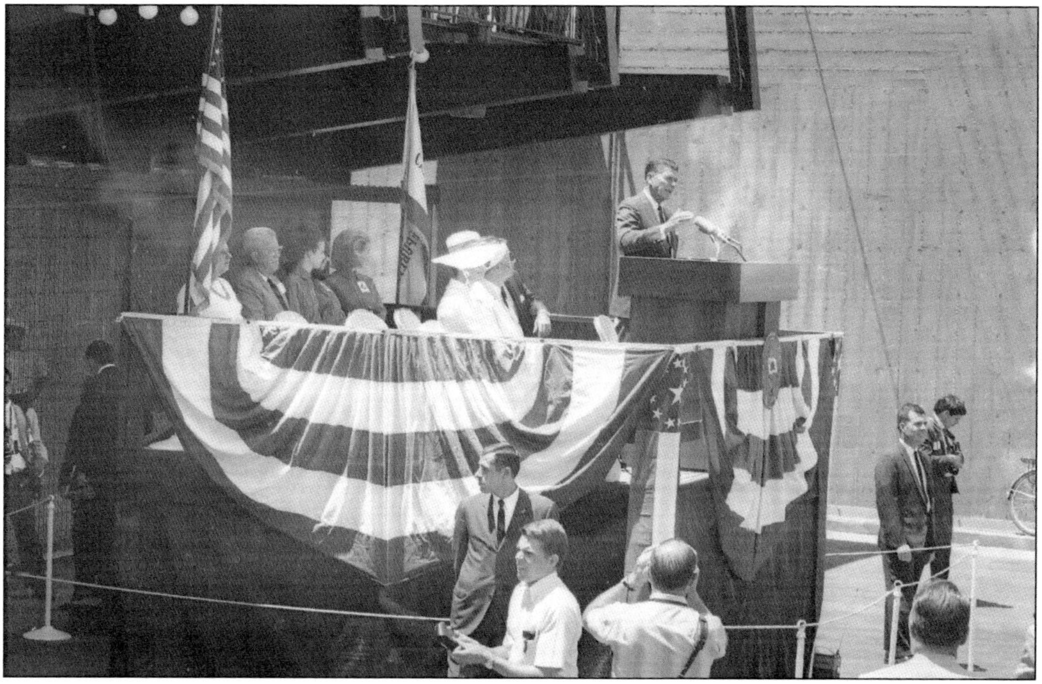

Gov. Ronald Reagan attended the opening day of Cal Expo on July 1, 1968. He is seen here on the stage at the front gate, giving a speech to mark the occasion. Governor Reagan did recognize that Gov. Edmund Brown was the man most responsible for Cal Expo, but was unable to attend. Not seen in this photograph is the crowd of over 9,000 in attendance. (CSH.)

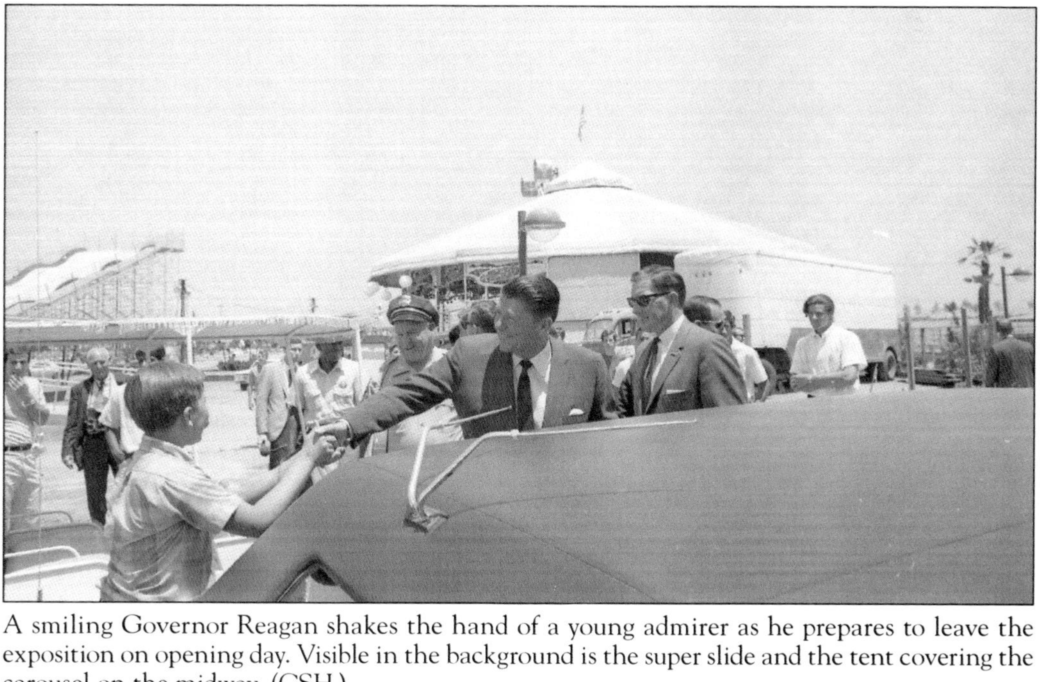

A smiling Governor Reagan shakes the hand of a young admirer as he prepares to leave the exposition on opening day. Visible in the background is the super slide and the tent covering the carousel on the midway. (CSH.)

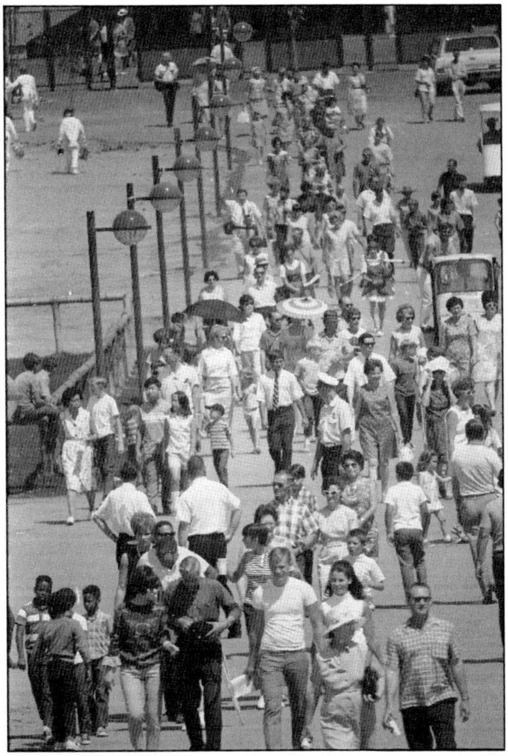

Seen here is part of the opening day crowd at the new Cal Expo. This view looks back toward the grandstand and was taken from the promenade, near the main gate. (CSH.)

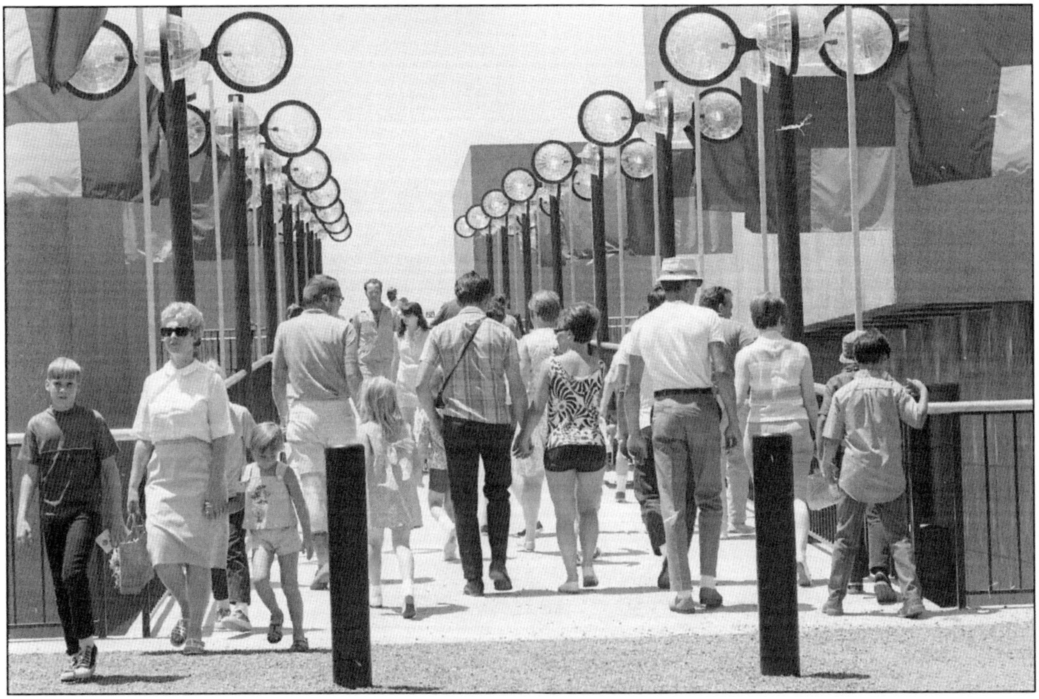

Seen here is opening day on the bridge from the promenade into the new Expo Center. The promenade runs through the main exhibition areas of Expo Center, the Counties Exhibit building, the racetrack and grandstand, and the midway. (CSH.)

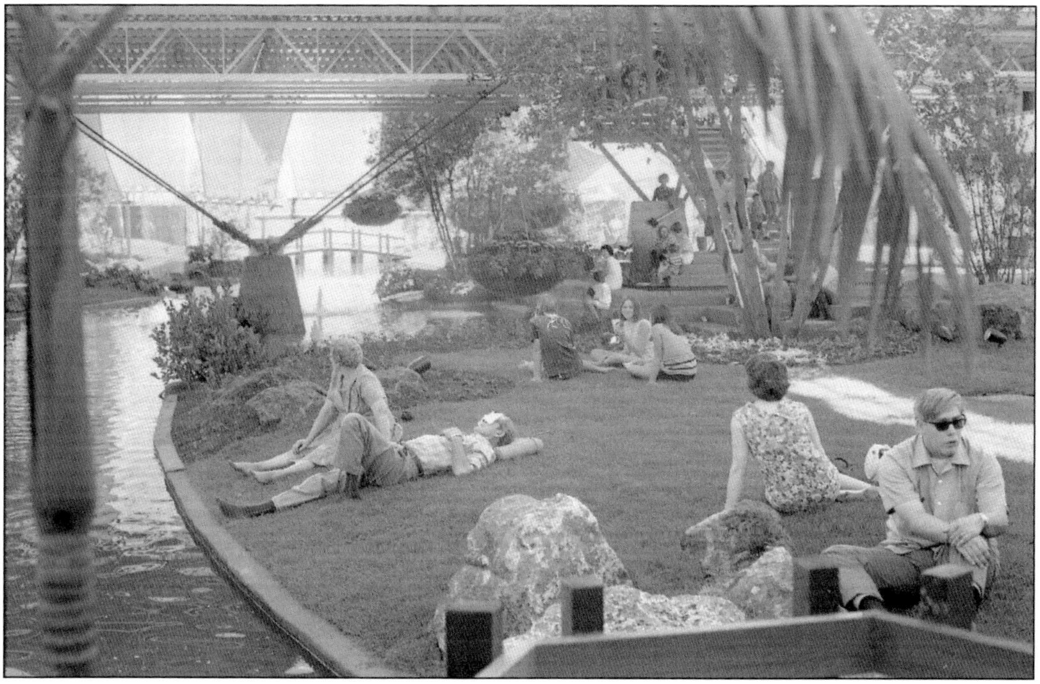

The long-standing State Fair tradition of giving your feet a rest continues at Cal Expo. Fairgoers are seen here in the new Floriculture Pavilion taking a well deserved break on the new grass in the shade of the tent. (CSH.)

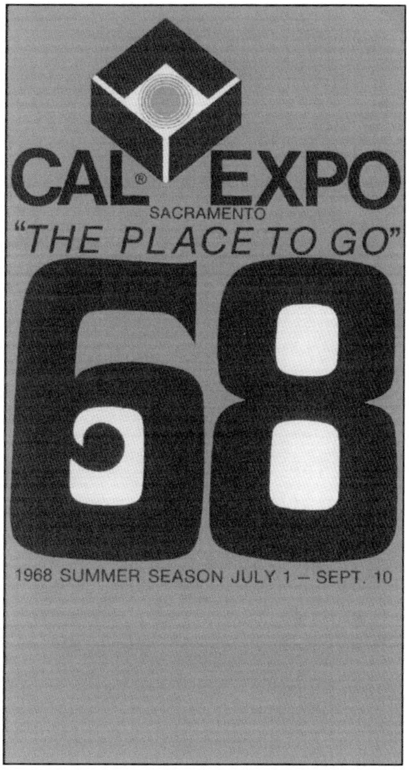

This is one of the many pamphlets produced to promote the new Cal Expo as "The Place to Go." The California Exposition was originally planned to be open nearly year round, incorporating the State Fair in August and other events the rest of the year. Thus, the pamphlet is for the "Summer Season." (CSH.)

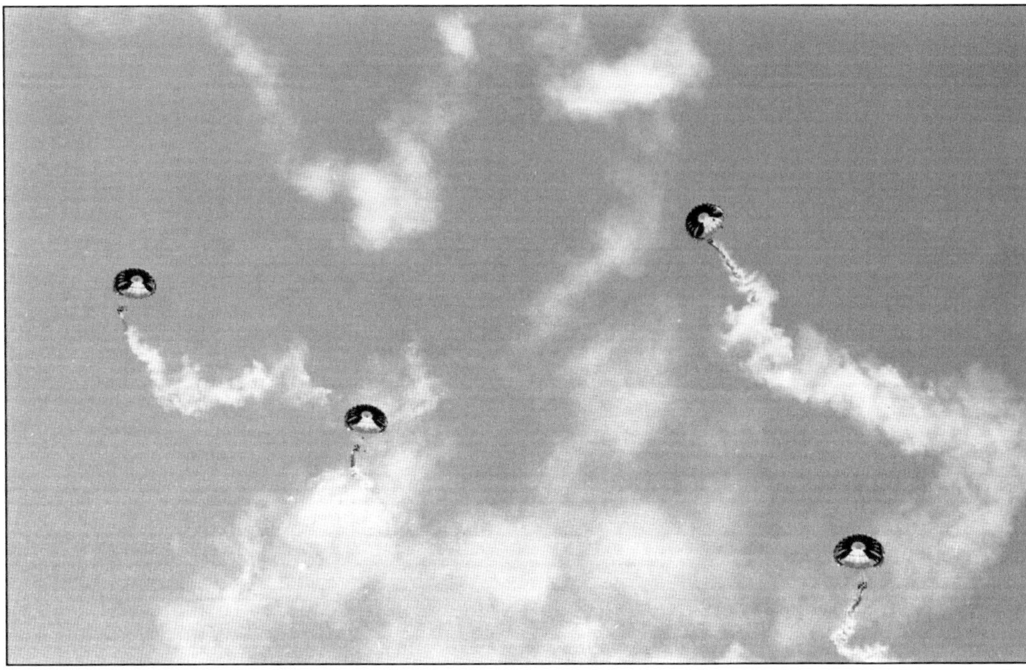

The United States Army elite parachute team, the Golden Knights, performed on opening day. Four of the members are seen here trailing smoke as they come in for a landing on the infield of the racetrack. (CSH.)

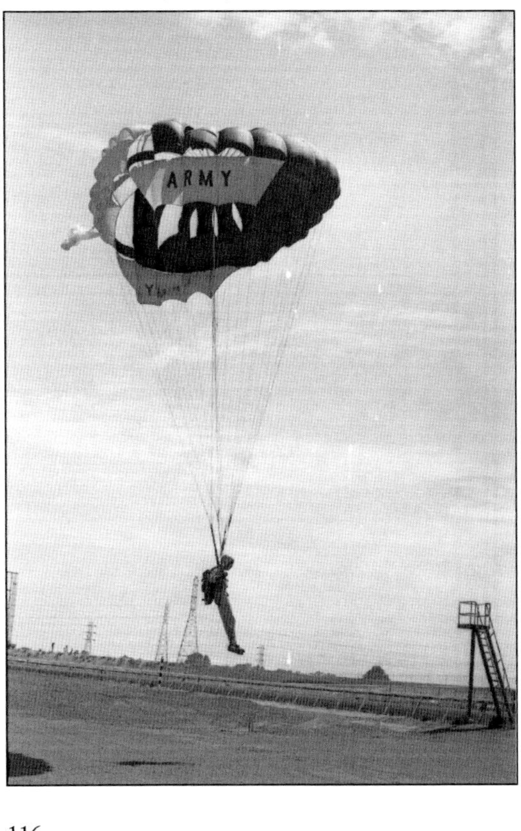

A member of the Golden Knights comes in for a perfect two-point landing near the back stretch of the racetrack on opening day. (CSH.)

Buck Owens performed at the grandstand at Cal Expo on August 3, 1968, as part of the first-year festivities. He is seen here backstage, signing one of his albums for two young fans. By all accounts, the show was well attended. (CSH.)

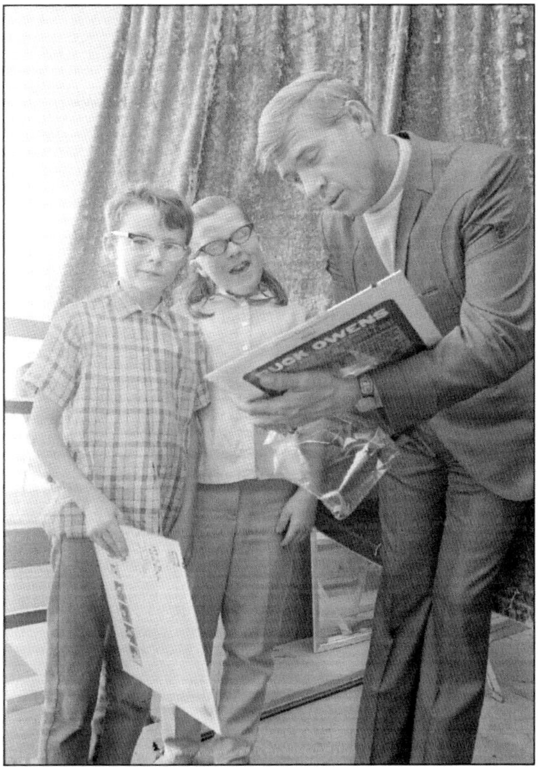

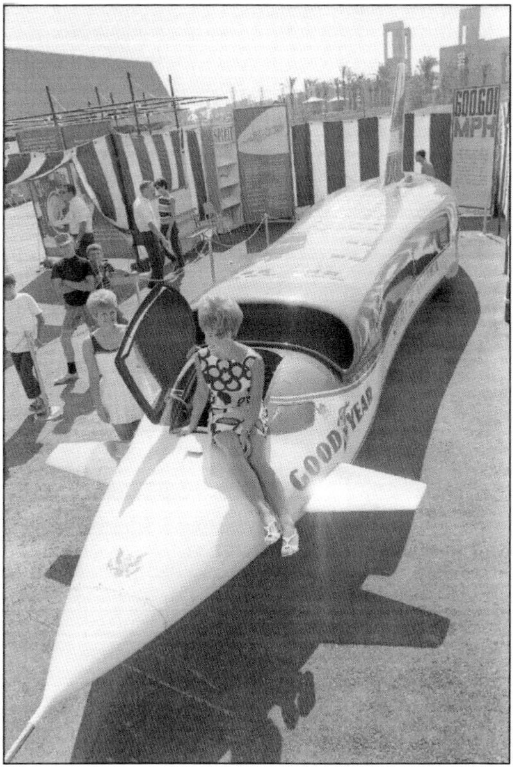

On November 15, 1965, Craig Breedlove set a land speed record of 600.601 m.p.h. at Bonneville Salt Flats. The record stood until 1970. Cal Expo exhibited the record-setting vehicle, "Spirit of America," during the opening season in 1968. It was a very popular exhibit among the men who attended. (CSH.)

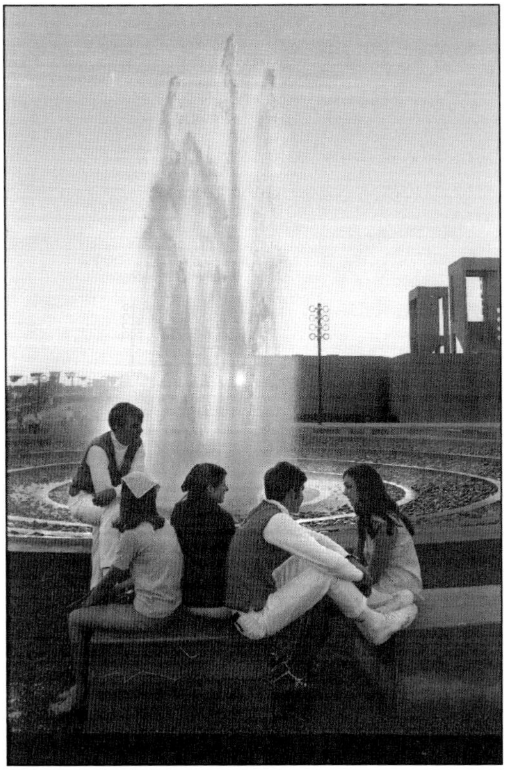

The new fountain at Cal Expo was quite popular, especially during the middle of a typical August day in Sacramento. This photograph shows a group of young people gathered at the fountain at sunset on August 28, 1968. Expo Center is visible in the background of this west-looking image. (CSH.)

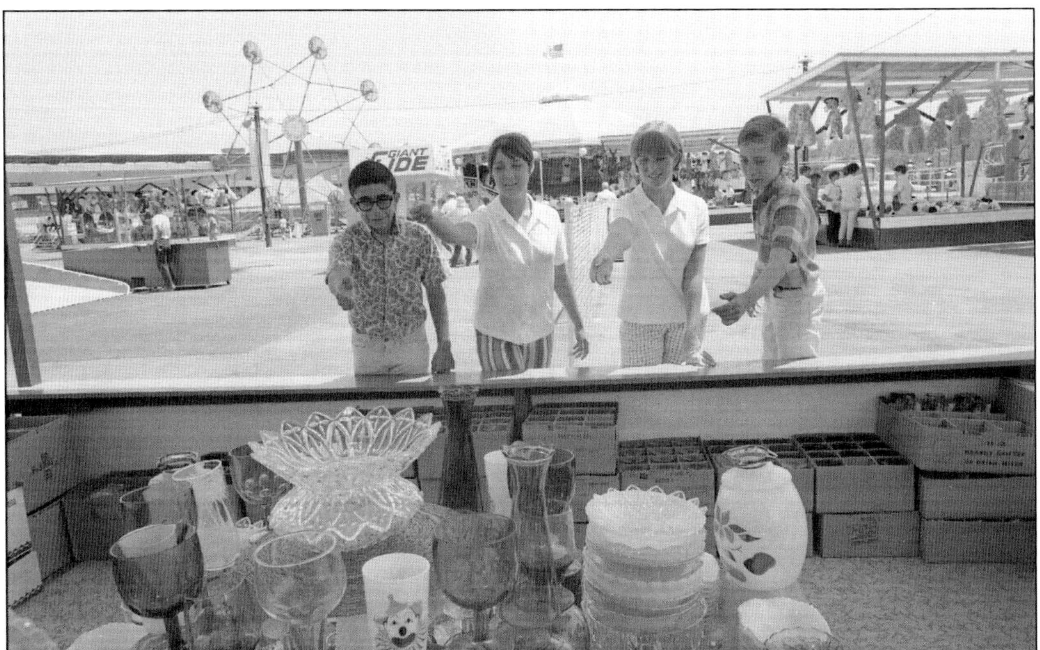

The dime toss is always a popular stop for kids on the midway. Attempting to win a vase or bowl are, from left to right, Frank Rienti, Cindy Loomis, Mary Roy, and Bob Brady. It is unknown what they won, if anything. (CSH.)

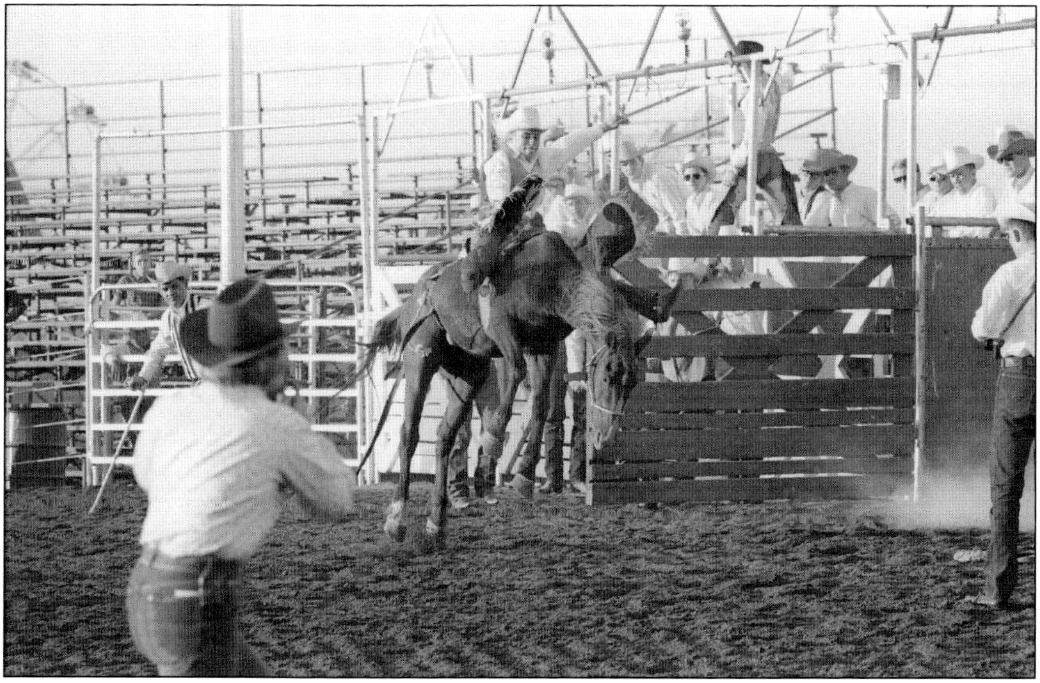

At the new Rodeo Arena, the first bronco-busting contest took place on July 3, 1968. This photograph vividly captures the action. Whether or not this contestant succeeded in staying on the horse for the required eight seconds is unknown. (CSH.)

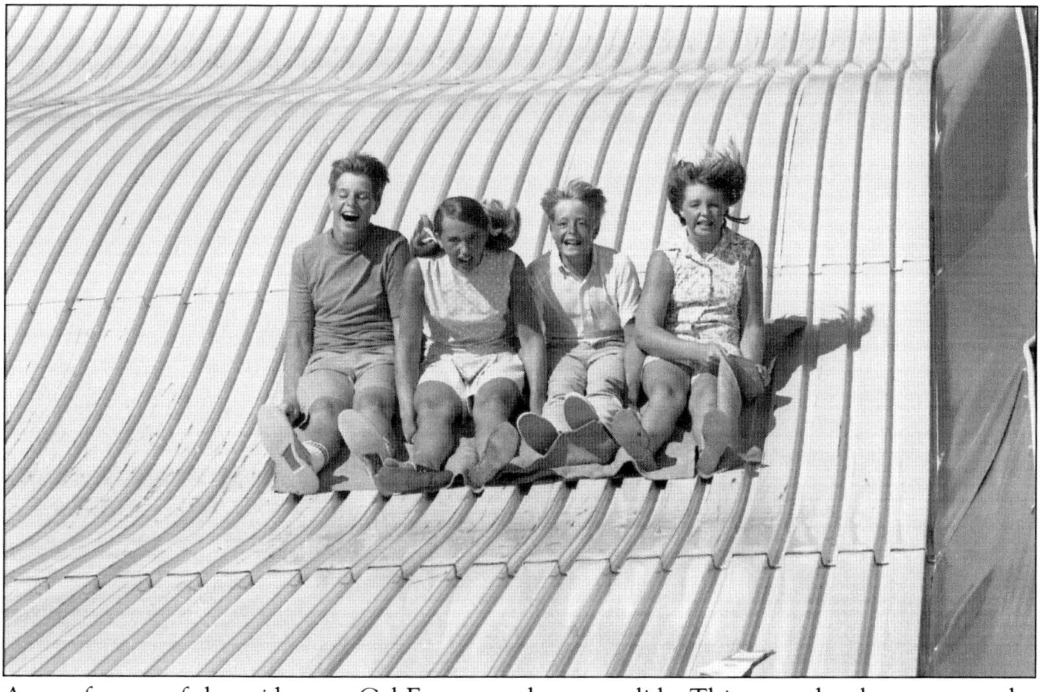

A new feature of the midway at Cal Expo was the super slide. This proved to be more popular than one might imagine. The sliders are unidentified. The same slide is visible in the photograph of Governor Reagan on page 113. (CSH.)

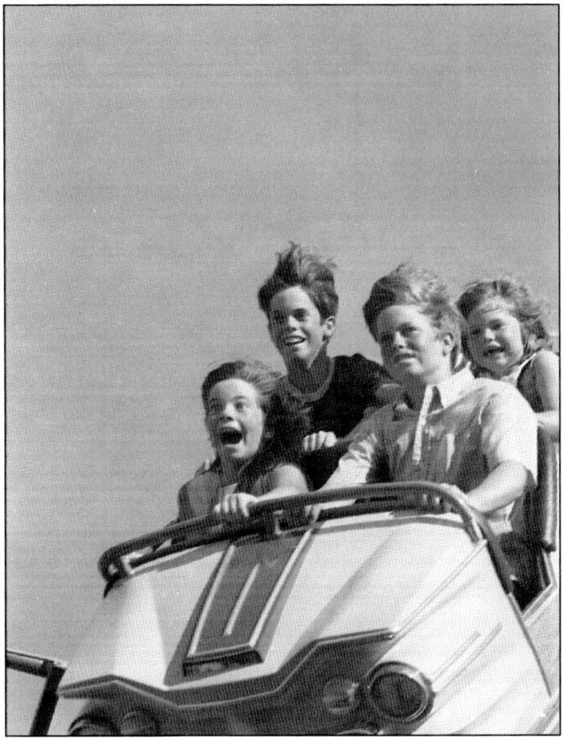

Midway rides will always be popular because nearly everyone enjoys the thrills they provide. This is plainly evident in this photograph from August 2, 1968. The expression on the boy to the left explains it all. This particular ride is called the Zyklon Roller Coaster. (CSH.)

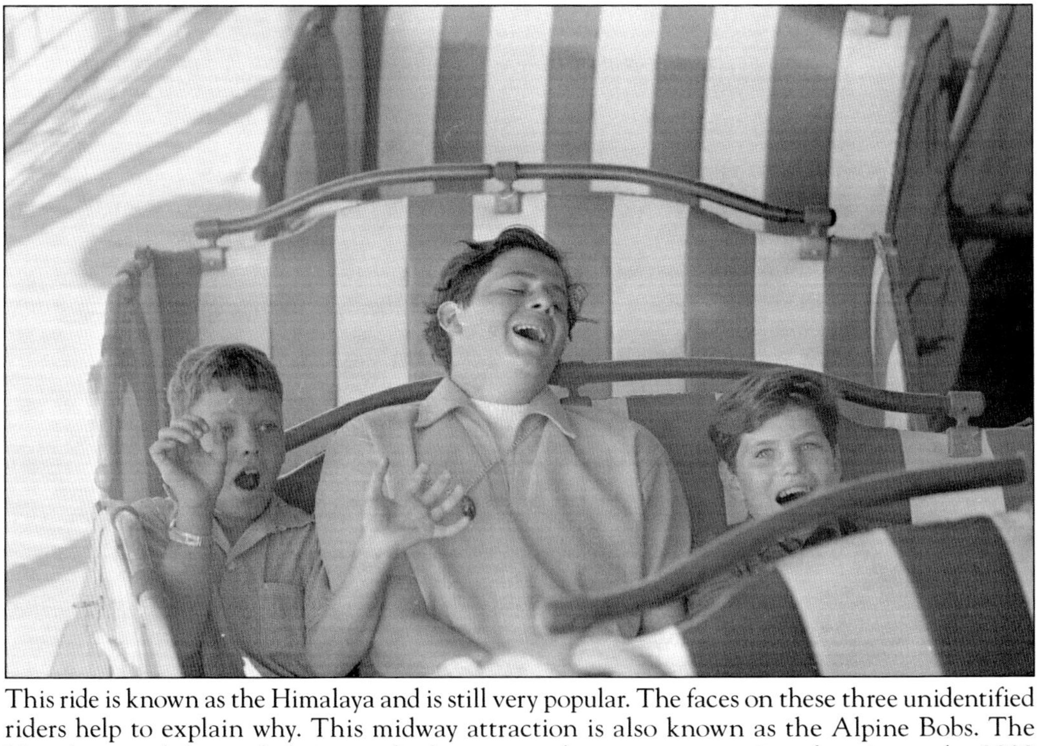

This ride is known as the Himalaya and is still very popular. The faces on these three unidentified riders help to explain why. This midway attraction is also known as the Alpine Bobs. The Himalaya, with better lighting and a larger sound system, was again a favorite at the 2009 California State Fair. (CSH.)

The space race was always a popular subject for exhibits. This exhibit from 1969 shows an authentic spacesuit worn by astronauts who flew in the Apollo missions to the moon. It is strikingly different from Aerojet's 1962 version of a spacesuit, seen on page 95. (CSH.)

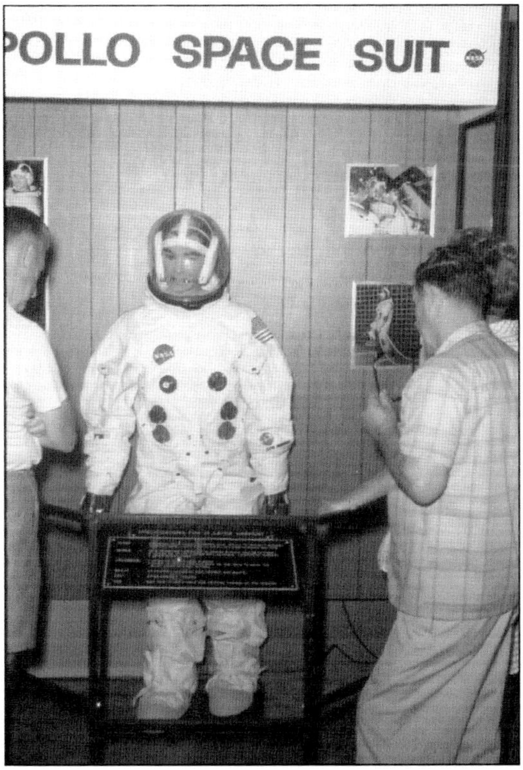

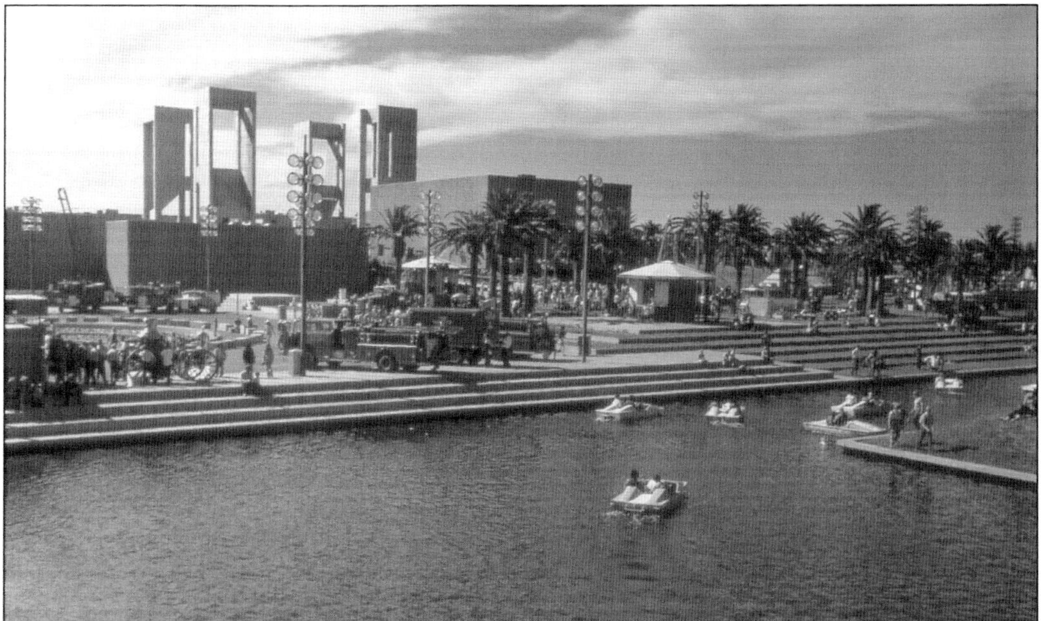

This photograph from August 1970 was taken from nearly the same spot as the image on page 110. On what appears to be the day to salute firemen, the grounds are a beehive of activity. Paddle boats are patrolling the waters of the lake and people are everywhere. This is what the planners of Cal Expo originally envisioned. (CSH.)

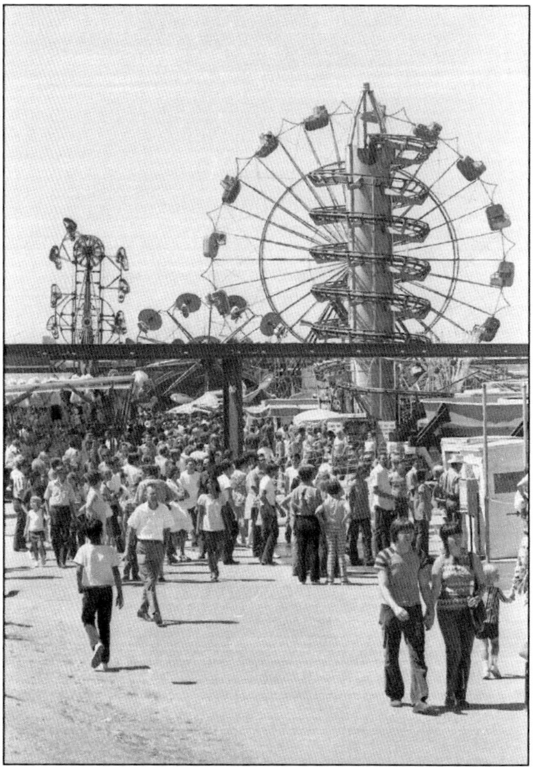

Seen here is the midway at Cal Expo as it looked in 1971. Many favorite rides are seen, including the Zipper. Also visible is the track of the monorail, which rides around and through the entire fairgrounds. (CSH.)

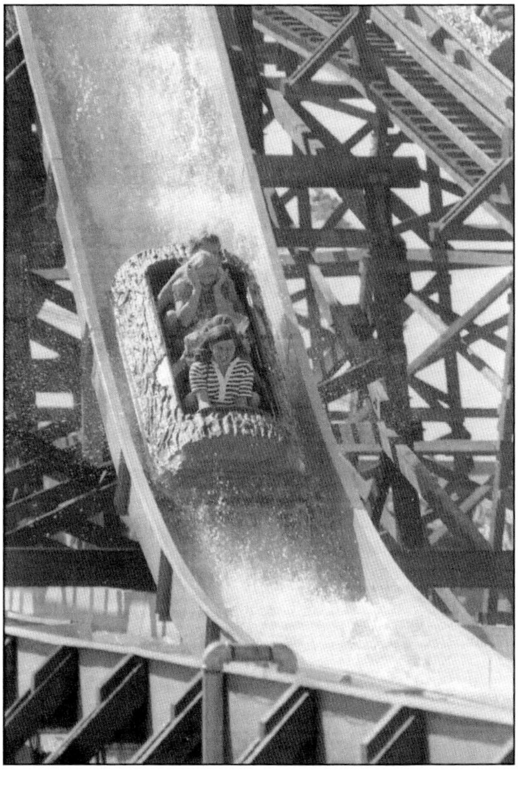

One of the most popular rides at the midway was the log flume. It was constructed in 1971, almost entirely of wood, which made it a bit rickety. The photograph was taken in 1971. It captures the moment a split second before the grand finale when the log hits the water at the bottom, soaking the riders and any unwary bystanders. (CSH.)

Livestock was not left out of Cal Expo. The two major youth organizations, 4-H and the Future Farmers of America, were active participants. In 1970, FFA member Conrad Bitter, of Madera, is receiving help grooming his sheep from Sacramento residents Lauren Wetterer (left) and Sue Backus. The base of the water tower is visible in the background. (CSH.)

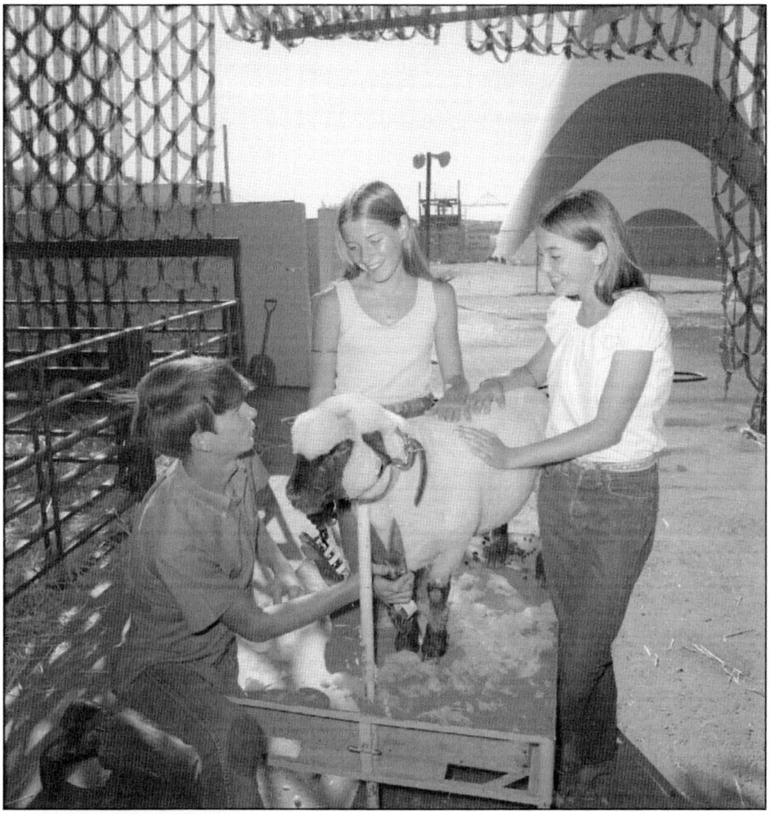

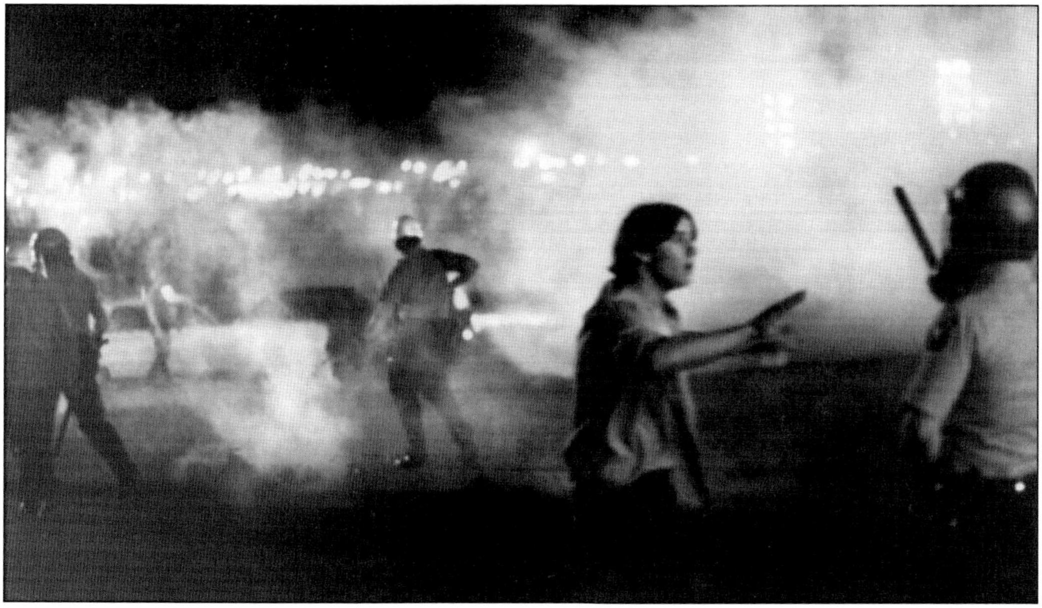

In what can only be called an anomaly, fighting broke out during the 1971 State Fair. The antagonists were a rowdy group of young people who did not want to leave at closing time. When the automatic sprinklers came on, they became enraged, blaming the police. The unusual event happened right at or after closing time and several dozen youths were arrested over three days. (CSH.)

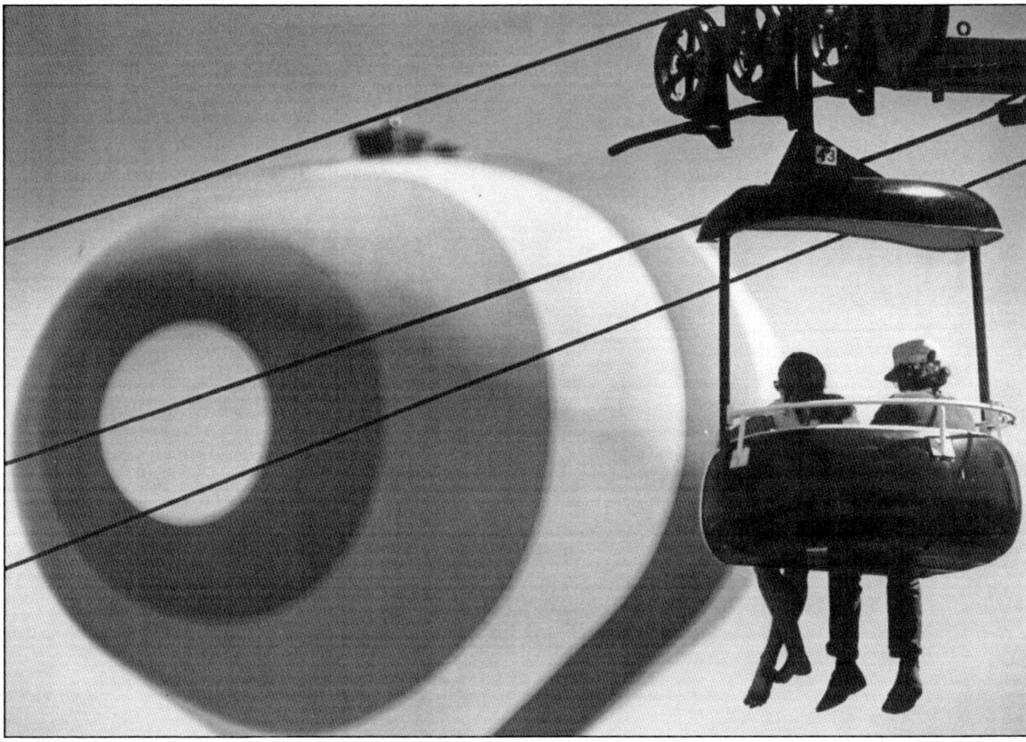

After the uncommon events of 1971, the State Fair returned to normal. This photograph from August 24, 1978, captures a gondola of the Sky Glider passing in front of the Cal Expo water tower. The Sky Glider traversed nearly the entire length of Cal Expo and gave riders spectacular views of the festivities and most of the Sacramento area. (CSH.)

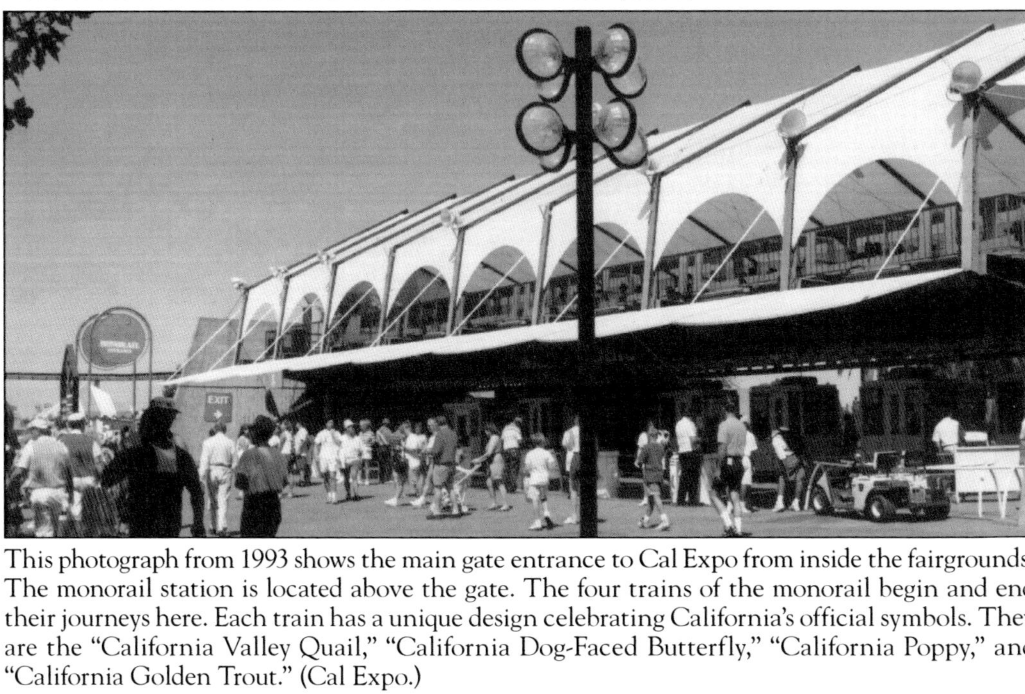

This photograph from 1993 shows the main gate entrance to Cal Expo from inside the fairgrounds. The monorail station is located above the gate. The four trains of the monorail begin and end their journeys here. Each train has a unique design celebrating California's official symbols. They are the "California Valley Quail," "California Dog-Faced Butterfly," "California Poppy," and "California Golden Trout." (Cal Expo.)

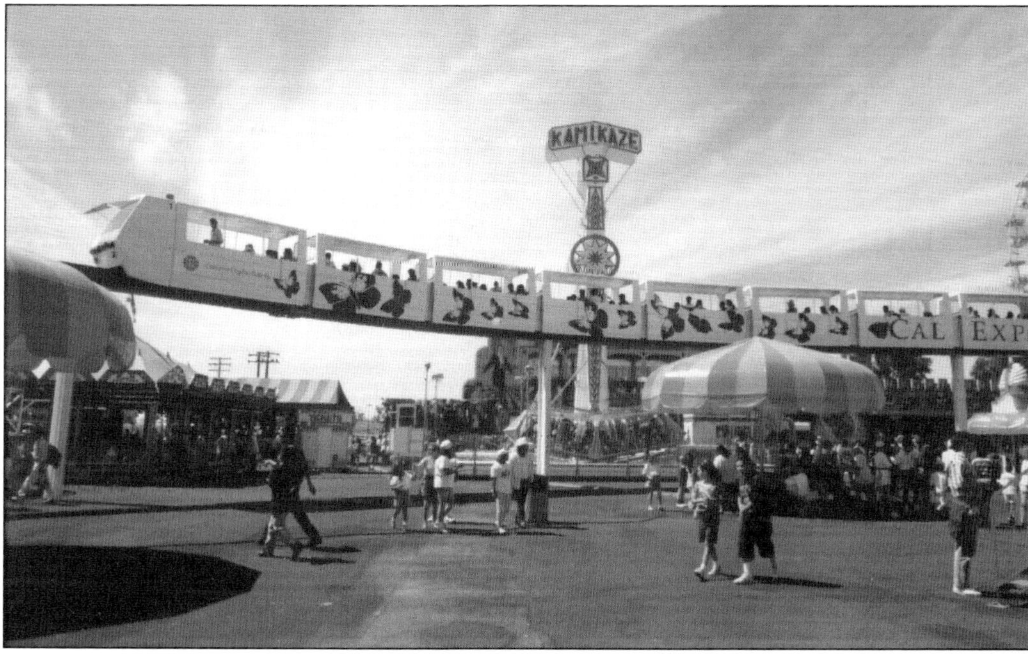

This photograph shows the monorail as it glides through the midway in 1993. The monorail's four separate trains run around and through all the major areas of Cal Expo, giving riders a rather intimate view of the festivities. The track is 7,000 feet long, or one-and-one-third miles. Seen here is the "California Dog-Faced Butterfly" design. (Cal Expo.)

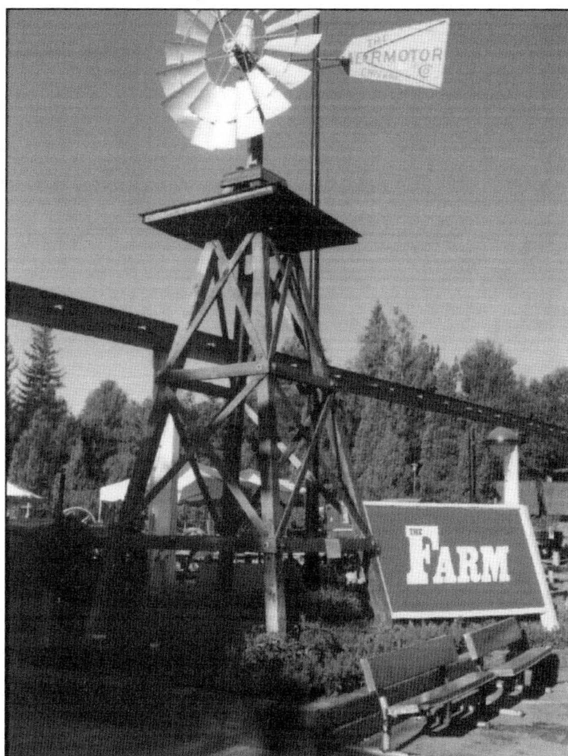

A major part of the mission of the California State Fair is education. The 1854 act that created the fair mandated that model farms be maintained to educate the general public. Cal Expo continues this mandate with "The Farm," a working model of a farm, seen here in 1994. New and innovative farming techniques, as well as the tried and true, are demonstrated here. (Cal Expo.)

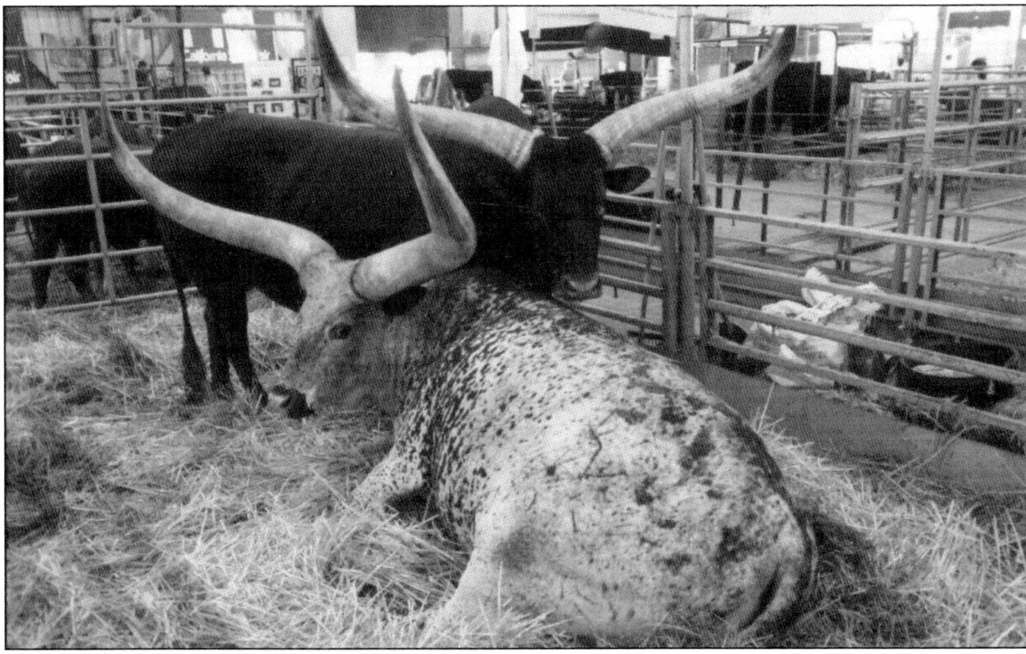

Part of the stock show in 1994 was a pair of Ankole-Watusi cattle. Native to Africa, the breed goes back at least 6,000 years in the Nile Valley. Images of this breed of cattle are seen in pictographs inside Egyptian pyramids. Their horns are noteworthy not just because of their six-foot length, but also their very large circumference. These two were a very popular attraction. (Cal Expo.)

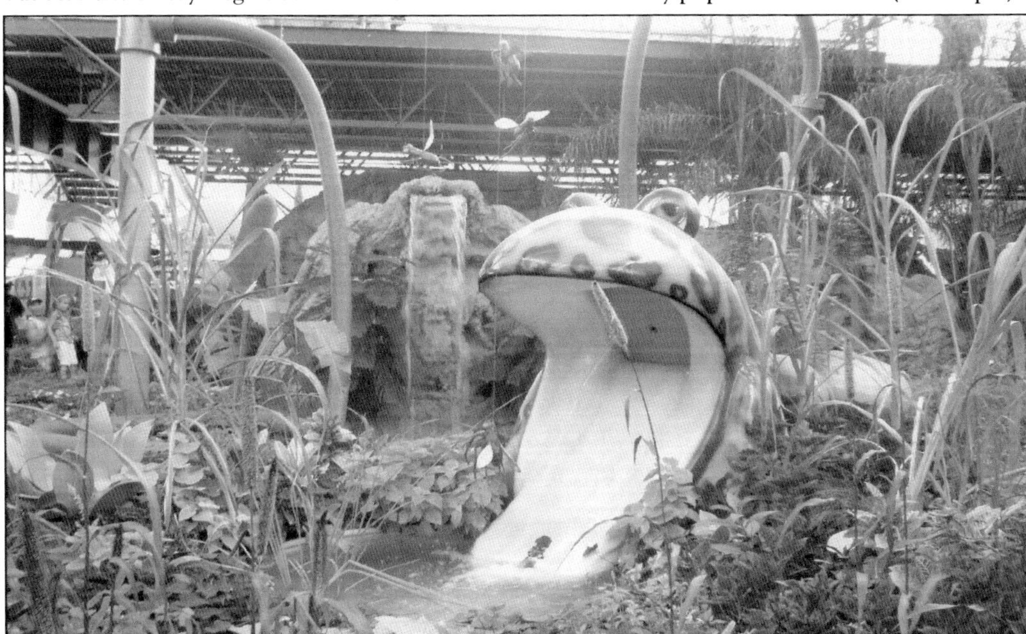

The Floriculture Pavilion is always colorful. In the past several years, the displays have highlighted the importance of the environment and ways to protect it, all in very imaginative ways. A frog awaits a meal in someone's yard in this delightful exhibit from 2009. The elevated walkway in the background leads to the Counties Exhibit to the right. (Author's collection.)

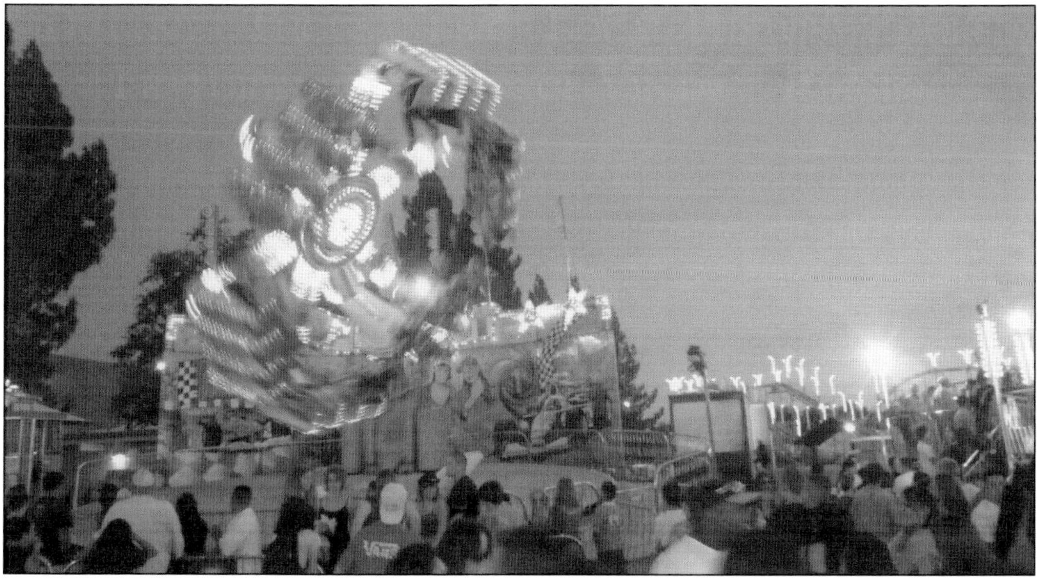

From the 2009 State Fair, this photograph captures one of the more invigorating rides on the midway in full flight. Not only are riders spun as if in a centrifuge, but the whole thing travels around a turntable and inverts the riders. As one might suspect, it is highly advised that you do not eat before attempting to ride it. (Author's collection.)

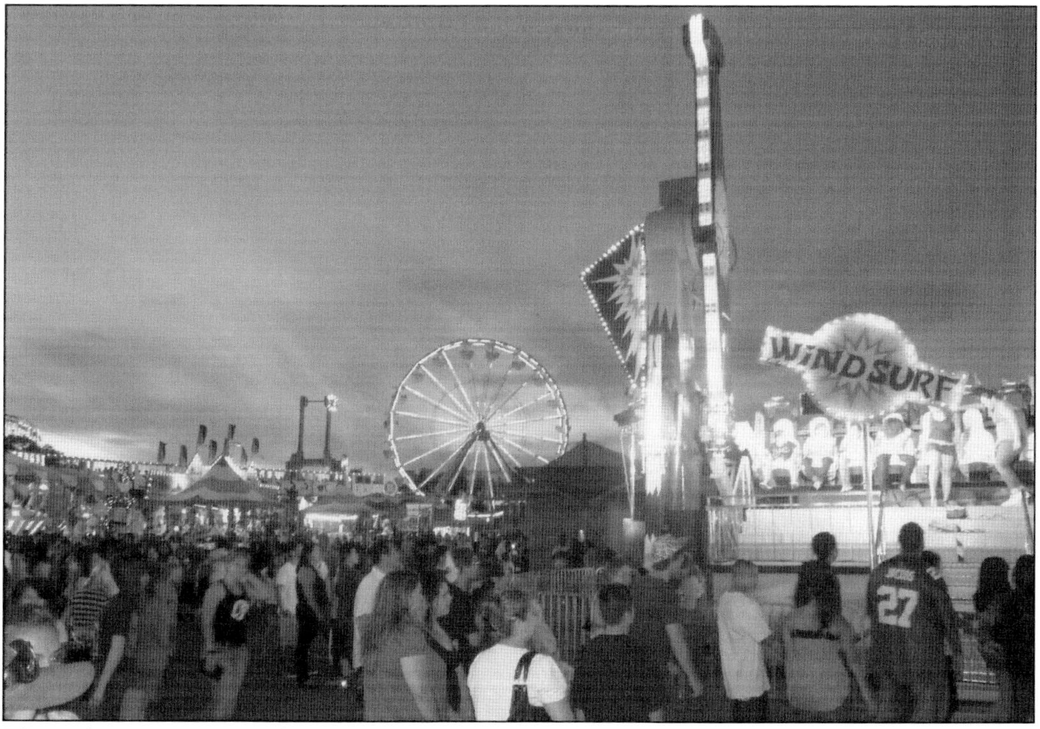

The midway continues to be one of the major attractions at Cal Expo. This photograph was taken at sunset during the 2009 fair. In the background is the giant Ferris wheel. It is one of the largest travelling Ferris wheels in the country and takes riders almost one hundred feet in the air. The view from the top is spectacular. (Author's collection.)

Discover Thousands of Local History Books Featuring Millions of Vintage Images

Arcadia Publishing, the leading local history publisher in the United States, is committed to making history accessible and meaningful through publishing books that celebrate and preserve the heritage of America's people and places.

Find more books like this at
www.arcadiapublishing.com

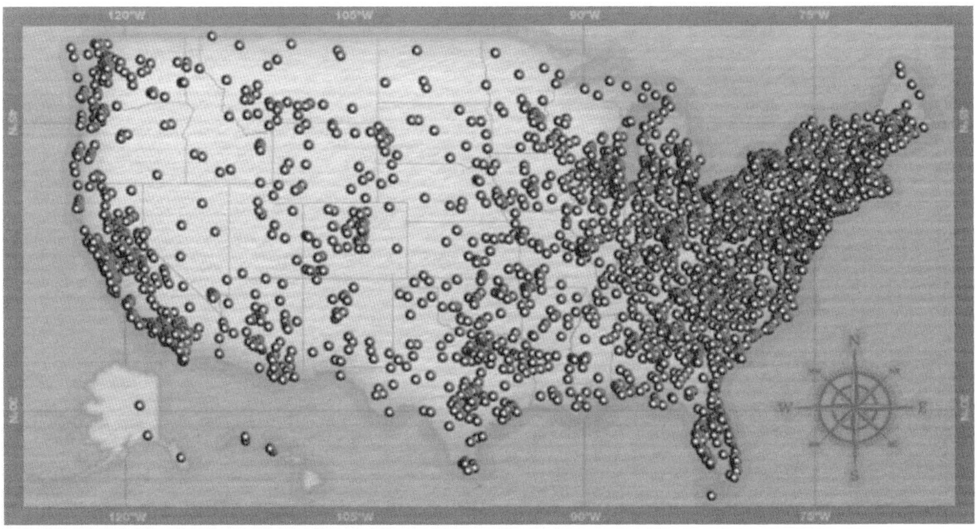

Search for your hometown history, your old stomping grounds, and even your favorite sports team.

Consistent with our mission to preserve history on a local level, this book was printed in South Carolina on American-made paper and manufactured entirely in the United States. Products carrying the accredited Forest Stewardship Council (FSC) label are printed on 100 percent FSC-certified paper.

MADE IN THE USA